*Marx's lost aesthetic*

The unveiling of A. Matveyev's memorial to Karl Marx in front of the Smolny Institute, Petrograd, 1918

# Marx's lost aesthetic

## Karl Marx and the visual arts

MARGARET A. ROSE

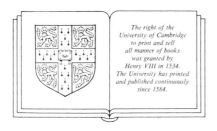

The right of the
University of Cambridge
to print and sell
all manner of books
was granted by
Henry VIII in 1534.
The University has printed
and published continuously
since 1584.

CAMBRIDGE UNIVERSITY PRESS

Cambridge
London   New York   New Rochelle
Melbourne   Sydney

Published by the Press Syndicate of the University of Cambridge
The Pitt Building, Trumpington Street, Cambridge CB2 1RP
32 East 57th Street, New York, NY 10022, USA
296 Beaconsfield Parade, Middle Park, Melbourne 3206, Australia

© Cambridge University Press 1984

First published 1984

Printed in Great Britain at the University Press, Cambridge

Library of Congress catalogue card number: 83–14319


*British Library Cataloguing in Publication Data*

Rose, Margaret A.
Marx's lost aesthetic.
1. Communist aesthetics
I. Title
700'.092'4   HX 521

ISBN 0 521 25666 6

# Contents

# Illustrations

# Acknowledgements

I should like to take this opportunity to thank all those who have assisted in the publication of this work, in particular the staff of the Cambridge University Press, especially the editors who supervised the production process, and Pauline Marsh, who subedited the book, the Alexander von Humboldt Stiftung, and the Deakin University Research Grants Committee. In addition, I should like to thank the Director of the Heinrich Heine Institute, Düsseldorf, Dr Joseph Kruse, and its librarian, Heike von Berkholz, for their assistance in completing the research for the study, the History of Ideas Unit of the Australian National University, Canberra, for the opportunity to spend some time there while completing the manuscript, Judy Barber and Beverley Bartlett for typing the first version of it, Dorothy Franklin for typing the final version, and Peter Wilson and Robert Filippi for their help with the preparation of visual materials. Every effort has been made to trace the owners of copyright of the illustrations and to give correct acknowledgement to them. Acknowledgement for the use of illustrative material is gratefully made to Her Majesty the Queen; the Bayerische Staatsgemäldesammlung, Munich, Alte and Neue Pinakothek and Graphics Collection; the Bildarchiv Preussischer Kulturbesitz, Berlin; Collection Mr and Mrs Eric Estorick; the Glasgow Art Gallery & Museum; Alexander Glezer; the Goethe-Museum, Düsseldorf; the Hermitage, Leningrad; the Kaiser Wilhelm Museum, Krefeld; the Kunsthalle, Hamburg; the Kunsthalle, Karlsruhe; the Kunsthistorisches Museum, Vienna; the Kupferstichkabinett und Sammlung der Zeichnungen, East Berlin; the Musée Communal de la Louvière; the Musée de l'Art Russe; the Musée du Louvre; the Museum für Kunst und Kulturgeschichte der Hansestadt, Lübeck; the National Gallery of Parma; the Pitti Gallery, Florence; the Rheinisches Landesmuseum, Trier; the Russian Museum, Leningrad; Schloss Charlottenburg, Preussische Kunstsammlung; the Staatliche Kunstsammlungen,

Dresden; the Staatliche Museen of the German Democratic Republic; the Städelsches Kunstinstitut, Frankfurt on Main; the Stadtgeschichtliches Museum, Düsseldorf; the Tretyakov Gallery, Moscow; the Vatican, Rome; and the Wallraf-Richartz-Museum, Cologne.

# Introduction

Most works published as studies of Marxist Aesthetics to date have either been concerned with applying Marx's theories to the narrative arts, or have taken a text-orientated approach to his comments on aesthetic theory. Very few of these works have, however, spoken of his contribution to aesthetic theory in relation to the visual arts of his own time. When the name of Marx has been called upon in discussions of the visual arts from a viewpoint other than that of narrative theory it has been largely in the context of the twentieth-century debate between Socialist Realism and Modernism, where again little notice has been taken of what Marx actually saw or thought of the visual arts.

In contrast to other studies, this book will attempt both to open up a new field of inquiry into what it was that Marx himself saw of the visual arts in nineteenth-century Germany, France, and England, and to ask how information gained from such an investigation may affect current as well as earlier twentieth-century views on what Marx's aesthetic theory might have been.

While the method used here is directed above all towards uncovering the historical background to Marx's treatment of the visual arts, it is also concerned with rescuing from oblivion a much-overlooked set of concepts in his work relevant to an understanding of his aesthetic theory. At this point that set of concepts may be broadly described as being based in the Saint-Simonist concept of art as an 'avant-garde' part of modern production able to lead, rather than simply reflect, social development.

Following on from the analysis in Part 1 of both this concept and of the visual arts in Marx's time, this avant-garde, 'productivist' theory of art is then traced forward to the early twentieth century, to its revival by those early Soviet artists of the 1920s known as the 'Constructivists', whose work was aimed at uniting art, science, and technology for the purpose of creating a socially useful and innovative form of artistic

1

production.[1] Given the large amount of documentation recently published on the art of the Russian avant-garde of the 1920s, less emphasis is put in this section of the book on illustrating the work of these artists than in the earlier section on Marx, where artists are spoken of who are not so familiar to us today. Instead emphasis is put on relating the lesser discussed theoretical bases of Soviet 'productivist' art to Marx's own 'lost' productivist aesthetic. This investigation of the theoretical links between the Constructivist avant-garde of the 1920s and Marx's 'lost' productivist aesthetic is also one which has of necessity to break new ground, since historians of Soviet art have generally assumed that Marx had legitimated not the avant-garde productivist artists of the 1920s but the Socialist Realism which displaced Constructivism from Soviet art history in the 1930s. While it will be introduced into Part 2 of this study in the context of analysing the fate of the avant-garde Constructivists and their theories, Soviet Socialist Realism will, however, also be related to the nineteenth-century visual art experienced by Marx in his native Germany, and its claims to be a Marxian Aesthetic will be critically reconsidered through an evaluation of those relations.

# PART ONE

# Visual art and aesthetic theory in Marx's early years

# 1

*Hellenes vs. Nazarenes*

The works of the Utopian socialist Saint-Simon, the Count Claude Henri de Rouvroy (1760–1825), had already been censored together with those of his Saint-Simonian disciples in Germany when Marx became acquainted with them in Trier in the mid 1830s.[1] Apart from being condemned in Trier itself by the Catholic Archbishop of Trier as morally subversive, Saint-Simonism was officially banned by a Federal German Diet in 1835 (in the wake of the 1830 revolutions which had spread out from Paris to threaten the German monarchic States) as dangerous to both the religious and moral well-being of the German nation. This was a ban which had arisen largely because Saint-Simonism had become associated in Germany in the 1830s with at least two kinds of emancipatory and potentially revolutionary programmes. The first of these was based on Saint-Simon's own attack on the feudal organisation of labour under modern industrialism, to which was related the idea that industrial labour could be emancipated from its outdated feudal controls by an avant-garde consisting of artists, scientists, and engineers. The second had to do with the quasi-religious ideas of 'Saint-Simonians' such as Enfantin who had attacked orthodox religion by speaking of the need for the 'liberation of the senses' and 'emancipation of the flesh' from the 'spiritualism' of Christian dogma.

Threatened by both kinds of Saint-Simonist demand for emancipation, the German monarchic States which had resisted reform in the early 1830s in the face of revolutions in France, Poland, and elsewhere, strengthened their censorship laws and combined to ban the import of the ideas which they saw as having contributed to the fall of the monarchy in France in 1830, and as being of danger to their own political power.

In addition to banning the works of Saint-Simon and his French disciples, the Federal German Diet of 1835 placed a ban on several German writers involved with Saint-Simonism or known to have introduced it to a German public. Amongst these German authors banned by the Federal Diet in 1835 was the writer who had perhaps done most to transmit the ideas of Saint-Simon and his school to Germany, the poet and essayist Heinrich Heine. As Georges Gurvitch writes,[2] Heine was one of several writers from whom the young Marx was to glean his knowledge of Saint-Simonism in the 1830s; others were the Trier socialist Ludwig Gall, whose *Was könnte helfen?* of 1825 had condemned the condition of the working classes in Germany, and the Berlin Hegelian Eduard Gans, whose *Rückblicke auf Personen und Zustände* of 1836 had praised the Saint-Simonians for criticising the continuing 'feudal' character of labour under industrialism.

It has already been recognised by critics that Marx developed this Saint-Simonist critique of the feudal nature of the relations of production under industrial capitalism in both his *Economic and Philosophic Manuscripts* of 1844 and the *German Ideology* of 1845–6. One purpose of this study, however, will be to show how, like Heine,[3] Marx can also be seen to have used the Saint-Simonist critique of modern feudalism together with its related concept of an alternative avant-garde in criticisms of the cultural politics then being practised by the Prussian monarchs of their time.[4]

For Heine, one of the most visible expressions of the existence of a feudal basis to the development of the artist in Prussia was the patronage given by the Prussian monarchs· Friedrich Wilhelm III (b. 1770, acc. 1797, d. 1840) and his son, Friedrich Wilhelm IV (b. 1795, acc. 1840, d. 1861) to the Romantic and 'Nazarene' artists who sought to revive the religious art of Germany's feudal Middle Ages. As, though rarely discussed now outside Germany, the German Nazarenes were the most influential group of painters working – and selling – in Marx's time in Prussia in the 1830s and 1840s, they are of central importance to an understanding of Marx's critique of the cultural politics of his time as well as to the description of other critiques, such as those given by Heine, which helped to form Marx's ideas on the patronage given to the arts in early nineteenth-century Prussia.

Founding members of the German Nazarene school, later given patronage by the Prussian monarchy in the 1830s, had included Franz Pforr, Friedrich Overbeck, Peter Cornelius, Rudolf and Wilhelm von Schadow, Friedrich Olivier, Philipp Veit, and Julius Schnorr von Carolsfeld. Although only later given the name 'Nazarenes', on account of the long hair which they had grown in the manner of their admired Dürer's Christ-like *Self-Portrait* of 1500, these artists had originally called themselves the 'Lukasbrüder', or 'Brethren of Saint Luke',

1. Albrecht Dürer, *Self-Portrait*, 1500 (Bayerische Staatsgemälde-sammlung, Munich, Alte Pinakothek)

To the German Nazarenes the work of Dürer and of other German and Flemish painters of the late Middle Ages reflected an age uncorrupted by religious dissent and represented an art free of the corrupt 'virtuosity' of the late Renaissance and after.

because, according to apocryphal tales, the Evangelist had himself been an artist and had therefore been made patron-saint to mediaeval art guilds.

Inspired by the Middle Ages, and by the life led by its monks, the 'Lukasbrüder' had taken up residence in a former Franciscan monastery, known as San' Isidoro, near Rome, in 1810. While studying the work of the masters of the early Italian Renaissance from their Roman monastery they maintained their interest in the art of Dürer, Cranach, and the Flemish artists of the late Middle Ages. Apart from their artistic value, the Middle Ages were particularly important to the German Nazarenes as a time before the Reformation in which art, religion, and life 'had been one'. In this romanticised view of Germany's past they followed the ideas and beliefs of the German Romantics, Novalis, Friedrich and August Schlegel, Tieck, and Wackenroder, the author of a work on the visions of an 'art-loving monk' which is supposed to have inspired them in their 'monk-like' life-style. Like these Romantic writers, the German Nazarenes also converted to Catholicism (if not already Catholic) as a sign of their faith in the Catholic Church as a symbol of the unity between art, life, religion, and State, which they considered to have been lost to Germany by its Protestant Reformation.

Peter Cornelius had been one of the first of the 'Lukasbrüder' to imitate the religious art of Germany's Middle Ages; he had been introduced to it by the Boisserée brothers, Sulpiz and Melchior, in 1803 before joining Pforr's group of artists in Rome. Apart from being shown the work of Dürer and Cranach by the Boisserées, Cornelius may also have seen the altar-pieces (then attributed to van Eyck) by Rogier van der Weyden which Goethe describes seeing in the Boisserée collection in Heidelberg in 1816, and from which he singles out for description a panel showing Saint Luke painting a portrait of the Madonna and Christ-child. Like this Saint Luke the German Nazarenes, or 'Brethren of Saint Luke', were, of course, to become famous for their paintings of the Madonna, while two at least – Steinle and Sutter – are also known to have painted her being sketched by Saint Luke himself.

Cornelius was to become one of the most successful of the German Nazarenes, commissioned by Ludwig of Bavaria and the Prussian monarchs Friedrich Wilhelm III and Friedrich Wilhelm IV to decorate palaces and public buildings with murals and frescoes. One further example of the favours bestowed upon Cornelius by the Prussian Court was that he had been appointed to the Directorship of the Düsseldorf Academy of Art in 1819. From here he was, though often absent elsewhere on commissions, to influence the growth of a Nazarene

2. Franz Pforr, *Raphael, Fra Angelico and Michelangelo on a Cloud above Rome* (Städelsches Kunstinstitut, Frankfurt on Main; photographer, Ursula Edelmann)

Three of the Italian painters admired by the German Nazarenes – Raphael, Fra Angelico, and Michelangelo – are depicted together on a cloud above Rome in this pencil-sketch by Franz Pforr. (Pforr also used the sepia-coloured paper used by Raphael and Michelangelo for their sketches for his drawing of them.)

school of painters who would be visited by artists from as far afield as
Russia, and who would dominate the German art world during the years
in which the young Marx was developing his theories of artistic and
economic production.

As suggested earlier, one of the writers who was both to influence the
development of the young Marx, and who was able (as a resident of
Düsseldorf) to observe the rise of the Nazarene school of painters at first

3. Peter Cornelius, *The Holy Family*, 1809–11 (Städelsches Kunstinstitut, Frankfurt on Main)

hand, was Heinrich Heine. Like Marx, Heine was at that time a subject of the Prussian State whose patronage the Nazarenes enjoyed (the Rhineland had been made a Prussian territory in 1815) and also had, according to his own account, been taught drawing in his youth by Lambert Cornelius, the elder brother of the Nazarene, Peter Cornelius. The subject of Prussian censorship rather than patronage, Heine later made several criticisms of the Nazarenes in his *Reisebilder*, in particular in the descriptions of a journey which he had made from Munich to Italy in the years 1828 and 1829. In the first of these *Reisebilder*, the *Reise von München nach Genua* of 1828, for example, he condemned the 'spiritualism' of Cornelius' pictures by describing them as so mournful that they looked as if they had been painted on a Good Friday.[5] To Heine Cornelius had resurrected the fifteenth century in the nineteenth as well as a 'sadness unto death'.[6] By 1828 Heine had, moreover, already come into contact with the ideas of Saint-Simon and the Saint-Simonians which he was to champion explicitly in the 1830s from his exile in Paris. From the point of view of his Saint-Simonian sensualism, he then dubbed the German Nazarenes 'spiritualists' on account both of their choice of religious subject-matter for their art, and of their attempts to thwart progress by reviving a feudal age antipathetic to the goals of nineteenth-century socialism. In wanting to return to the Middle Ages, the Nazarenes were, in Heine's opinion, denying all the principles of progress defended in Saint-Simonian theory as well as Saint-Simon's concept of avant-garde.

This concept of the artist as an avant-garde leader of men was particularly important to Heine as a writer who had been prevented by censorship from publishing in his own country; but it was also a concept which had originally, in the writings of Saint-Simon, represented a subversion of the traditional feudal hierarchy of leadership by replacing the leadership of King and Court with that of a union of artists, scientists, and 'industrialists'. As early as 1802,[7] in his 'Lettres d'un habitant de Genève à ses contemporains', Saint-Simon had included artists and scientists amongst those marching 'under the standard of the progress of the human mind', and had addressed some of them as the 'vanguard' of society as a whole:

> Scientists, artists, and all those of you who devote some of your power and resources to the progress of enlightenment: you are the section of humanity with the greatest intellectual energy, the section most able to appreciate a new idea, and most directly interested in the subscription's success. It is up to you to defeat the force of inertia. So mathematicians; as you are the vanguard, begin![8]

Even here, while specifically designating mathematicians as his vanguard, Saint-Simon spoke of scientists and artists in one breath as the leaders and protectors of their contemporaries, the class of property-owners, and what are then vaguely described as 'all others'. Following this early vagueness the concept of 'avant-garde' finally put forward by Saint-Simon was one specified as designating a vanguard of 'producers' involved in the spiritual leadership, as also in the actual construction of 'the new society'. So Saint-Simon wrote in his *Le Politique* on April 1819: 'Artists should also be considered as industrialists, as they are producers in many respects and among them they contribute greatly to the prosperity of our manufacturers by the designs and models with which they furnish the artisans.[9] Some six months later Saint-Simon wrote in the first part of his *L'Organisateur* of 1819 (the so-called 'Parabole politique'), that artists were also to be counted amongst the most essential 'producers' of society because they could make products of use as well as of aesthetic value.[10]

For this reason too artists were initially described as both 'producteurs' and 'industrielles' by Saint-Simon,[11] and were placed in the 'Chambre d'invention' at the head of his administrative pyramid, together with engineers and architects. There were in fact to be 200 engineers, 50 poets, 25 painters, 15 sculptors or architects, and 10 musicians in the 'Chambre d'invention' – a balance indicative of the emphasis placed on engineering in Saint-Simonism, and of how engineering was (in France at least) to become synonymous with the more successful and serious of the Saint-Simonians.

In arguing that artists too had an important role to play in developing the economic productivity of a nation, Saint-Simon was also echoing – though, as will be seen later, with some reservations – the Smithian, even Mercantilist,[12] ideas of the eighteenth century, which had seen art justified as having commercial possibilities in terms of both its own monetary exchange value and its value in improving the design and marketing of other commercial goods. As a part of his avant-garde of producers, artists were, however (in contrast to Mercantile theory) to play the further role of reforming the feudal nature of the relations of production which Saint-Simon saw the Jacobins of his time as having failed to reform. Given that Saint-Simon had called politics a 'science of production', this role of the artist-producer in reforming the vestigial feudal character taken on by labour in modern industrial societies was also to be a 'political' role. As leaders of the administration of his ideal society artists were furthermore to fulfil the ethical function of achieving greater social cohesion and happiness by assisting in the general economic productivity and well-being of their society. In addition to fulfilling the latter role, they were to use their artistic talents to 'hymn' the benefits of the new golden age to those who were not yet converted to their vision and purpose:

> They [the artists, the men of imagination] will lead the way in that great undertaking; they will proclaim the future of mankind; they will bring back the golden age from the past to enrich future generations; they will inspire society with enthusiasm for the increase of its well-being by laying before it a tempting picture of a new prosperity, by making it feel that all members of society will soon share in enjoyments which, up to now, have been the prerogative of a very small class; they will hymn the benefits of civilization and they will employ all other resources of fine arts, eloquence, poetry, painting, music, to attain their goal; in short, they will develop the poetic aspects of the new system.[13]

In contrast to this Utopian Saint-Simonist concept of the artist as producer, administrator, and moral guide, Heine saw the artist treated in his native Germany either as a servant or as a rebel to be silenced or banned. In fact, the year of Cornelius' appointment to the Directorship of the Düsseldorf Academy by the Prussian government had also seen the imposition by the latter of the notoriously strict 'Karlsbader Beschlüsse' or 'Carlsbad Decrees'. Although these were originally aimed at controlling radicalism within the universities, they were applied more broadly in the 1820s to the publication of works by authors critical of Prussia. The censorship introduced by the decrees, and regularly renewed thereafter through the 1820s, was also to help drive Heine into exile in Paris in 1831. As several of his works were banned in 1835 together with the philosophy of the French Saint-Simonians as endangering the 'moral safety' of the populace, it is perhaps not surprising that Heine was then to combine his support for the ideas of Saint-Simon and his followers with an opposition to both the Prussian censor and to those, who, like the German Nazarenes, enjoyed his protection.[14]

Apart from being based in his dislike of the Prussian system of patronage and in his contrary belief in the avant-garde role of the artist, Heine's criticism of the German Nazarenes was grounded in a Saint-Simonian antipathy to orthodox Christianity as both a feudal and an anti-materialist, spiritualistic philosophy. The catch-cry of the French Saint-Simonians of the 1820s had been that of the 'liberation of the flesh', by which was meant, amongst other things, the liberation of philosophy from theology, of materialism from spiritualism, and of sensualism from puritanism. Such a philosophical programme was clearly anathema to the Christian Prussian State, as well as antipathetic to the Idealist philosophy which at that time dominated its universities. As both an erstwhile student of Hegel (the Professor of Philosophy in Berlin from 1818 until his death in 1831, and the then doyen of German Idealist thought), and a follower of Saint-Simonism, Heine was able, however, on moving to Paris in 1831, to take up the role of intermediary between the Saint-Simonians in Paris and the Hegelians in Germany and to suggest a new and radical 'Saint-Simonian' reading of Hegel. The result of this new reading was, further, to translate Hegel's Idealist concept of progress into a more materialist concept, and his support of Romantic art into a 'Hellenistic' criticism of the same.

In his *Aesthetics* Hegel had traced the realisation of Spirit in the arts through the symbolic, classical, and Romantic stages of their development, and argued that in the symbolic stage there had been an 'abstract agreement' between form and idea, in the classical a harmony between the idea and its external manifestation, and in the Romantic, subjective period of art, the 'internalisation' of the idea in its coming to consciousness of itself. (Rationalism, as characterised by the Enlightenment, was excluded from the history of art by Hegel by virtue of its 'repression of imagery'.) Although his view of classical art could be said to have reflected Winckelmann's view that Greek art has represented a harmonisation of form and an 'edle Einfalt und stille Grösse', Hegel had also characterised the Greeks as limited by their 'bondage' through the senses to the physical world. Where Greek art was contrasted with Romantic in Hegel's *Aesthetics*, the Hellenic spirit was furthermore contrasted with the 'Judaic' spirit in his *Philosophy of History*, and the Judaic described as 'free of the sensuous' and as a spirit in which Nature is 'reduced to something merely external', while the Hellenic was described as existing in 'freedom of Spirit . . . conditioned by . . . some stimulus supplied by Nature'.

Although also critical of many of the Romantic artists and writers of his own time (he had criticised an 1828 exhibition of the Düsseldorf school of Nazarene artists in volume 3/3/3/1 of his *Vorlesungen über die Ästhetik* as too sentimental in its attempts to be poetic), Hegel had further described 'Romantic' art in general as representing the culmination of the history of art in his *Lectures on Aesthetics*, and praised many of the older examples of religious 'Romantic' art from the German Middle Ages and the Italian Renaissance. Hegel had also learnt much of what he knew of German and Flemish religious painting from Sulpiz and Melchior Boisserée, who were (in the early 1820s) in the process of making a collection of art for Friedrich Wilhelm III's new Berlin museum. These were the brothers who (as mentioned earlier) had already introduced the modern Romantic artist, the Nazarene painter Peter Cornelius, to their pieces of mediaeval German and Flemish art, and whose collection Goethe had described seeing in Heidelberg in 1816. The wide influence of these brothers may also be discerned in the fact that Hegel, in his *Lectures on Aesthetics,* followed Goethe's praise for Rogier van der Weyden's *Annunciation* with a laudatory description of that artist's *Three Kings Altar* (both were then attributed to van Eyck), as one of the best works of early German/Flemish 'Romantic' art yet seen by him.

It was, however, Raphael – idol of the German Nazarenes as also of

4. Lithograph by Johann Nepomuk Strixner, 1830, of the centre panel of a *Three Kings Altar* attributed to Rogier van der Weyden (Goethe-Museum, Düsseldorf)

their royal patrons, the Prussian monarchs Friedrich Wilhelm III and Friedrich Wilhelm IV – to whom Hegel gave his greatest accolade in his *Lectures,* by naming Raphael's madonnas as the most expressive pieces of Romantic art known to him and as the works in which Raphael had achieved the most beautiful representation of the Divine ever to have been made in the visual arts.

While to Hegel Raphael's madonnas had represented the high-point of Romantic and modern art because of their achievement in representing Ideal forms behind the everyday, phenomenal world, Heine rejected such art as reactionary. Thus, in his *Romantische Schule* of 1836, Heine attacked his teacher Hegel's defence of a spiritualistic subjective Romantic art as the culmination of art history as well as the Romantics of his time, whom he saw as having been wrongly justified by such aesthetics. Heine's criticism of the Romantic School of 1836 was, furthermore, one of those works in which he explicitly defended his own 'sensualistic' Saint-Simonian concept of the artist as avant-garde critic of the retrograde and spiritualistic in art and described the sensualism of Hellenistic art in Saint-Simonian terms as representing a higher form of art than that of the spiritualistic Romantics and Nazarenes.

Later (in his *Ludwig Börne* of 1841) Heine extended his use of the term 'Nazarene' to describe all those spiritualists of history whom he regarded as being opposed to the 'Hellenistic' ideals of freedom of expression and sensuous beauty. This use of the categories of Hellene and Nazarene, which was so opposed to the use made of them by Hegel in his comparison of the Judaic and the Hellenic, has been found again in the work of the Victorian critic Matthew Arnold. Heine himself, however, was to claim a few years later (in 1844), that the synthesis of Hegelian and Saint-Simonian ideas which he had made in the 1830s had influenced the Left Hegelian Bruno Bauer to develop his 'esoteric' reading of Hegel as a radical Hellenistic Jacobin, and to deny the 'official' or 'orthodox' Hegel who had defended Romanticism against Hellenism and the Prussian State against political Jacobinism. As Bauer's reinterpretation of Hegel as a 'radical Jacobin' was the subject of his 1842 tract on Christian art and religion for which Marx was asked to write, this reinterpretation of Hegel through Saint-Simonism by Heine is also relevant to an understanding of the background to Marx's and Bauer's critiques of Christian art and religion of the early 1840s. Because those critiques were concerned with the analysis of the visual arts, it is, however, also important to note that Heine had already suggested a synthesis of Hegelian and Saint-Simonian ideas in a review of the art of

5. Raphael, *Sistine Madonna*, 1513–14 (Staatliche Kunstsammlungen, Dresden)

Years before actually seeing it in Dresden in 1820 Hegel had received an engraving of the painting from the pupils of the Nuremberg 'Gymnasium' where he taught between 1808 and 1816.

the Paris Salon of 1831, in which he not only criticises the 'spiritualistic' religious art made popular in Germany through the work of the Nazarenes, but also contrasts it with the 'sensualistic' revolutionary art of French painters celebrating the July Revolution of 1830.

According to his own reports Heine had first visited the Paris Salon of 1831 in July, on the anniversary of the July Revolution of 1830; and it is above all his description of Delacroix's representation of that revolution in his *La Liberté guidant le peuple* (fig. 6) as a 'sensualistic', Saint-Simonian celebration of progress, in which Heine's attempt to translate the Hegelian concept of progress as the progress of Reason to greater self-consciousness into the Saint-Simonian concept of progress can best be seen, even though it is not explicitly but only metaphorically made there.

Whereas to Hegel history was to be understood as the progress of Reason to greater self-consciousness of itself (and Romantic art therefore the culmination of the history of art), the Saint-Simonist concept of progress was of progress towards greater material harmony and well-being, while the role of the artist was conceived of as the avant-garde introduction of that progress.[15] In addition, the Saint-Simonian conception of progress entailed the liberation of the senses and the translation of Idealist and spiritualistic theories of human society into materialistic concepts. It is therefore interesting to note in Heine's description of Delacroix's *Liberty* an emphasis on the 'sensualistic' character of Delacroix's celebration of revolution, which serves to translate the Hegelian symbol of the progress of Reason through history, the winged messenger Hermes,[16] into the more sensualistic image of Liberty as a 'winged messenger of love', and at the same time rejects the call of German Idealist aesthetics for a 'disinterested', self-reflexive form of art in favour of a Saint-Simonian concept of art as both the depiction and vehicle of avant-garde reform.

Describing Delacroix's Liberty as both a Venus and a Phryne or prostitute (in terms which echo Johann Jakob Wilhelm Heinse's description of the Venus di Medici as a Lais or Phryne,[17] as well as a passage from Hegel's *Aesthetics*[18]), Heine wrote:

> A great Thought approaches us from this picture. A crowd of people from the July days is represented, and in the middle, almost like an allegorical figure, a young woman rises up, a red Phrygian cap on her head, a rifle in one hand and a tricolour in the other. She strides over corpses, calling to battle, naked to her hips, a beautiful wild body, her face a brave profile, courageous suffering in its features, a strange

6. Eugène Delacroix, *Liberty Guiding the People*, 1831 (Musée du Louvre)

mixture of Phryne, fish-wife, and the goddess of Liberty. It is not quite explicit that she should represent the last; she seems much more to express the wild energy of the people, who are throwing off a heavy burden. I can't but confess that she reminds me of those peripatetic philosophresses and those winged messengers of love ('Schnellläuferin- nen der Liebe') or winged lovers ('Schnellliebende') who crowd the boulevards in the evening. I confess that the little chimney-cupid, who, with a pistol in each hand, stands next to this Venus of the streets, is perhaps not just dirtied by soot, and that the candidate for the Pantheon lying dead on the ground has perhaps spent the previous night dealing in counter-marks at the theatre . . .[19]

In contrast to the sad madonnas described in his *Stadt Lucca* a year earlier,[20] Heine's description of Delacroix's Liberty has made of her a 'Venus of the streets' who is the embodiment of the Saint-Simonian concept of the 'liberation of the senses' as well as of political liberation. In addition, Heine's praise for the sensualistic character of Delacroix's painting (for its colouristic qualities as well as for its depiction of the goddess of Liberty as a 'goddess of love') rejects the Idealist concept of an art which would transcend the sensual depiction of material reality for a sensualistic and political art aimed not at the perfection of a modern feudal State (as Hegel had suggested was a goal of the history of Spirit) but its overthrow. In that Hegel had argued that the history or development of art would also cease with the perfection of the State, Heine's choice of a Saint-Simonist aesthetic, with its emphasis on the avant-garde function of the artist, was that of an artist interested in preserving the freedom of his profession rather than in justifying its subjugation to State patronage or in approving its elimination.

In praising the sensualism of Delacroix's Liberty Heine not only repudiated Hegel's idea that the senses could bind an artist too closely to the material world, but also implicitly rejected the Idealist aesthetic views of Kant, who had both defined art as having to be free of any 'Tendenz' or political interest, and asked of it that it be able to liberate the subject from the limits placed upon his reason by his senses. In connection with these arguments Kant had written that while colour might be counted as belonging to the 'charm' of the work of art, and as 'enlivening the object for sensation', it alone could not be made worthy of 'contemplation', or 'beautiful',[21] and had added that the appreciation of painting, sculpture and architecture was not dependent upon that which 'gratifies in sensation', but upon that which 'pleases by means of its form'.

In his comments on Delacroix's *Liberté* Heine both praised its sensuous colouring and satirised the fears of his German audience that an art which would neither follow the classical rules of Idealist aesthetics nor avoid political content would lead to the destruction of a moral form of art as well as to the undermining of public morality in general:

> 'Papa', called a little Carlist, 'who is the dirty woman in the red cap?' 'Well, obviously', mocked the noble Papa with a sickly smile, 'well obviously, dear child, she has nothing to do with the purity of the lilies. It is the goddess of Liberty.' 'Papa, she doesn't even have on a blouse.' 'A true goddess of Liberty, my child, usually has no blouse, and is therefore very jealous of all people who wear clean linen.'

The moral condemnation of Delacroix's painting which Heine mocks, in this conversation between a Carlist and his child, as part of his satire on the Carlists who had been dispossessed of power by the July Revolution of 1830 (and who were, therefore, critical of its glorification by artists such as Delacroix) is also a parody of aristocratic and bourgeois art journals of the time which had condemned Delacroix's Liberty as a crude and unaesthetic figure. One article in the *Journal des Artistes et des Amateurs*, of 15 May 1831,[22] for example, had already condemned 'La Liberté', in terms similar to those put into the mouths of the Carlist and his child by Heine, as an indecent and dirty figure. As Heine was aware, the aristocrat's condemnation of Delacroix's Liberty as indecent might, however, have been equally applicable to the Venuses favoured by the artists of the *ancien régime*. Indeed Heine later wrote in the 1833 Postscript to his *Französische Maler* that another contemporary, de Maynard, had joked that the artists of the *ancien régime* had been surprised 'en négligé' by the revolution of 1789. (The bourgeois ethic which was responsible for the condemnation put by Heine into the mouths of the dispossessed aristocracy in 1831 was of course to survive well into the twentieth century – producing such ironies as the nineteenth-century American demand that reproductions of the Venus de Milo only be let into the home after being renamed 'The Goddess of Liberty', while in Montreal in 1927 a reproduction of the *Venus de Milo* used on a Palmolive soap poster was censored by a white patch across the breast, in accord with 'local censorship regulations'.[23])

One reason for Heine's attribution of a moralising and perhaps inappropriately 'bourgeois' prudery to the dispossessed Carlists in 1831 was that their opposition to the July Revolution of 1830 was for him, as a Saint-Simonian, an opposition to an anti-feudal but also 'sensualistic' and anti-puritanical revolution. Further to this, Heine described both aristocrats and Jesuits as spiritualistic opponents to that revolution in 1831, and also warned that just as they had once attempted to mask sensualism (in the manner, described by Gibbon and others, of the early Church's masking of the pagan gods), now they were themselves using that revolution as a mask, behind which they could conceal their true 'spiritualism' and antipathy to the freedoms granted in 1830, while also biding their time until the restoration of their power.

While in his 1831 report on the Salon Heine thus described a Jesuit 'masked' in secular dress amongst the viewers of Delacroix's *Liberty* as a warning that her liberty was still under threat, his 1833 Postscript to that report commented on how Louis Philippe and his bourgeois cabinet had themselves begun the masking of the revolution which had ensured them their place in government, and how the paintings inspired by July 1830 had already begun to disappear from the eye of the French public.

Significantly, the images used by Heine to condemn the 'masking' of the July Revolution by Louis Philippe in his 1833 Postscript are also those of a 'Hellene'. Asking how the art of democratic Greece could have survived in a situation similar to that being created by the July monarchy in France, Heine ironically suggested that the Spartacus statue standing in the gardens of the Tuileries should be immediately covered, in order to protect it from the inclement 'weather' which was to come. Using the word 'beschirmt' to suggest the idea of protection, Heine ironically indicated that the protection (or 'masking') to be given Spartacus by Louis Philippe (who was inevitably characterised by Heine – as by Daumier and other caricaturists of the time – as carrying the umbrella or 'Schirm' which had come to symbolise the bourgeois monarch) would in fact not be conducive to its survival, or to the survival of the revolutionary spirit and art it had come to represent. Similarly, the unfinished building of the Tuileries themselves is taken by Heine as a symbol of the unfinished work of the July monarchy which had in his view become more concerned with the building of street barricades (demanded from Louis Philippe by the Holy Alliance as an insurance against further revolution in France), than with the support of the new artistic and architectural programmes begun in the days following the revolution of 1830. For the Saint-Simonian Heine the end of those artistic and architectural programmes was representative of the July monarchy's growing suppression of the Utopian spirit of 1830, his 1833 Postscript to his Salon report of 1831 describing this as a 'counter-revolution from within' which had been accompanied by yet another Romantic spiritualisation of the sensualistic art of 1830–31.

Noting a return of the spiritualistic religious painting he had thought eliminated in 1831, and that the 1833 Salon had been hung so as to conceal the permanent exhibition of classical Greek and Roman art, Heine compared the Salon itself to a 'codex palimpsestus', a 'written-over text', in which the sensualism of former years was being masked, just as the revolution of 1830 was being masked in its 'cabinet' by its former political protagonists. Whereas in 1831 Heine had described artists such as Delacroix, Delaroche and Robert as having given the revolution 'flesh and blood' in their art (a copy of Delaroche's portrayal of Cromwell viewing the body of Charles I, described by Heine in his Salon report of 1831, was later to be one of the first works of Western art exhibited by the Soviets of 1917), he now, in 1833, saw the revolutionary artists of 1831 retreat from their revolutionary themes and return to the safer ground of religious history. Commenting on how the Salon had been reduced to self-caricature, Heine concluded his Postscript with a reference to a satirical but also cynically self-parodistic picture by Decamps of a monkey painting a historical scene. To Heine this picture not only represented the reduction of the revolutionary art of the Salon of 1831 to self-caricature, but also served as a reminder of the progress of those 'other long-haired artists', the spiritualistic German Nazarenes,[24] whom he had criticised earlier in his travel-sketches of 1828. Significantly, these Nazarenes were now enjoying the patronage of both the German Court and Prussia's ally the Tsar of Russia, who had, with the other members of the Holy Alliance, Prussia and Austria, demanded from Louis Philippe that he fortify Paris with the street barricades which Heine had described as having helped to divert the patronage of the State from earlier, more 'revolutionary', art projects.[25] It was, as will be discussed presently, for similar political reasons that Young Hegelians of the 1840s such as Marx were also to turn their attention to the increasing patronage given by their native Prussia to the religious art against which Heine had warned in the 1820s and 1830s.

# 2

## Feuerbach and the 'Nazarene' madonna

Heine's 1833 Postscript to his reports on the Salon of 1831 had, as we have seen, concluded with a reference to the growing strength of the German Nazarenes, whose neo-mediaeval and pseudo-religious art he had attacked in his Italian travel-sketches of the late 1820s. Although his criticisms of the Nazarenes were well known, Heine was, however, not the only writer known to the young Marx to have condemned the spiritualism of the German Nazarene School favoured by the Prussian monarchy in the 1830s, and to have done so with reference to the feudal politics of the latter and in defiance of the officially approved Idealist aesthetics of the time. One other critic of the Nazarene painters of madonnas to write in the 1830s, before Marx had begun his own critique of Christian art and religion, was the socialist writer Hermann Püttmann. Püttmann had been a friend of the young Engels in the late 1830s but was referred to later by Marx and Engels with some sarcasm in their *German Ideology* of 1845–6 as a 'True Socialist'. His *Düsseldorfer Malerschule*, published by Otto Wigand in Leipzig in 1839, had – while praising the followers of the more socially critical Düsseldorf artists Lessing and Bendemann – criticised the sentimental followers of Cornelius and Schadow who were still obsessed with painting the madonna and winged angels.

Püttmann's criticisms of such works, as sentimental and ridiculous attempts at reviving a form of religious art inappropriate to the modern nineteenth-century world, furthermore echo not only Heine's attacks on the Nazarenes, but the philosopher Ludwig Feuerbach's 1833 criticism of the false consciousness at work in the painting of madonnas. Feuerbach had written in a note in his *Geschichte der neueren Philosophie* of 1833 to his introductory comments on mediaeval art:

> Art is only apparently holy because her devotion is only an illusion;
> because while she is appearing to serve the Church, she is only working

7. Christian Köhler, *Poetry*, 1838 (Kaiser Wilhelm Museum, Krefeld)
Christian Köhler's allegory of Poetry of 1838 was based on an
imitation of Raphael's fresco by the then leader of the Düsseldorf
Nazarenes, Wilhelm von Schadow, and was itself imitated by other
Nazarenes. Püttmann wrote scathingly of Köhler's *Poetry* in 1839:
'*Poetry* is sitting – yes, she is sitting, even though she has wings, and
she is sitting on clouds . . .'

in her own interest. The artist who, for example, makes the Virgin the object of his art, treats her as an art object and no longer as an object of religion. In addition he will not have had the courage, the strength, the freedom, to let her out of the sacristy of his religious conviction and imagination, to externalise her out of the secretive, unspeakable realm of religious faith into the realm of the profane and the sensuous and actually make the beloved of his heart into a sensual pleasure-loving woman . . .

The comments made by Feuerbach in this footnote are ones which could apply to the art of his time – and especially to the madonna pictures of the Nazarenes – as much as to mediaeval art. In addition, they attack a basic assumption of Romantic aesthetics, that the artist should serve religion; a view put forward, for example, by the Romantic Friedrich Schlegel,[1] one of the earliest patrons of the German Nazarene artists, and stepfather to one of their number, Philipp Veit.

Whereas the Romantic Friedrich Schlegel had regarded art as the expression of a religious spirit in man, and Hegel had seen the religious paintings of Raphael and other 'Romantic' artists as the expression of a 'World Spirit' in human history, Feuerbach was to suggest in his *Essence of Christianity* of 1841 that man's 'sensuous human essence' is both expressed and alienated from him in the religious art of the Christian world.[2] Seen against the background of the Romantic and Hegelian defences of religious painting – as also against the background of the official patronage given the Nazarenes of his time – Feuerbach's emphasis in his *Essence of Christianity* on the importance of the visual character, or *Bildlichkeit*, of Western religion in the alienation of the human subject is also of importance as a clue to both the anti-Romantic, and anti-Hegelian, character of his criticism of Christianity. It is also important as an indication of the anti-Prussian critique entailed in the latter, which was to make the *Essence of Christianity* of use to both Bauer and Marx in their criticism of Prussia in the early 1840s and, in particular, in their 1842 attempts to offer a radical Left-Hegelian reinterpretation of Hegel's support for the Christian world and its arts.

To Feuerbach the anthropomorphic image of God offered by contemporary Christianity and its forebears could be seen both as a 'mirror of man' – as religion in general was to be seen as a 'mirroring of the human essence'[3] – and as an alienation of the human to an unreal and spiritualised realm of illusion. The *Bildlichkeit* of Western religion was therefore not only that which distinguished religion from philosophy,[4] but was also that part of the 'false consciousness' which made the alienated religious mind incapable of understanding its basis

8. Philipp Veit's *Introduction of the Arts into Germany through Religion*, completed between 1834 and 1836 (Städelsches Kunstinstitut, Frankfurt on Main) depicts the arts as a Raphaelesque madonna, and the Church as her patron. Another version of the theme was completed by Joseph Führich in 1846.

9. Friedrich Overbeck, *Triumph of Religion in the Arts* (Städelsches Kunstinstitut, Frankfurt on Main)

Like Veit's allegory of the *Introduction of the Arts into Germany through Religion* of 1836, Friedrich Overbeck's *Triumph of Religion in the Arts* of 1831–40 exemplified the ideal relationship between religion and the arts spoken of by Friedrich Schlegel. Though based on the form of Raphael's *Disputà*, Overbeck's allegory also has a madonna and child as its centrepiece.

in the material life of the human subject. For Feuerbach, as later for Marx and Engels, both Christianity and its art were to be understood as entailing an alienation of the human being from his sensuous, material 'species-being', and from the consciousness of his material existence.[5]

In addition to criticising the *Bildlichkeit* of the Christian religion Feuerbach elaborated on the criticism of the madonna paintings which he had made in 1833, and related them explicitly to his criticism of the alienation of human sensuality by the spiritualising *Bildlichkeit* of Christian thought:

> The monks praised modesty and repressed sexual love, but in place of that they had in heaven, in God, in the Virgin Mary, the image of woman – an image of love. They could do without real women the more an ideal imagined woman was the object of real love. The more meaning they placed on the negation of sensuality, the greater was the meaning of the Virgin Mary for them: she came to stand in the place of Christ, in the place of God. *The more the sensual is denied, the more sensual is the God, to whom the sensual is sacrificed* . . .[6]

Given the fame of the Nazarenes and the infamy of critics of their work such as Heine, it is interesting to speculate on how much Feuerbach may have been thinking of the brightly-coloured though doleful and 'spiritualised' madonnas of the Nazarene school then popular in Protestant Prussia when writing of how the monks had transferred their repressed sensuality to sensuous images of the Madonna. Many of the Nazarenes had, as already stated, become famous for their 'madonna-like' portraits and monk-life life-style.[7] They were, as mentioned in chapter 1, also believed to have been inspired in both their art and life-style by Wackenroder's romanticised account of the thoughts and visions of an art-loving monk in his *Herzensergiessungen eines kunstliebenden Klosterbruders* of 1796, where they would have heard the monk describe both the vision of the Madonna that Raphael is said to have had and a dream vision which he himself has had of Raphael and Dürer.[8]

The connection made by Feuerbach in 1841 between the spiritualised madonnas of the Christian Church and the repression of human sensuality had also been made by Heine in his *Stadt Lucca* of 1829–30. There, Heine had followed his description of the Nazarene art of his time as a pale imitation of its Italian Renaissance models[9] and a description of a Renaissance madonna as a 'Venus dolorosa'[10] with an ironic humanisation and revivification of a painted madonna as a real, flesh-and-blood woman,[11] and had then given an explicit criticism of 'anthropomorphic religion' in a manner which foreshadows Feuerbach's criticisms of the same in the 1830s and 1840s.[12] Later, in his verse satire *Atta Troll* of 1842, Heine further explicitly mentioned Feuerbach as one of those 'atheists' who (like himself) had described religion as an anthropomorphic projection of its believer's own human characteristics on to a supernatural being.[13]

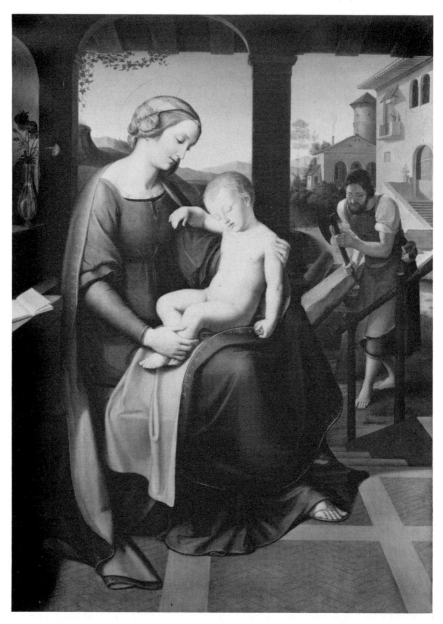

10. Wilhelm von Schadow, *The Holy Family beneath the Portico*, 1818 (Bayerische Staatsgemäldesammlung, Munich, Neue Pinakothek)

One of the most popular of the Nazarene 'madonnas' of its time.

Later still Engels was to comment on the political significance and contemporary relevance of Feuerbach's *Essence of Christianity* in his *Ludwig Feuerbach and the Outcome of Classical German Philosophy* of 1888. According to Engels the theological critiques written by Feuerbach and by Young Hegelians such as Bruno Bauer in 1840–1 had been in answer to the policy, taken up and put into practice by Friedrich Wilhelm IV on his assumption of the Prussian throne in 1840, of support for the pietists and ultramontanists opposed in theory and academic debate by the Young Hegelians. The continuing philosophical opposition of the Young Hegelians after 1842 to the officially legitimated theories of the Prussian monarchy had, so Engels writes, also concealed a politically radical bourgeois opposition to the feudal powers still dominant in Prussia at that time.

As a materialist Feuerbach also differed from those Hegelians (both 'Left' and 'Right') who had retained an Idealist belief in the primacy of criticism over political or social change; and his criticism of Christianity is not one which is couched in purely theological terms. Apart from challenging the established State religion of his time, the ideas expressed in *The Essence of Christianity* could have been compared by the Prussian censor to those Saint-Simonian ideas banned in 1835 and thought morally and politically subversive to the Christian Prussian State. Feuerbach had in fact expressed his fears about the censor to his publisher at the time of completing *The Essence of Christianity*. Earlier (in April 1835, in a letter to him from L. von Henning), some of his more radical ideas had also been compared to those of the Saint-Simonians; while in a letter written to Feuerbach in October 1843, Marx was also to comment on the similarity of Feuerbach's ideas to the materialism of the Saint-Simonian School. Writing that Feuerbach had done what Leroux (a Saint-Simonian) had claimed Schelling to have done – to have given the idea 'flesh and blood' – Marx praised Feuerbach and put down Schelling, the then Professor of Philosophy at Berlin, who had opposed both Feuerbach and Saint-Simonism.[14]

In that Feuerbach's materialism had in general taken over concepts of French materialism, he could indeed be said to have adopted ideas similar to those of the French Saint-Simonians, such as their belief in the necessity of ending the 'spiritualistic' suppression of material and sensual life. Like the French Saint-Simonians Feuerbach also specifically emphasised, in the conclusion of his *Essence of Christianity*, the importance of sexual love in the elimination of social and human alienation, and spoke of a new 'religion' in which men would live together without the need for false consciousness. Following his criticism of the spiritualising effect of alienated consciousness on man's human essence in the Christian religious imagination, he also turned to praise the 'sensualism' of the ancient Greeks, arguing that they had been men of Nature in their worship of elemental gods.[15]

In suggesting earlier in his *Essence of Christianity* that the *Bildlichkeit* of Christian religion had alienated humans from their senses and true human essence, Feuerbach had already transferred to Christianity the symptoms of that primitive *Bildlichkeit* which Hegel had associated with the Greek world. Whereas Hegel had seen the *Bildlichkeit* of Greek culture as having bonded the Greeks to the physical world, and Christian spiritualism as having liberated civilisation from that bondage, Feuerbach considered the sensuousness of the Greeks free, and the spiritualism of Christianity unfree and alienated from that which would make them free. For Feuerbach the latter was, moreover, the healing contact with the world of the senses and with Nature which had been known to the Greeks. In elevating Greek religion and art above that of Christianity in this way, he both reversed the order outlined by Hegel in his Philosophies of History and Religion and echoed Heine's elevation of the Hellene over the Nazarene in those works in which he had defended his Saint-Simonian aesthetic. The fact that that aesthetic was also concerned with defending the liberation of the senses against the German preference for an Idealist theory of aesthetics in which the goal of art was not the liberation of the senses, but the liberation of the subject from them,[16] is of course also relevant to understanding its and Feuerbach's appeal to the young Marx.

As we shall see in chapter 4 of this study, Marx in his *Economic and Philosophic Manuscripts* of 1844 was to use both Feuerbach and Saint-Simon for his own purposes and in his own manner, to develop a critique of alienated labour relevant to the philosophical and intellectual problems of his time, as well as to its material, economic problems.[17] Prior to that work, Marx had, however, begun a critique of Christian art for Bauer which would appear to have started out from Feuerbach's critique of Christian art as a 'fetishistic' alienation of the human essence, and to have aimed at condemning the mediaeval 'madonna-art' criticised by both Heine and Feuerbach, and revived in the nineteenth century by those painters given patronage by the Prussian and Bavarian monarchies.[18] Opposed to Marx and his companions, and representative for Marx of the anachronistic survival of feudal relations within industrialising societies which had previously been condemned by Saint-Simon and his followers, the philosophical, cultural and political policies of these monarchies were, as we shall see, to be attacked by Marx in various articles, from his reviews of parliamentary debates to his criticisms of the Idealist and Romantic philosophies which still held sway in Prussia in the early 1840s.

# 3

# Marx's lost aesthetic: the early years under Friedrich Wilhelm IV

While Feuerbach had transformed theology into anthropology and the criticism of Christianity into the criticism of the alienation of physical man, the legacy of Heine's reports on the Salon of 1831 was a politicisation of art criticism such as even the earlier, and more famous, Salon reports by Marx's 'favourite prose writer', Diderot, had not achieved.[1] This politicisation of art criticism, an expression of Heine's Saint-Simonian belief in the role to be played by the artist in social reconstruction, could have provided Marx with a model for his criticism of the legitimation of Romanticism in Prussia as a retrograde political aesthetic, as also with a basis for a materialist aesthetic with which to counter it. Hence it is interesting to note that the opposition which Heine made between the Nazarene and Hellene, the spiritualist and the sensualist, is one which is to be found throughout Marx's scattered writings on aesthetics, from his proposed criticism of Christian and Romantic art of 1841–2 to his praise of the eternal charm of Greek art in his *Grundrisse* Introduction of 1857, and is symptomatic too of a latent Saint-Simonian aesthetic in his work. Any study of Marx's 'aesthetic' thought must, however, not only consider the aesthetic debates of his time, but also look at the art and architecture which would have been seen by him while he was sharing in these debates.

With respect to Marx's experience of the visual arts produced and given patronage in his time, it is not unimportant that two of the professors whose lectures he attended while a student at the Friedrich Wilhelm University in Bonn in the Winter Semester of 1835–6 and the Summer Semester of 1836 were the Romantic critic and writer A. W. von Schlegel and the Professor of Art History, Eduard d'Alton. Although much is known about A. W. von Schlegel (the brother of Friedrich Schlegel), very little appears to have been written about d'Alton, at least in connection with Marx. (While Lifshitz, for example, mentions in his 1933 study of Marx's 'philosophy of art' that Marx listened to lectures in

11. Portrait of Karl Marx in his student years at Bonn

Bonn on 'modern art', he does not name d'Alton; and though the latter is named by Nicolaievsky and Maenchen-Helfen in their biographical study of Marx, they do not tell us anything about him or his lectures.)[2] Accounts of d'Alton can, however, be gleaned from comments made by contemporaries like A. W. von Schlegel, who edited some essays by d'Alton on his collection of art and a list of the works contained in it after d'Alton's death in 1840, and Gaedertz, a friend of Goethe, with whom d'Alton had been acquainted. From such sources we learn that Joseph Wilhelm Eduard d'Alton, born in Aquileja on 11 August 1772, was an engraver of anatomical and zoological drawings for a series of works on various types of animals by the naturalist and zoologist Dr. C. Pander; had engraved fifty-two plates for a study entitled *The Natural History of the Horse* after the English painter Stubbs between 1810 and 1816 (the horse was a popular subject of military art in Prussia at the time); and had spent the last years of his life as Professor of Archaeology

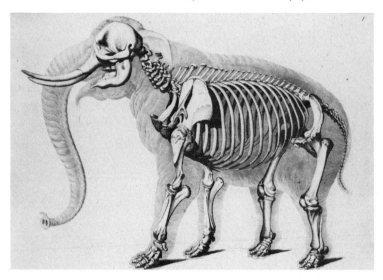

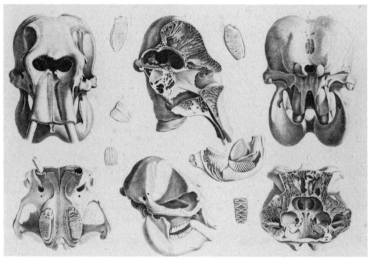

12.a,b Engravings of the body and skull of an elephant made by Eduard d'Alton for his and Dr. C. Pander's *Skelete der Pachydermata* (published Bonn, 1821)

D'Alton completed engravings for several such works in the 1820s, but left the series to be completed by his son Johann Eduard d'Alton in 1831, while he turned to lecturing at the University of Bonn on the art of 'modern', post-classical Europe. (The style of the engravings generally followed that taken by Stubbs in his *Natural History of the Horse*.)

and Art History at the University of Bonn, lecturing on the art of 'modern' (post-classical) Europe, from the Flemish and German masterpieces of the Middle Ages to the Renaissance, and engraving copies of the masterpieces in his own collection.

The list of paintings collected by d'Alton which A. W. von Schlegel edited in 1840 included a *Venus and Cupid* by Pontormo after Michelangelo, a Correggio, a portrait of a man by Tintoretto, Annibale Caracci's *Head of St Francis, Holy Magdalene* and sketch of a madonna and child, a Castiglione, a self-portrait by Poussin, a portrait of the family Olden-Barnefeld by Rubens, and a study by him of heads of the Christ-child and the child John the Baptist of the *Madonna with the Lamb,* and, from the school of Rubens, a portrait of King Philip IV of Spain. Other paintings named in the list of the collection edited by Schlegel included Van Dyck's *Head of St John the Baptist,* a portrait of an astrologer by Rembrandt, a Franz Hals portrait of a man in red with greyhound and several lesser known examples from the Flemish school of the time of Johann Breughel.

According to Schlegel it was the more important of these works – the Pontormo, the Correggio, the Caraccis, and the Rubens – on which d'Alton lectured to students such as Marx at Bonn, and of which he engraved copies and wrote explanations of the kind given in the essays edited by Schlegel in 1840. Schlegel's Foreword to his edition of d'Alton's collection expressed his pleasure at the presence of paintings by Pontormo, Correggio, and Annibale Caracci (an admirer of Raphael mentioned previously by A. W. von Schlegel in volume 2, number 1 of the journal *Athenaeum* of 1799 and praised in Wackenroder's *Herzensergiessungen),* while d'Alton's essay on Rubens (as reproduced by Schlegel) suggests that d'Alton too preferred the religious works of the great Renaissance painters and their followers to all others.

The German Nazarenes had of course shared Caracci's devotions to St Francis and the Madonna as well as his devotion to Raphael, and it is relevant here to note also d'Alton's reference to Raphael in his essay on Rubens. Like A. W. von Schlegel in his Introduction, d'Alton refers in that essay to the ability of the works of both Rubens and Raphael to 'spring as a whole from the Idea' to form 'an organic unity', and shows that he was sympathetic to the praise for Raphael which came from fellow professors such as Hegel and from the German Nazarenes, as well as to the theories of organic unity developed by Romantic theorists who had given their patronage to the Nazarenes.

Evidence that d'Alton may have been sympathetic to the Nazarenes themselves comes, moreover, from claims made by H. Schrörs in his

13. Annibale Caracci, *Pietà with Saints* (National Gallery of Parma)
Annibale Caracci (1560–1609), an admirer of the art of Raphael,
completed several studies of St Francis in his life-time, including this
study of the saint kneeling before the figure of the dead Christ of 1585.
St Francis is also juxtaposed with the figure of Mary Magdalene,
kneeling to the left of Christ, while the transfiguration scene above (a
popular device with Caracci) depicts the cross on which Christ had
been crucified.

book on the frescoes of the old Bonn Aula (*Die Bonner Universitätsaula
und ihre Wandgemälde* of 1906), that both August Wilhelm von
Schlegel and d'Alton supported the painting of frescoes by the Nazarene
Peter Cornelius and his school for the Aula of the Bonn University in the
1820s.[3] The fact that Marx must have seen these frescoes while a
student at Bonn in the mid-1830s, and had thereby had first-hand
experience of the patronage given to Nazarene artists in his day, is also
significant – especially given the criticisms being written of the

14. Wilhelm von Schadow, *Portrait of Agnes d'Alton* (Kunsthalle, Hamburg)

This portrait of Eduard d'Alton's daughter-in-law (the daughter of the sculptor Christian Daniel Rauch), was painted around 1825 by the then head of the Düsseldorf School of Nazarene painters, Wilhelm von Schadow, and further illustrates d'Alton's connections with the German Nazarenes. The portrait now hangs in the Kunsthalle, Hamburg. Later, Agnes' daughter and d'Alton's grand-daughter, Eugénie, married the Nazarene artist Felix Schadow (1819–61), the son from the second marriage of Gottfried Schadow, the father of Wilhelm.

Nazarenes by Heine, who was much admired by the young Marx at that time, and Marx's return to Bonn to write his critique of Christian art in 1842.[4]

The frescoes spoken of by Schrörs in his book as having been supported by d'Alton and Schlegel had originally been commissioned from Peter Cornelius by the Prussian Minister von Altenstein in 1822 on behalf of the monarch Friedrich Wilhelm III, after whom the recently refounded university had been named. Cornelius appointed several of his students to assist him in the design and execution of the frescoes, and it was originally decided by them that four should be begun – on the subjects of Theology, Philosophy, Jurisprudence, and Medicine – and that they should follow the design and spirit of Raphael's famous *Disputà* and *School of Athens*.

The frescoes which Marx was to see in Bonn on his arrival there in 1835 were classic examples of Nazarene art. Jakob Goetzenberger's fresco *Philosophy* of 1829–33, for example, had not only imitated the design of Raphael's *School of Athens*, but had also placed Dürer and Raphael – the two great idols of Nazarene art – standing together (as in the vision dreamed by Wackenroder's monk) in the centre, where Raphael had placed the figures of the great Greek philosophers. In addition to depicting Raphael holding his 1508 fresco of Philosophy

15. Raphael, *Disputà*, 1508–9 (Vatican, Rome)

16. Raphael, *School of Athens*, 1509–10 (Vatican, Rome)

(Wackenroder had also described Dürer and Raphael contemplating examples of their own art in his *Herzensergiessungen*) Goetzenberger placed an allegorical female figure representative of unveiled Truth above those of Raphael and Dürer as the central figure of the fresco in the manner of Raphael's more religious *Disputà*.

As well as these self-referring artistic allusions to his models Raphael and Dürer (Goetzenberger has depicted Dürer in the manner of the latter's 'Nazarene' *Self-Portrait* of 1500, and Raphael in the manner of the self-portrait on the right-hand edge of *The School of Athens*), Goetzenberger gave special prominence in his fresco to those philosophers who could be regarded as having justified the self-referential, Romantic character of the art aspired to by the German Nazarenes at that time, or whose opinion (like Goethe's) they particularly valued. Thus the front left foreground of *Philosophy* is taken up by the seated figures of Goethe and Hegel, while the right foreground depicts the standing figures of Schiller and Kant.

Goetzenberger had earlier been a painter of madonnas in the style of Raphael, but his allegorical depiction of Truth in his fresco of

Philosophy is less of a traditional Nazarene madonna than that of Karl Hermann's allegory of Religion in his *Theology* fresco of 1824–5. Although also painted in the style of Raphael's *Disputà* and *School of Athens*, and although giving prominence to contemporary theologians and pietists approved of by the Prussian monarchy, Hermann's fresco had at first displeased Friedrich Wilhelm III, who wished to see more of a reconciliation between the theologians of different faiths depicted than was shown in Hermann's mural. Like his son, Friedrich Wilhelm IV, Friedrich Wilhelm III envisioned a reconciliation of the differing

17. Jakob Goetzenberger, *Philosophy*, 1829–33 (Old Aula, Bonn University); cartoons of fresco, Kunsthalle, Karlsruhe

18. *Theology*: fresco designed (1824–5) for the Old Aula of Bonn University by Karl Hermann, and executed by him with the assistance of Jakob Goetzenberger and Ernst Förster

religious factions in Germany, and (as with the establishment of a Prussian Academy for the Arts in the Rhineland in Düsseldorf[5]) had seen the new foundation of the university at Bonn in 1818 as another step towards the reunion of Catholic and Protestant Germany.[6]

As later letters from Marx make plain, he had intensely disliked his Bonn professors, as well as the ideas and policies for which they had stood. When Marx moved from Bonn to the University of Berlin in 1837, he was to find professors of similar ilk to those he had left, as well as an academy dominated by the same school of Nazarene artists he had seen favoured in Bonn. In 1841 the new monarch, Friedrich Wilhelm IV, appointed the Nazarene artist Peter Cornelius to a new commission in Berlin as a sign of his favour, and shortly afterwards (in December 1841) issued a new censorship instruction intended to give added protection

19. Ferdinand Theodor Hildebrandt, *Portrait of Prince Friedrich of Prussia* (Stadtgeschichtliches Museum, Düsseldorf)

Prince Friedrich Wilhelm Ludwig of Prussia was appointed Protector of the *Kunstverein* for Rhineland–Westphalia in 1829, following Friedrich Wilhelm III's foundation of the new Academy of Arts for the Rhineland in Düsseldorf, and held the post until the death of Friedrich Wilhelm IV in 1861. The strong links forged between the Prussian monarchy and the Nazarene school of painters in Düsseldorf in these years is exemplified in this portrait (*circa* 1830) of the modern but armoured Prussian Prince by Hildebrandt, a favourite artist of Friedrich Wilhelm, whose portrait he also painted in this manner.

20. Hildebrandt's and Pistorius' 1829 *Portrait of Princess Luise Wilhelmine of Prussia* with her sons Alexander and Georg (Stadtgeschichtliches Museum, Düsseldorf) not only depicts a madonna-like Princess but contains within it a picture of a Prussian on horseback and a stained glass of the Virgin herself.

to both Church and State from the jibes of writers and journalists of persuasions similar to those of Marx and his Young Hegelian friends.

Taking up the role of the journalist, Marx published his first article in February 1842 against the censorship instruction of December 1841, and condemned the instruction for its 'Romantic' protection of religion,[7] claiming Friedrich Wilhelm IV's 'Romantic hatred of free speech' to be a betrayal of the Enlightenment State to which Prussia had aspired under Frederick the Great, rather than the rebirth of the spirit of the latter which the new monarch pretended to represent.

Friedrich Wilhelm IV was in fact to provide the young Marx with many examples of patronage antipathetic to Marx's ideals and favourable to the religious and Romantic artists of the time in the coming years of his reign. Apart from his own encouragement of the German Nazarenes and patronage of their art, Friedrich Wilhelm IV also continued his father's policy of using both political and cultural patronage to tie the citizens of Prussia, as well as of other territories, closer to the Prussian State, and to bring together the Protestant and Catholic factions separated since Germany's Reformation.

It was as a part of his ultramontanist policies, as well as out of a pietistic love of mediaeval Christian art and religion, that Friedrich Wilhelm IV also began in the 1840s to take an interest in events such as the reconstruction in Trier of the second-century Roman Gate, the Porta Nigra, and of the Catholic Simeonstift which had been built on to the Porta Nigra in the eleventh century. Later Marx was of course to satirise the monarch's participation in the restoration of Catholic monuments in Trier in the conclusion of his *Eighteenth Brumaire* of 1852, when he compared Napoleon III's assumption of the mantle of Emperor with Friedrich Wilhelm IV's restoration to the Catholic Cathedral at Trier of the relic of the 'Holy Cloak'. At home in Trier in the 1830s Marx had also experienced the renewal of archaeological

21. Johann Anton Ramboux, lithograph of the Porta Nigra imagined as a museum for classical art, 1825–30. (Rheinisches Landesmuseum, Trier)

22. Ramboux was also a painter of frescoes; this is a sketch for a fresco depicting a grape harvest for a

interest in the city's ancient Roman ruins, together with the Archbishop of Trier's ban on the 'dangerously' sensualistic philosophy of the Saint-Simonians. As the most famous of Trier's Roman ruins, the Porta Nigra, had had its Catholic *Stift* built on to it by the Catholic Bishop Poppo in the eleventh century, it was itself as much a monument to Germany's mediaeval Christian past as to its pagan Roman heritage, and for this reason too it may well have been that Marx's first experience of the struggle between a Hellenism sympathetic to artistic freedom and a Romanticism antipathetic to Hellenism, of which he was to write in later years, was first made in Trier in the 1830s.

Romanticised depictions of Trier's Porta Nigra and *Stift* were also made in Marx's time in Trier by the Nazarene follower Johann Anton Ramboux (1790–1866). Ramboux had returned to Trier from Italy in 1822 and worked there until 1832, painting its landscape and architecture in the Italianate manner which he had learnt from the Nazarenes in Italy. Later, as curator of the Wallraf-Richartz-Museum in

23. Johann Anton Ramboux, sketch for a fresco for Trier Cathedral (East Choir), never completed because of lack of funds (Kunst-museum, Düsseldorf)

24. The Berlin which Marx entered as a student in 1837 was one dominated by classical architecture and monuments. The university (founded in 1809) was itself housed in a former palace of classical design, and was typical of the type of architecture favoured in the time of Frederick the Great and still promoted under his successors.

Cologne, Ramboux worked with others on the restoration of Cologne Cathedral, and edited collections of lithographs of the art of the Italian Renaissance and of his own madonna pictures.

Travelling to Berlin as a student in 1837, Marx again found a mixture of classical and Romantic architecture, but where in Trier he had met the Roman imitation of the Greek, he now saw Greek art as understood and celebrated by the Enlightenment State of Frederick the Great.

For Heine, who had admired the classical lines of Langhans' Brandenburg Gate in his *Briefe aus Berlin* of 1822, the symbol of Friedrich Wilhelm IV's Romantic negation of the German Enlightenment of the eighteenth century and of its 'Hellenist' tendencies was the monarch's plan to begin the rebuilding of Cologne Cathedral, stopped, as Heine wrote, by the 'good sense' of Luther in the sixteenth century.[8] Goethe's *Von deutscher Baukunst* of 1772 was but one of several works, published in Germany before Friedrich Wilhelm IV's accession, which had praised mediaeval German 'Gothic' architecture as a lost national German art-form. For both Friedrich Wilhelm IV and his father

25. One of the most famous of the classical monuments built in the time of Frederick the Great was the Brandenburg Gate, designed by C. G. Langhans and completed in 1794.

Friedrich Wilhelm III Prussia was to lead the revival of this national German art. It was also with this goal in mind that Friedrich Wilhelm III commissioned the architect Karl Friedrich Schinkel to design a new museum for Berlin to house his collection of national German art. So although Schinkel designed his museum in imitation of the classical Greek and Roman designs favoured in the time of Frederick the Great, the museum itself (opened in 1830) became home to a collection of national art which gave precedence to the mediaeval German and Flemish painting and modern Christian art-works favoured by Friedrich Wilhelm III and his advisers.

Some of the art collected for the new Berlin museum had moreover been collected by Friedrich Wilhelm IV while still Crown Prince. Caspar David Friedrich's Romantic *Monk by the Sea* was, for instance, bought by Friedrich Wilhelm IV while Crown Prince, and is characteristic of the Romantic art favoured by him both before and after he became King.

Yet Friedrich Wilhelm IV was known not only as a collector of Romantic art and patron of its artists, but as an artist in his own right.

26. This romanticised depiction of the interior of Cologne Cathedral was engraved by Sulpiz Boisserée after a work by Georg Moller in *circa* 1821, before plans were put into action by Friedrich Wilhelm IV for its completion.

27. Lithograph of the portrait by Franz Krüger, *King Friedrich Wilhelm IV in the Berlin Palace* (Bildarchiv Preussischer Kulturbesitz, Berlin)

This portrait by Krüger (nick-named 'Pferde-Krüger' for his numerous paintings of horses and military parades) shows the monarch in a favourite role, as a collector of Gothic and Romantic art.

28. Caspar David Friedrich, *Monk by the Sea, circa* 1809 (Schloss Charlottenburg, Preussische Kunstsammlung)

Taught drawing and painting by the Court architect Karl Ludwig Krüger (not to be confused with Franz Krüger mentioned above), and inspired by the neo-Gothic architecture then favoured by his favourite architect, Karl Friedrich Schinkel (1781–1841), the Crown Prince Friedrich Wilhelm spent much of his youth drawing 'fantastic landscapes' and designing Gothic temples.

While the Gothic churches designed and drawn by the Crown Prince were in imitation of Schinkel's Gothic cathedrals and drawings (the latter's *Gotischer Dom am Wasser* of 1813–14 is one example, but exists now only in copies such as that by Wilhelm Ahlborn of 1823), his 'fantastic landscapes' drawn before 1828 seem to have been executed in imitation of the Romantic neo-classical sets designed by Schinkel for operas such as Mozart's *Zauberflöte,* Spontini's *Olimpia,* and the Romantic writer E. T. A. Hoffmann's *Undine.*

Several years prior to the Crown Prince's composition of his 'fantastic' sketches, in 1812, the Prince's tutor Ancillon had complained of his seventeen-year-old charge that he was rarely to be seen without a pencil in his hand, and that although sketching might be good practice for a future Schinkel, the State did not 'after all' consist in a Gothic temple, and a people was never ruled by means of 'romantic pictures'. Despite this warning from the definitely 'unromantic'

Ancillon (who is reported to have said after visiting Italy that he had been 'overfed' with marble), the Romantic Prince Friedrich Wilhelm continued his sketching, and, in 1828, succeeded in persuading his father to allow him to visit Italy, the scene of his artistic fantasies.

29. Schinkel's theatre set for the first act of Spontini's opera *Olimpia*

30. A 'fantastic landscape' by the Crown Prince Friedrich Wilhelm of Prussia of *circa* 1828, reproduced by Ludwig Dehio in his 1930s study, *Friedrich Wilhelm IV von Preussen: ein Baukünstler der Romantik* (Bildarchiv Preussischer Kulturbesitz, Berlin)

The guide chosen for Friedrich Wilhelm's Italian journey to Florence and Siena in 1828 was Carl Friedrich von Rumohr, an authority on the mediaeval art of Tuscany, whose *Italienische Forschungen* had begun to appear in Berlin in 1827. In these *Forschungen* von Rumohr had praised the art of Giotto and Raphael, two of the 'heroes' of the German Nazarenes who moved to Italy after 1810. Although he is said to have criticised the Nazarenes privately as poor imitators of Raphael's work, he also acted as patron to some of their number, for instance, in taking the Nazarene landscape artist Franz Horny (1798–1824) with him to Italy in 1816, and in helping to finance Horny's further training with J. A. Koch and Peter Cornelius.[9]

Like von Rumohr, and like his father Friedrich Wilhelm III, Friedrich Wilhelm IV was a great admirer of the paintings of Raphael, and was also a champion of Raphael's latter-day imitators, the German Nazarenes then working in Italy. Furthermore, while one commentator, von Reumont, has claimed that the young Friedrich Wilhelm admired and was influenced by the German Classicist painter Johann Christian Reinhart (a painter of heroic Italianate scenes then also living in Rome), the sketches of Italy done by the Prussian Crown Prince himself after

31. Johann Christian Reinhart, *Classical Landscape*, 1810 (Hermitage, Leningrad)

32. Franz Horny, *View of Olevano*, 1822 (Kupferstichkabinett und Sammlung der Zeichnungen, East Berlin)

1828 can best be compared to those of Nazarenes who had studied and painted in Italy in the 1820s, such as Friedrich Olivier, Julius Schnorr von Carolsfeld, Theodor Rehbenitz, or Rumohr's protégé, Franz Horny.

Given Friedrich Wilhelm IV's patronage of both the 'Gothic revival'

33. Theodor Rehbenitz, *Perugian Steps, circa* 1823 (Museen für Kunst und Kulturgeschichte, Lübeck, Graphische Sammlung)

34. Friedrich Olivier, *Alley in Olevano*, dated 1822 (Bayerische Staatsgemäldesammlung, Munich)

and the neo-religious art of the Nazarenes of his time, it is particularly interesting to note his tutor von Rumohr's *Italienische Forschungen* amongst the list of books which Marx spent the Winter of 1841–2 reading for his contribution to the works being planned by Bruno Bauer on Hegel's teachings on religion and art. Hegel too was acquainted with von Rumohr and (though criticising his emphasis on the need for art to find its forms in Nature) had endorsed his praise for Raphael as one of the greatest religious painters of modern times in his *Lectures on Aesthetics*.[10] Bauer, however, as mentioned previously, wished Marx to join him in 1842 in reinterpreting Hegel's support for the religious 'Romantic' art, still given patronage in their time by the Prussian monarchy, in a treatise on Hegel's 'hatred' of Christian religious art. In planning this project in 1842 Bauer had also been reaffirming the 'Left' Hegelian position taken in his *Last Trump* of 1841, in which he heretically interpreted Hegel's work as that of a radical 'Jacobin Hellene', as part of an attack on the orthodox Hegelianism officially approved in Friedrich Wilhelm IV's Prussia at that time.

Prior to the *Last Trump*, and at that time he is said to have 'converted' Marx to Hegel after Marx joined the *Doktorenklub* of the University of

35. Sketch by the Crown Prince Friedrich Wilhelm of Prussia of an Italian scene, June 1832 (Bildarchiv Preussischer Kulturbesitz, Berlin)

Berlin in 1837,[11] Bruno Bauer had been a member of a branch of Young Hegelians who were then still to the 'right' of David Friedrich Strauss. By 1840 this group had, however, developed its own 'esoteric', Left Hegelian reading of Hegel, which opposed the 'official' reading of him as the apologist of the Prussian State and as the legitimation of its support – in politics and art – of Romanticism. By this time Bauer too had changed from the position held by him in 1837 to the 'esoteric' reading of Hegel which saw him not as the defender of Romanticism he had first appeared to be, but as a 'Jacobin' Hellene.[12]

Like other Young Hegelians of the 'Left', Bruno Bauer not only identified the Hellene with the French Jacobin (where representatives of German Classicism such as Goethe and Schiller had turned against the excesses of the French Revolution and the Jacobinism inspired by it), but also condemned the prosaic Old Testament 'Nazarene' morality of Judaism and Christianity defended by more conservative Hegelians as being in opposition to these new ideals. In addition, he defined Hellenism as a 'religion of beauty, art, freedom, and humanity'.[13] The sympathy to Christian art of the orthodox Hegel was the subject to which Bauer then specifically turned in his treatise entitled *Hegels Lehre von der Religion und Kunst von dem Standpunkt des Glaubens ausbeurteilt (Hegel's Teachings on Religion and Art Judged from the Standpoint of Faith)*, for which Marx was to have written his interpretation of the 'radical' Hegel as a critic of Christian art and religion. Although Marx never finished that interpretation for Bauer, Bauer's own piece was published anonymously (as his *Last Trump* had been the previous year) in Leipzig in 1842 by Wigand, the publisher of both Feuerbach's *Wesen des Christentums* of 1841 and Püttmann's *Düsseldorfer Malerschule* of 1839.

In his tract on Hegel's teachings on religion and art, Bauer set out to create a radical Hellenistic Hegel as an antitheme to his criticism of the orthodox Hegel's support for Christian art and religion by exploiting the ambiguity of certain of Hegel's statements on Greek art. Thus Hegel's claim that Greek art was limited through the sensuous character of its depiction of the beautiful in Nature to a depiction of the material world, and had therefore not been as capable as the Romantic artist now was of bringing Spirit to its realisation of itself, was to enable Bauer to argue that Hegel had admired both the wholeness of the Greek character,[14] and the sensuous nature of Hellenistic art,[15] and to ignore the rest of Hegel's argument that this sensuousness was a limitation to the development of Spirit. In noting that Hegel had praised a Greek statue of the Phryne in his *Ästhetik*, Bauer went on to praise the 'unchristian' character of his appreciation of Greek art, and to argue for an antitheses between the points of view of Hegel and of those orthodox pietists who had thought themselves justified by his theories in condemning Greek art as both immoral and unartistic.[16]

In this way Bauer argued that Hegel had preferred Greek art, and the Hellenism regarded by some Prussian authorities and censors as morally dangerous', to the spiritualistic and religious art preferred by the pietists of the time. (A second improved edition of Hegel's *Aesthetics* published in 1842 was to pour fuel on to the disputes which were now raging over this issue.) Above all, however, Bauer's reinterpretation of Hegel's aesthetic preference for Romanticism over Greek art had the political aim of suggesting that Hegel had not looked for the death of sensuous art in the service of the development of Spirit to either Absolute Consciousness or to its 'Objective' form in the Prussian State,[17] but had supported a form of art in which the principle of material life had been celebrated over that of the death of matter, and the freedom of the artist preferred to his subjugation – or elimination – by State patronage.

Read as a Hellenist, Hegel became for Bauer a way of attacking both the conservative reading of the Hegelian aesthetic as a defence of the Prussian State as it then existed and the Romanticism supported by the latter in preference to writers such as himself.

The section into which Marx's contribution to Bauer's work on Hegel's teachings on art and religion was to go had originally been called 'Hegels Hass gegen die religiöse und christliche Kunst und seine Auflösung aller positiven Staatsgesetze' ('Hegel's hatred of religious and Christian art and his dissolution of all positive State laws'), a title which in itself indicates that Marx was originally to have followed Bauer in offering a 'radical', Young Hegelian interpretation of Hegel as a 'Hellenist' who was antipathetic rather than sympathetic to the spiritualism of State-approved Christian art. Marx's contribution was, however, as mentioned previously, never completed or published in its intended form, having first of all (according to Marx) grown almost to book length, and then into a criticism of Christian art, different from that requested by Bauer, and followed by an epilogue on Romantic art.[18] Finally Marx wrote to Ruge on 27 April 1842 that he was sending him four articles for his journal: '1) "On Religious Art", 2) "On the Romantics", 3) "The Philosophical Manifesto of the Historical School of Law", 4) "The *Positive Philosophers*" '.

Although only the third of these was ever published (in a supplement to the *Rheinische Zeitung* of 9 August 1842), all four of the topics mentioned by Marx can be said to have had some connection with the criticism of Friedrich Wilhelm IV's 'political Romanticism' with which Marx was to concern himself in early 1842 in his articles on the censorship instruction of December 1841, written at the same time as he was working on his treatise for Bauer. Later, in October 1842, Engels also criticised the political Romanticism of the Prussian monarch in an article entitled 'Friedrich Wilhelm IV, King of Prussia'.[19] There Engels spoke critically of the Prussian King's attempts to found his State on a 'Christian–feudalist' basis, while also attacking the King's Romanticism and his support for the philosophical Romanticism of the Historical School of Law. Heine had also attacked that school from a Saint-Simonian perspective in the 1830s,[20] while Ruge himself had launched an attack on the political Romanticism of the times in 1840, the year of Friedrich Wilhelm IV's accession to the Prussian throne.

Both Heine and Engels had, furthermore, connected their criticism of Friedrich Wilhelm IV's Romanticism with his strengthening of the censorship of writers critical of official Prussian policy, while Marx, as just noted, had connected his attack on Friedrich Wilhelm IV's strengthening of the censorship with the monarch's 'feudal Romantic ways' in articles written for the *Rheinische Zeitung* in 1842. Given a complaint made by Marx to Ruge in a letter of 5 March 1842 that the King's new censorship instructions would also make the publication of his treatise on Christian art difficult, and the linking of Christian art to State law in its title, it is also likely that Marx had made some connection between Romantic Christian art and censorship in that work. Because the new censorship instruction discussed by Marx in his *Rheinische Zeitung* articles of early 1842 was specifically directed toward protecting the Christian religion from any critical attack, Marx may, however, have believed that his discussion of Christian art alone would be enough to have his work banned.

That Marx's analysis of Christian art might by itself have upset the pietist hierarchy in Prussia at the time is a possibility supported both by the nature of the arguments on Christian art which are to be found in his essays of 1842, and by the types of books used by him at that time for his treatise on Christian art. As Mikhail Lifshitz has argued in his 1933 study of Marx's philosophy of art, Marx's reading for his contribution on Christian art for Bauer suggests that that contribution would originally have followed a path from the study of the religious and fetishistic art of Asia and of Greece to the Christian art of the Romantics of his own time, and have attempted to link the latter with the former pagan arts. The works which Marx mentions reading in 1842, and from which he excerpted passages now published in the new *Marx-Engels-Gesamtausgabe*,[21] consisted in fact of a mixture of works on pagan and Christian art, and also indicate that Marx may have been interested in working on the opposition between the Hellenistic and the Nazarene with which both Heine and Bauer had been concerned in their analyses of the politics of contemporary aesthetic debate and practice. The works read by Marx in Bonn in 1842 for his treatise on Christian art were (apart from Rumohr's *Italienische Forschungen* of 1827–31):

Christoph Meiners, *Allgemeine kritische Geschichte der Religionen (General Critical History of Religions)* (2 vols., Hanover, 1806–7);

J. Barbeyrac, *Traité de la morale des Pères de l'Église (Treatise on the Ethics of the Fathers of the Church)* (Amsterdam, 1728);

Benjamin Constant, *De la religion (Of Religion)* (Paris, 1826);

Charles Debrosses, *Über den Dienst der Fetischgotter oder Vergleich der alten Religionen Egyptens mit der heutigen Religion Negritens (On the Idolisation of Fetishes; or Comparison of the Old Egyptian Religions with Contemporary Negro Religion)* (translated Berlin, 1785 from French of 1760. A study of the fetish basis of religion);

C. A. Böttiger, *Ideen zur Kunst-Mythologie (Ideas on Mythology in Art)* (2 vols., Dresden and Leipzig, 1826–36); and

J. J. Grund, *Die Malerey der Griechen oder Entstehung, Fortschritt, Vollendung und Verfall der Malerey. Ein Versuch (The Painting of the Greeks, or the Origin, Progress, Completion and Decay of Painting)* (in two parts, Dresden, 1810–11).

In addition to these works Marx was of course also reading and rereading works by Hegel and Feuerbach on art and religion, while we may also surmise (from, for example, the fact that Marx's library contained an 1841 edition of Saint-Simon, and that he was to mention the latter in following years), that he was also, at this time, rereading Saint-Simon. Some of the ideas which Marx noted from the writers listed above for his Bonn Notebooks in 1842 were ones which he could furthermore have found in some form in Hegel, Feuerbach, or Saint-Simon. Even Debrosses's work on the fetish character of pagan art, which is thought to have suggested to Marx some of his later ideas on the fetish character taken on by commodities under capitalism, offered an argument which Marx could also have found in Feuerbach, while Debrosses, Grund, and Böttiger had all also attributed the fetish character of ancient art to Christian art, as Feuerbach was to do in his criticism of the *Bildlichkeit* of Christian religion in his *Essence of Christianity* of 1841.[22]

Other clues to the development of Marx's arguments towards a criticism of Christian art and religion at this time are, as mentioned earlier, to be found in the articles and essays written at the same time or shortly after Marx's involvement with writing his tract on Christian art and religion for Bauer. Marx's 'Debates on freedom of the press' written for the *Rheinische Zeitung*, for 5 May 1842, for example, not only deal with a criticism of the 'Romanticism' of the King, but also centre on an attack on the love of all things mediaeval in his contemporary Prussia and conclude with a reference to Goethe's 'Verschiedene über Kunst'. The particular reference he makes to that text is, moreover, to a passage in which Goethe had commented that an artist could only succeed in painting female beauty when he had already loved it once before in a human being, a comment which can be seen to be related to Marx's interest in the sensuous and material bases of the painting of female beauty by the madonna-painters of both the Middle Ages and of his own time. It is a comment which may also be connected with a reference made by Marx a fortnight later, in an article on the 'Debates on freedom of the press' of 19 May 1842, to a painting by Rembrandt of a madonna as a peasant woman, in that Goethe had also mentioned that work in a commentary on Falconet of 1776, and compared its representation of motherly love with Raphael's in his madonna pictures. Where Hegel was later to praise Raphael because he was able to depict a 'transcendental' type of love with his madonnas (in his chapter on Romantic art in his *Vorlesungen über die Ästhetik*), Goethe had praised both Raphael and Rembrandt on account of their ability to represent natural motherly love. This was a point much closer to Marx's interest in uncovering the sensuous, materialist basis to the painting of the Madonna in Western art than Hegel's, and Marx's reference to it is an indication of his interest, at that time, in developing a critique of religious painting which would also serve to uncover a more 'Hellenistic' side to the arguments put forward by Hegel in the defence of the Romantic religious art of the West in his *Ästhetik*. Goethe's argument that paintings of the Madonna (by either Rembrandt or Raphael) could be seen to be based in the artist's experience of sensual love may also, that is, have suggested to Marx a way of interpreting the 'orthodox' Hegel's less materialistic analysis of Raphael's madonna pictures in a more materialistic manner, in the way suggested by Bauer in his 'esoteric' interpretations of the orthodox Hegel as a concealed but radical Hellene.

Soon after giving up his planned treatise on Christian art and religion in July 1842, Marx was also to write an article for a supplement of no. 191 of the *Rheinische Zeitung* of 10 July 1842, in which he set out to mock a correspondent of the *Kölnische Zeitung* for believing that he could justify State religion by claiming that even in its 'crudest form' as 'childish fetishism' it could 'raise man above his sensuous desires'. Arguing in reply that fetishism does not raise man above sensuous desire, but is, on the contrary, the 'religion of sensuous desire', Marx attempted to demonstrate the irony of a defender of a Christian State religion's himself suggesting that there had been in that religion a fetishistic stage usually only attributed to the pagan world.

Proceeding to a defence of Greek civilisation (Marx's article had begun moreover with an ironic comment on the fact that some of his readers may not be 'Hellenes'), Marx then turned his attention towards a more extended criticism of the *Kölnische Zeitung* correspondent's defence of Christianity as a more 'scientific' and progressive religion than that of the Greeks.

Marx's support for 'Hellenism' against the 'Nazarene' religion defended in the *Kölnische Zeitung* was, of course, in this article, but a part of his overall critique of the *Kölnische Zeitung*'s defence of Christianity as a defence of the recent censorship instruction's added protection of the Christian religion from his and others' jibes. Yet while the general aim of Marx's articles for the *Rheinische Zeitung* of 1842 was an attack on the new censorship instructions put out by Friedrich Wilhelm IV at the end of 1841 – and his attack on Christianity an attack on the added protection given it as the State religion by those instructions – the specific comments made by him in those articles also reflect the study of the history of pagan and Christian religion made for his unfinished critique of Christian art and religion, as well as the background to that study of the renewed censorship laws which were by then already affecting his own publications and career. The subject of fetishism referred to by Marx on 10 July 1842 is moreover taken up again in the conclusion of his 'Debates on the law on thefts of wood' of October 1842. There it is again treated as a negative symptom of alienated sensuousness, suggesting that if Marx had treated Christian art and religion in his treatise for Bauer as having fetishised religious objects in the manner suggested by Feuerbach in his *Essence of Christianity*, then he would (in contrast to the correspondent for the *Kölnische Zeitung* whom he attacked in July) have criticised it and its contemporary forms.

Articles such as those written by Marx for the *Rheinische Zeitung* in 1842 give, in short, both political reasons for Marx's criticisms of the 'mediaevalism' then popular in Prussia and indications that his treatise on Christian art and religion for Bauer would have argued that Christian culture had been based on a primitive fetishistic treatment of objects and had been a development away from the standard of civilisation of the Hellenic world rather than a progression beyond it. Not being concerned like Gibbon or other eighteenth-century rationalists to defend his own society as more rational than that of the early Christians who had replaced the declining culture of the Roman world with their own irrationalist system of beliefs, Marx in 1842 would appear to have been interested in using the insights of those such as Böttiger and Grund, who followed Gibbon into the way in which Christian art and religion had taken over and transformed the cultures of classical Greece and Rome, to argue that Christianity had taken over the most irrational, fetishistic aspects of the pagan religions it had thought it was replacing, and without progressing to the higher stage of civilisation indicated by classical culture itself in its more heroic historical moments.

In his reading of Marx's 1842 excerpts Lifshitz has also suggested that Marx's notes from Debrosses on the lack of artistry in ancient religious and fetishistic art, and from Grund on the lack of artistry in mediaeval art, indicate that Marx intended to apply the Christian criticism of fetishism in Greek art to Christian art itself. Lifshitz goes on to suggest that the tenor of these notes echoes that of Bauer's pamphlet – that the Hellenistic spirit was to be contrasted with a spiritualistic religious outlook 'based on oppression and submission' – and summarises Marx as believing with Grund and those others excerpted by him, that, for instance:

> Christian art of the post-classical period reproduced on a new level the aesthetics of Asiatic barbarism. There was a contact between Christian and Oriental culture. Arbitrary elongation and broadening of forms, love for the colossal and grandiose, characterized the art of both cultures. In classical art, form and artistry are essential; but the religious view strives after simple quantity, formless matter . . .

and that

> Christian architecture sought exaggeration and loftiness; yet it was lost in barbaric pomp and countless details . . .[23]

The excerpts made by Marx from Grund's *Malerey der Griechen* had, however, not only included the above point, that mediaeval Christian Gothic architecture had sought 'exaggeration and loftiness' but had 'lost itself in barbaric pomp and countless details' (Marx's excerpt reads: 'Die gothische Baukunst versteigt sich in sinnliche Höhe und verirrt sich in dürftige Kleinheit'), but had also noted Grund's criticism of the overuse of the madonna in Christian art. Moreover, if it is the case that Marx's excerpts from Grund were, as claimed by the editors of the new *Marx-Engels-Gesamtausgabe,* made after Marx had excerpted his notes from Rumohr's work, *Italienische Forschungen* of 1827–31,[24] then they could also be read in context as adding to Marx's reading of Rumohr, and to his criticism of the 'institutionalisation' of the religious art in Prussia to which Rumohr (as tutor to Friedrich Wilhelm IV) could be seen to have contributed, and of which the Nazarene 'madonna-painters' favoured by Friedrich Wilhelm IV had been such an integral part.

Where Hegel had noted and supported Rumohr's praise for the art of Raphael, Marx in his excerpts from Rumohr noted Rumohr's comments on the similarities to be found between Greek pagan art and Christian painting, and, specifically, his comments on the similarities between the clothing of the Christian madonnas and those of Roman matrons. In noting these comments, rather than Rumohr's praise for Raphael, Marx may well have been choosing passages from Rumohr which would allow him to reinterpret Hegel's praise for Raphael's madonnas as admiration for figures similar or related to those of pagan art. Indeed, Hegel himself had already compared a Christian madonna to an Egyptian Isis and a Greek faun in his *Lectures on Aesthetics,* while also, however, holding to his view that the Christian artist had done better in representing the divine spirit behind both motherhood and world history. While Rumohr had also not made his comments on the similarities between Christian and pagan art for the purpose of criticising or mocking Christian religious art (he had, as Hegel noted, been concerned to show how all great art – ancient and Christian – found its forms in Nature, but not to criticise it for that), the excerpts made by Marx from Grund suggest that he may well have been thinking of both using Rumohr's comparison to give a more radical reading of Hegel's praise of the Christian madonna, and of interpreting Rumohr's comments through the more critical eyes of Grund. Further to this Marx was later, as we shall see, to reject explicitly the argument put by Rumohr in the Third Part of his *Forschungen* that Raphael was not the imitator of Michelangelo, as other critics had described him, but an original genius, by arguing in his *German Ideology* of 1845–6 that the view of Raphael as an individual genius was misleading and symptomatic of a false view of artists in general.[25]

Returning to Marx's excerpts of 1842, it appears that Marx moved from his study of Rumohr's 'Raphaelite' *Italienische Forschungen* and Grund's more critical comparisons of Christian and Greek art in his *Malerey der Griechen* to the study of Debrosses's late eighteenth-century analysis of the fetishistic roots of all religion, and to Böttiger's *Ideen zur Kunstmythologie* of 1826. Following the bias of his previous excerpts toward the remarking of similarities between Greek and Christian art, Marx excerpted from the first part of Böttiger's *Ideen zur Kunstmythologie* of 1826 a passage on the way in which the Greeks had idealised men as gods and anthropomorphised gods as men in their art. The latter point was one which Marx could also have seen applied to Christian art by Feuerbach in his *Wesen des Christentums* of 1841, but it is particularly interesting, in view of the official (and 'fatherly') patronage given the Nazarine artists at that time, that Marx must also have read Böttiger's related comparison of the Greek idealisation of men and anthropomorphisation of gods with the art of Raphael and his school, in which Böttiger had described Raphael's depiction of God the Father in his *Vision of Ezekiel* of 1518 as an example of a 'spiritualised' idealisation of man in art.[26]

What we find, then, in Marx's excerpts from Böttiger, Grund, and Debrosses are ideas on the fetishistic origins of Christian art on which

36. Raphael, *Vision of Ezekiel* (Pitti Gallery, Florence)

Feuerbach could be said to have based his philosophical analysis of the fetishistic character of Christian religion, but which also indicate that Marx, like Feuerbach, may have been planning to attack – by means of a materialist analysis of their 'sensual base' – the paintings of mediaeval and Renaissance art which had been made popular again in his own time by the Nazarenes and their royal patrons, and which had been praised by what Bauer had termed the 'orthodox' Hegel. One further suggestion that Marx may have been given the task of critically reinterpreting both the orthodox Hegel and the mediaeval Christian painting supported by his defenders as part of his brief from Bauer is also to be found in Bauer's parody of a pietist's attack on Feuerbach for his criticism of the Madonna in the first part of his book *Hegels Lehre von der Religion und Kunst*, to which Marx was to have contributed his essay. Feuerbach of course had implicitly criticised the madonnas of mediaeval Christian art made popular again in his time (and Marx's) by the German Nazarenes in his *Essence of Christianity*. As that book had also provided Marx and Bauer with the means to interpreting those art works and their pietistic religious elements in a 'radical' manner – as being based in the suppression of sensualistic pleasure – this reference to Feuerbach by Bauer in his attempted 'esoteric' analysis of Hegel's views on religion and art also suggests that Bauer may have set Marx the task of arguing both that the orthodox Hegel was secretly a radical, 'sensualistic' Hellenist, and that pietistic art was an alienation or masking of that sensualism.

Here it is also important for an understanding of Marx's development of a critique of alienation in 1844 that where most of the art historians whom he studied in Bonn in 1842 had concentrated on the way in which mediaeval or Renaissance Christian artists had (in Heine's or Gibbon's terms) transformed the pagan Greek gods into Christian saints or devils,[27] Feuerbach had attempted to show how the Christian depiction of the gods was not only a fetishistic anthropomorphisation of the Divine, but also an alienation of human sensuality. This point also distinguishes Feuerbach from art critics such as Böttiger who had, for example, concluded (on page 213 of his study), that the anthropomorphisation of God in Christian art had helped preserve the Holy in art, as in religion in general. As Böttiger's initial distinction between 'Sabaismus' and 'Fetischismus' – as the religions of the spiritual and material worlds respectively – had led him to attribute the development of writing to 'Sabaismus' but the development of the visual arts to the fetishists, he had also implied (intentionally or unintentionally) that the visual arts in general, whether pagan or Christian, could be linked to fetishism; though he had not drawn consequences critical of Christianity from this fact, as Feuerbach was to do in his critiques of Christian art and religion. In fact, Böttiger (who was, like Rumohr, acquainted with Hegel) had, in general, not gone as far as Feuerbach in his analysis of the fetishistic character of Christian art, though he had suggested connections between Greek and Christian painting which may well have served Marx in his task of uncovering a radical 'Hellenistic' side to Hegel's defence of Christian and Romantic painting. As Bauer had also argued in his companion tract to Marx's that in the eyes of the pietist, art was the 'magic of the devil',[28] Marx may also have been using the excerpts he had made from Böttiger, Grund, and Debrosses, to argue that Hegel could not have defended Christian art if he had truly been the pietist his supporters had claimed him to be, as that art too could be seen to have had a sensualistic, if alienated, pagan base condemnable for all true pietists.

Given the fragmentary nature of the excerpts made by Marx in Bonn in 1842 for his treatise on Hegel's hatred of the Christian religion, its art, and the laws protecting it, it is of course not possible to come to any firm conclusions about his intended argument for the work. As a letter from Marx to Ruge of 20 March 1842 suggests, Marx was also by early 1842 moving beyond both Bauer and Feuerbach toward his own political analysis of Romanticism under Friedrich Wilhelm IV. While his essays on the 'Debates on freedom of the press' of May 1842 suggest that this move was one towards a more political analysis of Friedrich Wilhelm IV's patronage of Romantic artists and writers[29] (Marx was to break with Bauer in 1843–4 over such issues as Bauer's failure to understand or explicitly condemn the political nature of censorship), Marx's own experiences with the Prussian censor when editor of the *Rheinische Zeitung* in 1843 were to radicalise his views even further, and to lead him to look behind the politics of the censor toward their economic base.[30]

In turning to questions of economic production in his *Economic and Philosophic Manuscripts* of 1844 Marx nevertheless returned again to Saint-Simon and to his criticism of those 'feudal' systems in which the exploitation of production and of the modern workers could be said to be concealed. In returning to Saint-Simon, Marx also however combined Saint-Simon's theories with those of Feuerbach. From this combination of ideas Marx was then to attempt an analysis of the alienations produced by the dominance in economic production of the feudal relations condemned by Saint-Simon, which could also provide an explanation of the alienation of the aesthetic senses and of the artistic producer and his products which Marx had obliquely attacked in his criticisms of the Prussian treatment of the artist in his essays on censorship of 1842, and with which he had seemingly also been concerned in his planned 'Feuerbachian' critique of Christian art for Bauer.

Turning to the study of economics, Marx moved from the study of the 'unproductive' role which he saw given to art in Prussia to the study of economic production and to the theories of Saint-Simon's literary discussant, Adam Smith. Despite the apparent change of emphasis to questions of economic production, we shall, however, find in Marx's *Economic and Philosophic Manuscripts* of 1844 a concept of artistic production which reappears in his *Grundrisse* Introduction of 1857, and which demonstrates the way in which Saint-Simon's conception of production as encompassing artistic as well as economic production was to lead Marx to develop a critique of the unproductive role of art under feudalism in his time within a broad theory of material production in general.

# 4

## Marx's 'Economic and Philosophic Manuscripts' and the development of a 'productivist' aesthetic

Marx's 1844 *Economic and Philosophic Manuscripts* were written in Paris between January and August 1844 in answer to the silence of both German Idealism and English political economy on the social forms of alienation suffered, in Marx's view, by the new class of workers created by industrial capitalism in Europe. Although fragmentary in nature,[1] Marx's 1844 *Manuscripts* show him developing a theory of alienated labour which goes beyond Feuerbach's theory of alienated consciousness, and which also appears to utilise ideas gleaned from Saint-Simon. Hence where Feuerbach distinguishes man from the beasts in his *Essence of Christianity* on the basis not of religion, but of the human consciousness which was for him alienated in the Christian religion, Marx distinguishes man from the animal world by virtue of the fact that man could both plan and produce his own environment, as in fact Saint-Simon had claimed that men were able to do in works such as his *L'Industrie* and his *Nouveau christianisme*. In that Marx added to Saint-Simon – via Feuerbach's concept of alienation – a critique of how under capitalist industry production could lead to the alienation of the worker from his world, he also began the process of refunctioning the philosophies of these two thinkers through each other, though, as will be seen later, with some resulting problems for the Saint-Simonist concept of avant-garde.

In Marx's refunctioning of the arguments of Saint-Simon and Feuerbach in his 1844 *Manuscripts*, Feuerbach's theory of the alienation of man's sensuous 'species-being' by a spiritualistic religion is of course also linked to a materialist interpretation of Hegel's theory of the 'alienation' of Spirit in its 'self-objectification' in history, and to Moses Hess' theory of the alienation of the human essence by the sense of 'having'. In this way too, Feuerbach's own 'Saint-Simonian' cry for the liberation of the senses is connected by Marx to a criticism of the alienation of the human senses (which are also understood as the 'aesthetic senses') by a 'sense of having' – a new sense which Marx claims has been created by the rule of private property and the growth of the capitalistic mode of production.

It is through the use of such arguments that Marx also comes to write his own version of Feuerbach's criticism of the alienation of human sensuousness in the spiritualistic anthropomorphism of the Christian religion, and not within a study specifically or only concerned with either the Christian religion or its art, but in a treatise on the alienation of the human worker and his aesthetic senses through the alienation of his labour by the rule of private property. Following Moses Hess' essay on the alienating effect of the rule of money on the 'human essence', as well as Feuerbach's theory of alienated consciousness, Marx claims in his *Economic and Philosophic Manuscripts* that the natural human senses – that is, of sight, hearing, taste, touch and smell – have all been alienated by the sense of 'having'. Next Marx argues – by way of his arbitrary identification of this sense of 'having' with the bodily senses – that the solution to the alienation of all the senses (of both their physical and aesthetic functions) will be the 'overcoming' of private property:

> The overcoming of private property means therefore the complete emancipation of all human senses and aptitudes, but it means this emancipation precisely because these senses and aptitudes have become human both subjectively and objectively. The eye has become a human eye, just as its object has become a social, human object derived from and for man. The senses have therefore become theoreticians immediately in their *praxis*.[2]

The end of the alienation of our senses will, according to these terms, also mean an end to the fetishisation of both human qualities and objects: 'just as its object has become a social, human object derived from and for man'. Objects will in this way again become useful for the human worker working in accord with the needs of his human nature. Objectification – as it occurs in human labour – will no longer necessarily also be alienation (as it had been in Hegel's philosophy of Spirit), production will again be artistic, the object 'human' (and therefore also 'beautiful'), and the appreciation of artistic value no longer dominated by the sense of 'having'.

There is also a fair amount of Saint-Simonian Utopianism to be found in these passages, so that it is interesting to note that the increasing commercialisation of life spoken of by Marx in his *Manuscripts* with respect to the alienation of the aesthetic senses had also been commented on by Heine in an article on the art of the Salon of 1843, written one year previously, that is, to Marx's *Manuscripts*.[3] In his report on the art shown in that Salon Heine had written on how the paintings exhibited in the Salon appeared to him to mirror both the new Industrialism of the age and its obsession with money. Even the sacred pictures appear to Heine to be really allegories of financial life – one tortured Christ figure looking to him like the director of a 'collapsed share firm forced to report to his shareholders on its demise'. Interestingly, Marx has also written in his *Manuscripts*, in images similar to those used by Heine, that the man 'burdened with care and in need could have no sense for the finest play', while the dealer in minerals 'sees only the mercantile value, but not the beauty and the unique nature of the mineral'.

While we have seen Saint-Simon used by Marx to oppose the Idealist theories of those such as Hegel who had regarded artistic production as something separate from other forms of production, we shall now see Marx use him to oppose the ideas of English political economy, and, in particular, those of Adam Smith, to argue that artistic production need not be judged solely by its production of mercantile value, and to suggest, as in the passage just quoted, that those who do subject art to laws of increased productivity and profit are unable to appreciate aesthetic value. While Smith had distinguished between productive and unproductive labour in, for instance, chapter 3 of his *Wealth of Nations*, on the 'accumulation of capital, or of productive and unproductive labour', and had implied that artistic labour was to be described as 'unproductive' when it had produced no lasting products of economic value, but productive if productive of profit, Marx suggests in his *Manuscripts* that such an attitude to artistic labour is itself symptomatic of senses alienated by the 'sense of having', as well as instrumental in the alienation of the aesthetic senses of others.

As later works such as *Capital* and his *Theories of Surplus Value* show, Marx was unable to accept as a general principle Smith's distinction between productive and unproductive labour when the consequence of this was that 'productive' labour was defined only by the amount of profit or economic value generated by the exchange of the products of that labour. In fact, as Marx pointed out in these later works, 'productive labour' was for Smith labour which could produce 'surplus value', or more value than that given to the worker for the time taken to produce the goods of exchange. To Marx a poet such as Milton was 'productive' even when his work was to fail to make an economic profit for either himself or another. Marx, however, both made the point that labour as such should not be defined as productive or unproductive only on account of its exchange value, and suggested that as artistic production was productive of goods in the same sense that other labour could be, the sale of the products of such labour for the profit of another was essentially also a case of the capitalist system of economic exchange alienating rather than constituting the productivity of the artist.

The implication that art could be the victim of alienation as much as could the natural world was an argument which was to some extent to contradict the Saint-Simonist concept of avant-garde productive art developed elsewhere in Marx's work, but it was also to function there as part of that materialist 'productivist' aesthetic in repudiating the belief held by the Kantian Schiller that art could represent a non-alienated area outside production which was simply able to educate man to a realm beyond his alienated state. To Marx, such a belief ignored the importance of also analysing and ridding the material life of *its* alienations – of the alienation of labour and of one worker from another and from their own human nature which was its result. So too, a description by Marx in *Capital,* volume 3 of the realm of freedom which was to be created by the shortening of the working-day, which has often been read – because of its 'Schillerian' language – as a return to the ideas of Schiller, must rather be understood as being primarily concerned with the questions of material production raised by Marx in the preceding sections of *Capital.*[4]

In general, Marx's *Manuscripts* also cannot be read without some recognition being made of the Idealist theories being transformed there, and here the work of David McLellan and others has been of great importance. McLellan comments on the presence, for example, of Schiller in this part of Marx's *Manuscripts:* 'The idea of man's alienated senses finding objects appropriate to them, the attempt to form a connection between freedom and aesthetic activity, the picture of the all-round man – all these occur in Schiller's *Briefe.*'[5]

Marx had of course also given a materialist 'twist' to Schiller's Idealism in his *Manuscripts* by making the liberation of the worker a liberation *to* a fully 'sensual' life rather than away *from* it as conceived of by Schiller, for whom the senses, through which man perceived the physical world around him, were part not of the realm of freedom, but of necessity. So too, where the idea of the 'aesthetic education' of man as a means to his liberation is also based for Schiller in the Kantian idea of the 'disinterestedness' of art, Marx's description in his *Manuscripts* of a free association of producers freely working to serve their own *needs* argues that non-alienated (liberated) labour is not free because it is 'disinterested', but because it is *serving* the needs of the labourer. By implication, artistic labour, for Marx, also serves the *needs* of the labourer and his community. Although such passages have received relatively scant attention, the concept of art as serving needs (a concept also expressed by Heine in his Salon of 1831) is one which has been accepted within the Marxist aesthetic, and has continued to distinguish it from others, but particularly from the Idealist aesthetics of Kant and Schiller, which were still influential in Marx's time. Kant had written, in his analysis of the Sublime in his *Critique of Judgement,* that

> we may . . . readily concede to Epicurus that all gratification, even that which is occasioned through concepts excited by aesthetical ideas, is *animal,* i.e. bodily sensation.

He had, however, added that this concession could be made

> without the least prejudice to the *spiritual* feeling of respect for moral ideas, which is not gratification at all but an esteem for self [for humanity in us], that raises us above the need of gratification, and even without the slightest prejudice to the less noble [satisfactions] of taste.[6]

In this way Kant had distinguished the question of the satisfaction of the physical senses from the question of the moral valuation of the human essence which 'raises' the subject 'above the need of gratification'. For Marx, who had defended the materialism of Epicurus in his doctoral dissertation of 1841 as 'dynamic', and who was in 1844 defending the materialism of Feuerbach and Saint-Simon as modern forms of dynamic materialism, the true satisfaction of the physical and aesthetic senses which was to result from their 'liberation' was, however, to entail the satisfaction of the subject's human essence as a material being.[7]

In his Introduction to his *Critique of Judgement,*[8] Kant had defined 'taste' as the faculty by means of which an object could be called 'beautiful', and had then, in his 'Analytic of the Beautiful',[9] distinguished between the 'pleasant, the beautiful and the good', as, respectively, that which 'gratifies a man', that which 'merely pleases him', and that 'which is esteemed [or approved]' by him and to which he 'accords an objective worth'. Following his introduction to this ethical moment Kant had then described taste as 'the faculty of judging an object or a method of representing it by an entirely disinterested satisfaction or dissatisfaction'.

Predictably Kant was (like Hegel after him) also to make a distinction between art and handicraft (the production of 'use objects'), and to prefer the former to the latter. Hence he wrote in the section 'Analytic of the Sublime' of his *Critique of Judgement:*

> Art also differs from handicraft; the first is called 'free', the other may be called 'mercenary'. We regard the first as if it could only prove purposive as play, i.e. as occupation that is pleasant in itself. But the second is regarded as if it could only be compulsorily imposed upon one as work, i.e. as occupation which is unpleasant [a trouble] in itself and which is only attractive on account of its effect [e.g. the wage].[10]

Ironically, the very factor which Marx was to consider operative in the creation of alienated 'unpleasant' labour – its alienation by means of the wage paid for it by another, who will, for this wage, appropriate the product of the worker's labour – is given by Kant as the one reason for the labour of the artisan's being bearable and even 'attractive' to him, even though, to Kant, such handicraft is also for this reason different from 'true' art, which was for him always to be 'disinterested' art, free from the service of needs where handicraft was not. For this reason too neither William Morris' idealisation of the work of the mediaeval artisan nor the Constructivists' Saint-Simonian programme for a new union of art and technology would have been acceptable to Kant, to whom art objects and use objects were intrinsically opposite.

Although most modern 'Marxist' theories of art have rejected this Kantian distinction between art and use object – as also the idea that art must be seen to be 'disinterested'[11] – one notable exception to this rule has been Herbert Marcuse, who has joined Kant to Freud by interpreting the Kantian opposition between production and aesthetic play as an opposition of a reality to a pleasure principle. In addition to this sleight of hand Marcuse offers a Schillerian, Kantian reading of Marx in his *Eros and Civilization* of 1955,[12] which enables him to claim that Schiller's concept of freedom – which had seen freedom as won through the 'disinterested' activity of aesthetic perception of the Beautiful – was not wholly 'idealistic', because it introduced the idea of freedom into reality. Further to this twentieth-century reinterpretation of what reality meant to Schiller (which appears to identify reality with social life), Marcuse claims that art is able to comment on alienation because it is itself 'non-alienated'. Later, however, he was to describe this form of non-alienation as a 'second alienation'. Writing in his chapter 'Art and revolution' in his *Counter-Revolution and Revolt*, Marcuse explained:

> The affirmative character of art was grounded not so much in its

divorce from reality as in the ease with which it could be reconciled with the given reality, used as its decor, taught and experienced as uncommitting but rewarding value, the possession of which distinguished the 'higher' order of society, the educated, from the masses. But the affirmative power of art is also the power which denies this affirmation. In spite of its [feudal and bourgeois] use as a status symbol, conspicuous consumption, refinement, art retains that alienation from the established reality which is at the origin of art. It is a second alienation, by virtue of which the artist dissociates himself methodically from the alienated society and creates the unreal, 'illusory' universe in which art alone has, and communicates, its truth.[13]

The 'second alienation' which is supposed to save art from alienation as such is then for Marcuse still an escape from the world of production into one of pleasurable illusion.

To Marx illusion was of course not necessarily pleasurable, and although Marcuse's arguments suffer from the absence of any indication from Marx himself of a solution to the problem created by his synthesis of the Saint-Simonian concept of the artist as an avant-garde reformer with the Hegelian concept of an all-pervading type of alienation, they also appear to have ignored wilfully Marx's stress on the 'productive' character of art – and on its similarity to other forms of production – as well as how *both* his theory of alienation and his concept of an avant-garde, 'productive' type of art depend on that materialist emphasis on the primacy of production. For Marx, who made specific reference to Saint-Simon in his 1844 *Manuscripts* as having recognised the importance of looking at industrial labour and its social effects where others such as Fourier had continued to concentrate their attention on the agricultural form of labour written about by the eighteenth-century Physiocrats[14] – art was, as it had been for Saint-Simon, an integral part of production in general, and was therefore to be liberated together with man the maker from the distortions which he saw as characteristic of industrial capitalism. To valorise art as a form of escapist illusionism and as an alternative to production would have been (and, in fact, clearly was), for Marx, to revive the type of art and artistic politics practised by the German Nazarenes and protected by Friedrich Wilhelm IV in his time, as also to eliminate one possible way to the reformation of the alienating elements in production under which art itself might be made to suffer.

Although never able to explain clearly how art could function both as a part of the alienation produced in capitalist societies, and as a means to the reformation of the forces producing that alienation, Marx was to persist in his development of a materialist and productivist aesthetic, as also in the development of his criticism of the forms taken by economic production under industrial capitalism. A study of his later works – from his *German Ideology* of 1845 to his *Grundrisse* and *Capital* – will also show that having written in his *Introduction to a Critique of Hegel's Philosophy of Right* of 1843–4 that the criticism of heaven, of religion, and of theology would turn into the criticism of earth, of law, and of politics, Marx may well have added with reference to his own work that the criticism of artistic production would turn into a criticism of production in general. This was at least what was to happen in works such as his *German Ideology* and *Grundrisse,* in which, as we shall see in the following chapter, the concept of artistic production used by Marx in his early writings – from 1842 to 1844 – plays an important role in the development of his critique of the processes of production in general, as well as in the formulation of concepts basic to a materialist and 'productivist' aesthetic.

# 5

# Towards an outline of artistic production, or the 'charm' of a materialist aesthetic

## Introduction

Although Marx had spoken of a future form of non-alienated labour in terms of artistic activity in his *Economic and Philosophic Manuscripts* of 1844, he had not yet offered a fully developed analysis of art as a form of economic production subject to the demands – and alienations – of other forms of production. As seen in the last chapter, the ideal of a non-alienated 'artistic' form of production functions for Marx in his 1844 *Manuscripts*, in contrast to his antagonist Adam Smith, as an as yet unrealised alternative to the economically productive – and alienated – forms of labour encouraged by industrial capitalism. In contrast, further, to Kant and Schiller, existing art did not for Marx represent an 'Ideal' separate from and transcending the real world of economic production, but a product of the same alienating conditions under which economic production has taken place. The liberation of the senses from their state of alienation is thus a problem which for Marx remains attached to that of ending the alienation of labour, and, as just seen, receives as little solution as that other problem in the *Manuscripts* as we now have them.

While rejecting Adam Smith's definition of 'productive' art as art productive of exchange value only, Marx was to develop his own 'Saint-Simonian' concept of art as a form of socially important production in both his *German Ideology* of 1845 – in which he also discusses Saint-Simon and his followers at some length – and in his *Grundrisse* Introduction of 1857. It is in his *German Ideology*, furthermore, that Marx speaks of Raphael – the artist lionised in Marx's time by the German Nazarenes – and argues against what he calls, with reference to the cultural politics of his own time as well as to those of

Raphael's Renaissance world, 'an elitist view of art as something only to be created by great individuals'.[1] To Marx and Engels in 1845 the communist organisation of labour was, as in Marx's 1844 *Manuscripts*, both to liberate the senses of each citizen and to allow 'anyone in whom there is a potential Raphael to be able to develop without hindrance'. Looking back from this Utopian future to the past, Marx and Engels also made the point that the system under which art had previously been produced was one in which the individual artist was both limited by the demands of the market and dependent on the assistance of other managerial or entrepreneurial figures – an idea which might also remind one of Marx's and Engels' earlier statements against the patronage given by Friedrich Wilhelm IV to those artists who had supported the Christian Prussian State. Here, however, Marx set out not only to criticise the system of patronage in the arts, but also to demythologise the Romantic concept of the artist as an original genius (as expressed by Rumohr in his defence of Raphael), and to criticise the related concept of 'uniqueness' which he saw defended in Stirner's concept of private property. Hence he wrote that 'whether an individual like Raphael succeeds in developing his talent depends wholly on demand, which in turn depends on the division of labour and the conditions of human culture resulting from it'.

The passage on artistic talent in the *German Ideology*, to which we have been referring, begins, moreover, by alluding to Stirner's critique of the 'organisers of labour' (that is, Utopian socialists such as Fourier and Saint-Simon), who had opposed what they saw to be the 'anarchy of production under capitalism' with a reorganisation of labour. It reads in full:

> He [Stirner] imagines that the so-called organisers of labour wanted to organise the entire activity of each individual, and yet it is precisely among them that a difference is drawn between directly productive labour, which has to be organised, and labour which is not directly productive. In regard to the latter, however, it was not their view, as Sancho imagines, that each should do the work of Raphael, but that anyone in whom there is a Raphael should be allowed to develop without hindrance. Sancho imagines that Raphael produced his pictures independently of the division of labour that existed in Rome at the time. If he were to compare Raphael with Leonardo da Vinci and Titian, he would know how greatly Raphael's works of art depended on the flourishing of Rome at that time, which occurred under Florentine influence, while the works of Leonardo depended on the state of things in Florence, and the works of Titian, at a later period, depended on the totally different development of Venice. Raphael as much as any other

artist was determined by the technical advances in art made before him, by the organisation of society and the division of labour in his locality, and, finally, by the division of labour in all the countries with which his locality had intercourse. Whether an individual like Raphael succeeds in developing his talent depends wholly on demand, which in turn depends on the division of labour and the conditions of human culture resulting from it.

In proclaiming the uniqueness of work in science and art, Stirner adopts a position far inferior to that of the bourgeoisie. At the present time it has already been found necessary to organise this 'unique' activity. Horace Vernet would not have had time to paint even a tenth of his pictures if he regarded them as works which 'only this Unique person is capable of producing'. In Paris, the great demand for vaudevilles and novels brought about the organisation of work for their production, organisation which at any rate yields something better than its 'unique' competitors in Germany. In astronomy, people like Arago, Herschel, Encke and Bessel considered it necessary to organise joint observations and only after that obtained some fruitful results. In historical science, it is absolutely impossible for the 'Unique' to achieve anything at all, and in this field, too, the French long ago surpassed all other nations thanks to organisation of labour. Incidentally, it is self-evident that all these organisations based on modern division of labour still lead only to extremely limited results, representing a step forward only compared with the previous narrow isolation . . .

The exclusive concentration of artistic talent in particular individuals, and its suppression in the broad mass which is bound up with this, is a consequence of division of labour. If, even in certain social conditions, everyone was an excellent painter, that would not at all exclude the possibility of each of them being also an original painter, so that here too the difference between 'human' and 'unique' labour amounts to sheer nonsense. In any case, with a communist organisation of society, there disappears the subordination of the artist to local and national narrowness, which arises entirely from division of labour, and also the subordination of the artist to some definite art thanks to which he is exclusively a painter, sculptor, etc., the very name of his activity adequately expressing the narrowness of his professional development and his dependence on division of labour. In a communist society there are no painters but at most people who engage in painting among other activities.

It is interesting to note in this passage that Marx has not only taken Raphael, the hero and model of the German Nazarenes, as an example of the falsity of the concept of 'uniqueness' as applied to the work of the artist, but has compared him with Horace Vernet, whose paintings had hung together with Delacroix's *Liberty* in the Salon of 1831 and been described by Heine in his Saint-Simonian and anti-Nazarene reports on that Salon.

Heine had mentioned Vernet several times in both his Saint-Simonian reports on the Salons of 1831 and 1833, and in his *Lutezia* reports of 1843, and it is also likely, as suggested earlier, that Marx had known the first of Heine's Salon reports, and been aware of the opposition Heine had set up there between the spiritualism of Raphael and his nineteenth-century acolytes, the German Nazarenes, and the 'sensualism' of the new French art of 1831. Marx had of course met Heine in Paris in 1843, and continued to exchange pieces of work with him over the following few years of their acquaintance. In 1850 Marx was, moreover, to compare 'Raphaelite beauty in which all pictorial truth is lost' with the 'real form' and 'strong colours' of Rembrandt,[2] just as Heine had earlier (in chapter 11 of his *Memoirs of Schnabelewopski*) heretically compared the vibrant art of the Dutch painter Jan Steen with the art of Raphael, but at the same time predicted that Jan Steen's religion of joy would only come to be appreciated with the demise of the spiritualistic religions which had preferred the portrayal of suffering and sorrow in art.

In contrast to Stirner's praise for the 'uniqueness' of Raphael, Marx uses Vernet as a contemporary example of how the painter had actually to work in a workshop not unlike those of artisans and handicraftsmen.[3] Having 'demystified' Stirner's concept of the 'Unique', Marx uses this instance to criticise the idea that artistic labour can only be done by 'unique' and separate individuals. In his criticism of the divisions of labour affecting artistic production, but especially in Marx's final claim that in a communist society 'there are no painters but at most people who engage in painting among other activities', we find, moreover, an identification of artistic production with other forms of labour and production which echoes the identification made between them by Saint-Simon in his *L'Industrie*, and which also serves to undermine the concept of a community of priest-like artists as projected by the Saint-Simonians Enfantin and Barrault in the 1830s and criticised elsewhere in *The German Ideology* as a betrayal of Saint-Simon.[4]

In looking forward to a time in which art would be one with other forms of production, and in developing his argument that artistic production could be seen as determined by forces similar to those determining other forms of production, Marx above all brought attention back from the art object to the process of its production and opened the way for the elimination of the theoretical division between art and technological labour as it had been enshrined in German aesthetic theory by Kant, Schiller, and Hegel. It is therefore interesting to note that it is the theories of these thinkers – of Kant, Schiller, and Hegel – which are again 'refunctioned' in Marx's next attempt at an analysis of the processes involved in artistic production, in his *Grundrisse* Introduction of 1857, and translated into a materialist aesthetic in which artistic and material production are seen to be subject to the same laws and conditions of material life.

### *1857: the 'charm' of a materialist aesthetic*

As Marx had been asked in 1857 to contribute an article on aesthetics to the *New American Cyclopedia,* and had evidently been reviewing F. T. Vischer's *Aesthetics* (the sixth and last volume of which was published in 1857) and E. Müller's history of ancient Greek aesthetics at the same time as he was writing his *Grundrisse* Introduction, it is perhaps not surprising that one of the central questions of that Introduction was of how a technically advanced age such as that of Marx could still be charmed by Greek art. While that question may also have had some relevance to his own concern with writing an article on aesthetics at the same time as he was supposed to be completing a study of modern economics, the answer he gives to it in his *Grundrisse* Introduction of 1857 is to be found in large part in his opening remarks on how the uneven development within the arts, and between them and their societies, contains for us the important historical lesson of how our own social development from the 'childhood' of the ancient world has been a matter of changes in material production. He wrote:

> (8) The point of departure obviously from the natural characteristic; subjectively and objectively. Tribes, races, etc.
> (1) In the case of the arts, it is well known that certain periods of their flowering are out of all proportion to the general development of society, hence also to the material foundation, the skeletal structure as it were, of its organization. For example, the Greeks compared to the moderns or also Shakespeare. It is even recognized that certain forms of art, e.g. the epic, can no longer be produced in their world epoch-making, classical stature as soon as the production of art, as such, begins; that is, that certain significant forms within the realm of the arts are possible only at an undeveloped stage of artistic development. If this is the case with the relation between different kinds of art within the realm of the arts, it is already less puzzling that it is the case in the relation of the entire realm to the general development of society. The difficulty consists only in the general formulation of these contradictions. As soon as they have been specified, they are already clarified.

Let us take e.g. the relation of Greek art and then of Shakespeare to the present time. It is well known that Greek mythology is not only the arsenal of Greek art but also its foundation. Is the view of nature and of social relations on which the Greek imagination and hence Greek (mythology) is based possible with self-acting mule spindles and railways and locomotives and electrical telegraphs? What chance has Vulcan against Roberts & Co., Jupiter against the lightning-rod and Hermes against the Crédit Mobilier? All mythology overcomes and dominates and shapes the forces of nature in the imagination and by the imagination; it therefore vanishes with the advent of real mastery over them. What becomes of Fama alongside Printing House Square? Greek art presupposes Greek mythology, i.e. nature and the social forms already reworked in an unconsciously artistic way by the popular imagination. This is its material. Not any mythology whatever, i.e. not an arbitrarily chosen unconsciously artistic reworking of nature (here meaning everything objective, hence including society). Egyptian mythology could never have been the foundation or the womb of Greek art. But, in any case, a mythology. Hence, in no way a social development which excludes all mythological, all mythologizing relations to nature; which therefore demands of the artist an imagination not dependent on mythology.

From another side: is Achilles possible with powder and lead? Or the Iliad with the printing press, not to mention the printing machine? Do not the song and the saga and the muse necessarily come to an end with the printer's bar, hence do not the necessary conditions of epic poetry vanish?

But the difficulty lies not in understanding that the Greek arts and epic are bound up with certain forms of social development. The difficulty is that they still afford us artistic pleasure and that in a certain respect they count as a norm and as an unattainable model.

A man cannot become a child again, or he becomes childish. But does he not find joy in the child's naiveté, and must he himself not strive to reproduce its truth at a higher stage? Does not the true character of each epoch come alive in the nature of its children? Why should not the historic childhood of humanity, its most beautiful unfolding, as a stage never to return, exercise an eternal charm? There are unruly children and precocious children. Many of the old peoples belong to this category. The Greeks were normal children. The charm of their art for us is not in contradiction to the undeveloped stage of society on which it grew. [It] is its result, rather, and is inextricably bound up, rather, with the fact that the unripe social conditions under which it arose, and could alone arise, never return.[5]

Two major points made by Marx here are:

1. That art demonstrates the unequal development of economic and artistic production within society, and, therefore, of production in general

and

2. that the reason for the continuing charm of Greek art in the face of the demise of its particular social context can be found in the first point, in the implication that art has a role to play in human history in letting us understand the historical character of the material production and development of our societies.

The first of these points, the argument for seeing an uneven development between art and its social base, is not only important to Marx's development of the idea that art can have explanatory value in materialist terms, but also implies a rejection of any simplistic identification of art and the object represented in it – of art as merely the reflection of society. While still claiming a reflectionist function for art John Hoffman suggests a similar reading,[6] interpreting Marx's statement on the uneven development of material production relative to artistic development as a definite connection between art and society, but as one made in terms of an uneven relationship rather than as a simple parallelism: 'Artistic production can only be meaningfully understood in relation to (and as a reflection of) the material conditions of social life, but this relationship should not be seen as a simple parallelism.' As Hoffman points out,[7] Marx's *Grundrisse* Introduction further suggests that the uneven relationship between art and its base is itself due to the social conditions (Marx calls them 'unripe') in the base. With this claim Marx also rejects the Idealist view of Greek art of, for example, Schiller, that it had come from a world in complete harmony with itself. Similarly, our perception of the art of the past is understood by Marx to be the perception of a reflection of our childhood, as also of the processes of historical change themselves. The cognitive function of such art is hence much more than representational reflection (of 'showing that') – it is for Marx clearly also a matter of 'showing how'. It may well be for this reason too that such art is for Marx something which can both have 'eternal charm' and remain as an ideal before us and be both a 'norm and an unattainable model'. For like any statement which is to show us how some other statement or occurrence functions, Greek art, when understood as a way of making us comprehend historical change, may function as a norm for how we should try to understand other statements made in the past, but it is itself 'unattainable' in the sense that the knowledge it aims for (in this case, how our past has given rise to the present) can never be complete so long as history and the study of history is incomplete. This would at least be the logic of Marx's epistemological interpretation of the function of Greek art as that of showing us *how* we, and our art, have developed as a part of material history. Reproducing the truth of an earlier art 'at a higher stage' is, in Marx's materialist interpretation (despite the Idealist sound of its terms) a matter of reactivating the art of our past as something which tells us the 'how' of our historical–cultural development.

It should be said that such an epistemology of art is also at least intentionally materialist in deputing art to be the interpreter of its and our relationship to its material base, and in designating its 'consumption' as reflective of the material conditions in which it occurs. This materialist bias is also basic to Marx's reinterpretations and refunctionings of Idealist aesthetics in the above text, where both Hegel and Schiller are refashioned for a materialist aesthetic of artistic production. (The *Aesthetics* of Vischer which Marx was to review in 1857 was, moreover, a neo-Hegelian work in which some of the Idealist ideas refunctioned by Marx in his *Grundrisse* Introduction had been discussed.) In line with Marx's materialist reinterpretation of Idealist aesthetics, Hegel's comments on the end of the ancient epic in the course of the progress of Spirit towards greater self-consciousness of itself in world history thus becomes the basis – at the beginning of Marx's Introduction – for an analysis of the material reasons for its demise. Marx writes:

> It is even recognized that certain forms of art, e.g. the epic, can no longer be produced in their world epoch-making, classical stature as soon as the production of art, as such, begins; that is, that certain significant forms within the realm of the arts are possible only at an undeveloped stage of artistic development.

Not only Hegel's explanation of the disappearance of the epic in terms of the growth to self-consciousness by Spirit, but also his explanation of the difference between the Greeks' attribution of natural phenomena to the gods and modern man's explanation of them 'scientifically' in terms of universal laws and forces is 'refunctioned' by Marx in his next paragraph. Hegel had written in Part 2 of his *Lectures on Aesthetics*, in the section on the 'Ideal of Classical Art':

> We moderns, with our prosaic reason, explain physical phenomena by universal laws and forces; human actions, by personal wills. The Greek poets, on the contrary, saw, above all in these phenomena, their divine author. In representing human acts as divine acts, they showed the diverse aspects under which the gods reveal their power.

Marx of course wrote:

> Is the view of nature and of social relations on which the Greek imagination and hence Greek mythology is based possible with self-acting mule spindles and railways and locomotives and electrical telegraphs? What chance has Vulcan against Roberts & Co., Jupiter against the lightning-rod and Hermes against the Crédit Mobilier? All mythology overcomes and dominates and shapes the forces of nature in the imagination and by the imagination; it therefore vanishes with real mastery over them.[8]

Hegel's explanation of modern man's difference from the ancient Greeks in terms of his rational explanation of physical phenomena 'by universal laws and forces' – by, that is, the ever-increasing self-consciousness of Reason in history – is opposed by Marx with an explanation made in terms of material production, in terms of the technological advances which have actually tamed or harnessed Nature. Marx's refunctioning of Hegel is also self-consciously ironic in its final identification of the demise of Hermes with the rise of the 'Crédit Mobilier', and is not unlike the identification made by Heine in his 1831 review description of Delacroix's *Liberty*. Hermes, as mentioned previously, with reference to Heine's review, was the god chosen by Hegel to symbolise the progress of his World Spirit through history. Here, countered to the 'Crédit Mobilier' – the free flow of credit encouraged by French Saint-Simonian bankers of the 'enrichissez-vous' conviction of the 1840s and 1850s – Hegel's god is shown to have been outdated by the progress of industrial capital. By implication, Saint-Simon would appear still to be more relevant to Marx's theory of production than Hegel, just as his concept of artistic production has begun to prove more informative about the production of material history than Hegel's concept of art as the 'träumendes Spiegelbild ihrer Zeit', as a 'mirror reflection of its age'. This would seem to be implied in Marx's arguments, even if Marx's reference to the 'Crédit Mobilier' encouraged by Saint-Simonian followers is also an ironic reminder to the reader of the way in which the latter had finally aided rather than undermined the growth of inequality under industrial capitalism in France.[9]

It is clear when Marx agrees with Hegel that 'all mythology overcomes and dominates and shapes the forces of nature in the imagination', but then adds that 'it therefore vanishes with the advent of real mastery over them', that he is referring too to Hegel's Idealist explanation of the mythological. Yet one disadvantage of Marx's use of Hegel in this way (as with his use of Schiller) must be the resulting vagueness of some of his statements. Marx did not in fact complete or publish this Introduction, one should remember, because, as he writes in his Preface to the *Grundrisse* of 1859, he did not want the reader to be introduced to his work by proceeding from the general to the particular; rather, Marx decided, the particular must lead into the general to avoid the tendencies of the Idealist manner he was countermanding. Here it should be remembered too that the section on artistic production discussed above is the last of the sections in the Introduction as left by Marx, and is in fact unfinished. The discussion of Shakespeare which is mentioned, for example, is never forthcoming, at least within the Introduction itself. It should also be observed that the notes occur within a section of the Introduction, entitled 'Production, means of production and conditions of production and distribution; the connection between form and state and consciousness on the one hand and relations of production and distribution on the other: legal relations: family relations', and are number 8, the last of its points. They may therefore also connect with other arguments, such as that in point 2 'on the relation between the previous idealistic methods of writing history and the realistic method' which are not necessarily developed in the Introduction as we now have it, or connected with all the points with which they might originally have been intended to connect. (For instance, the 'realist' method of history spoken of in 2 appears to contrast with previous Idealist methods, yet Hegel's aesthetic ideas might however best be read both as Idealist and realist in the sense that art was to reflect reality as an expression of the Ideal.) Despite these problems and the lack of explicit connections between its various points, Marx's *Grundrisse* Introduction might furthermore best be read with the possible interconnection of its points in mind.

We have already investigated an example of how Marx had (covertly) proceeded to reinterpret Hegel's Idealist method of writing history in point 8, but as point 2 also specifies that the Idealist method of history in question is that of 'the history of religion and states', it may also be suggested that point 8 be read with this additional rider to Marx's criticism of Idealist history in mind. Clearly point 8 is also relevant to the 'history of religion and of states' even in its rewriting of Hegel, whose philosophy of State Marx had already discussed in the 1840s, but it could also be relevant to much more yet to come – to a critique, for example, of the religious misuse of art, or of its political misuse.

Point 6 might also be said to be related to point 8 in describing the 'unequal relation' between the development of material production and art, as also in its next point (relative to Marx's ironic treatment of

Hegel's Hermes) that 'In general, the conception of progress is not to be taken in the sense of the usual abstraction.'[10] Yet there is a difficulty created by a comparison between the sixth and eighth point relevant to our investigation of the development of a concept of artistic production in Marx's work. This difficulty resides in the fact that in point 6 there is a distinction made between art and the development of material production, while the role attributed to art in 8, of making the historical character of material production clear, acts to qualify this distinction, giving a role to art within the development of material production – a move possibly also made necessary by point 2. With this shift the argument also changes (in point 8), from a discussion of the mentality of the artist to that of the audience. Thus, in the first part of his argument, Marx explains on the example of the Greeks how great art can be produced in a materially primitive society, and what its relationship was to the physical world around it, and in the second part, its reception by the modern reader in modern times. Here the work of art is, further, no longer seen in contrast to the physical world, or in uneven development with it, but as part of the modern understanding of the development of material history through these uneven developments.

What is happening here is that Marx is beginning to talk of art in terms of both its production and its consumption – the moment in the production cycle which the *Grundrisse* themselves will discuss at length as important to the reproduction of production. In this sense too, the concept of artistic production is developed further in Marx's work as a moment important in the reproduction of the material history of modern society. This concept of reproduction is, however, also introduced in the Introduction within a refunctioning of Idealist aesthetics and, seemingly, in its terms. In his final paragraph Marx writes, returning to the language of Schiller's essay 'On Naive and Sentimental Poetry': 'A man cannot become a child again except that he become childish. But does he not find joy in the child's naiveté, and must he himself not strive to reproduce its truth on a higher level?'[11]

Schiller – many of whose aesthetic ideas had been taken over by Hegel, including his belief that Greek art represented a 'naive' harmony of idea and form – had defined the naive 'as a childlike character found exactly where it is not to be expected', and had contrasted true naivety with that which is 'ungezogen', or 'unruly', as Marx also does when contrasting unruly and precocious children with the normality of the Greeks. Schiller's implication that the discovery of the naive in the Greek world is 'unexpected' may at first also seem to pre-empt Marx's point that we find an uneven development between Greek art and its society, even though Schiller then also explicitly suggests that he finds them in harmony. What is unexpected about finding the naive in the Greek world is, however, for Schiller, its conjunction with an apparently highly developed civilisation, where for Marx the uneven development evident in Greek society was between its sophisticated culture and its 'primitive' mode of production.

Next Marx appears to take up Schiller's distinction between the childlike and the childish in distinguishing between the childlike Greeks and the childishness of those who would want to bring that childhood back. In stressing the historicity of the naive, and in substituting pleasure for loss as the reaction of those comprehending this aspect of it (its place in the historical past), Marx, however, unlike Schiller, rejects the sentimental itself as negatively 'childish'.

In addition to calling the Greeks childlike in the sense that they represented to him the childhood of modern, 'sentimental' man, Schiller, in contrast to Marx, had given a synchronic rather than a diachronic explanation of their relationship to ourselves by suggesting that they metaphorically represent our own lost childhood relationship to Nature, as well as a goal to be regained 'on a higher level'.

> Sie sind, was wir waren, sie sind, was wir wieder werden sollen. Wir waren Natur, wie sie, und unsere Kultur soll uns, auf dem Wege der Vernunft und der Freiheit, zur Natur zurückführen. Sie sind also Darstellung unserer verlorenen Kindheit, die uns ewig das Teuerste bleibt; daher sie uns mit einer gewissen Wehmut erfüllen.

> (They are, what we were; they are what we should become again. We were part of Nature, like them, and our culture should lead us back to Nature through the path of Reason and Liberty. They are therefore a representation of our lost childhood, which always remains the most dear thing to us, so that they fill us with a certain nostalgia.)[12]

Although Marx had spoken earlier of looking back with pleasure instead of 'Wehmut', or nostalgia, to the lost childhood represented by the Greeks, we have seen that he had also spoken (as had Schiller), of 'reproducing its truth on a higher level'. This, as we have also seen, was, however, the 'truth' – greater to Marx than the Ideal Truth offered by Schiller or Hegel – of the historical character of material development, and of its contradictory progress through all levels of society from the production of art to the production of the most simple use objects. In his *Grundrisse* Introduction Marx thus rewrote both Schiller and Hegel into a materialistic aesthetic concerned with the historical place of art in moments of historical production, and with the epistemological role of the reception of art in allowing us both to understand the development of those moments and to 'reproduce' them. In this sense too the art admired by Marx in his Introduction is one concerned with satisfying the material needs of its receiver. It hence also offers the very opposite to the 'disinterestedness' of the ideal form of self-reflexive 'sentimental' art envisaged by Schiller as being able to reproduce the truth of Greek art 'on a higher level'. To sum up this argument, the 'higher level' taken by Marx's aesthetic is also one related to reflexivity, to the 'showing how' of historical development, but in that this reflexivity is also involved for Marx in the reproduction of the historical materialist method as well as its objects, it is for Marx a higher-order moment of reflection within a materialistic framework.

Because of such arguments Marx's *Grundrisse* Introduction marks yet another rejection in his work of Romantic aesthetics, and a defence of the Hellenistic against what Heine had called the Nazarene.[13] To Romantics such as the Schlegels, as to Schiller and Hegel, the ancient Greeks had represented a society in harmony with Nature, undisturbed by the inner strife of modern societies, but at the same time incapable, because of their primitive harmonious relationship with Nature, of achieving the heights of the subjective freedom of the modern poet. Also opposed to the ideals of 'edle Einfalt und stille Grösse' (of 'noble simplicity and quiet greatness') of Wincklemann's theory of classical art, Romantic art was conceived of by the Schlegels and Novalis as breaking down the barriers between genres as well as those between imagination and reason, and of achieving a 'syncretic' and 'self-reflexive' union of each. The 'self-reflexivity' praised by Marx was, on the other hand, related not to an Idealist but to a materialist epistemology, and not to a religious, Christian form of art, but to that of the Greeks.

Read against the background of his time, Marx's comments on the eternal charm of Greek art in his *Grundrisse* Introduction reflect not only a preference for ancient art as a model for his own concept of art, but also a certain continuing political antipathy of the Hellene to the Nazarene, as shown in his earlier political statements against the Prussian monarch Friedrich Wilhelm IV. In fact, London was, at the time Marx was writing his *Grundrisse,* the centre of a 'revival' of the art of the German Nazarenes by English Pre-Raphaelites who had been inspired by them,[14] such as Sir Charles Lock Eastlake, whose 1855 version of his *Christ Lamenting over Jerusalem* of 1841 is illustrated here (fig. 37).

Like the German Nazarenes with whose work he was acquainted,

37. Sir Charles Lock Eastlake, *Christ Lamenting over Jerusalem*, 1855 version of 1841 original (Glasgow Art Gallery & Museum)

Eastlake had spent several years in Rome (between 1816 and 1830) and had, like them, been inspired by the works of the early Renaissance Italian masters. He had also, together with other Pre-Raphaelites like William Dyce, been favoured with the patronage of the Prince Consort, Prince Albert, who had also bought several examples of Nazarene art for Queen Victoria. One was a pencil sketch of Overbeck's *Triumph of Religion in the Arts* (fig. 9). In addition Albert had received the Nazarene artist Ferdinand Olivier's *Journey to Emmaus* cycle of 1827 as a gift from Friedrich Wilhelm IV and could still be seen, on Marx's arrival in London in 1849, to be an ally of the Prussian King.

Albert may even have admired the work of the German Nazarenes while a student in Bonn during the time Marx was developing his critique of Christian art, having attended Eduard d'Alton's lectures on modern art history in Bonn in 1837–8, just two years after Marx had heard them. Evidence of Albert's attendance at d'Alton's Bonn lectures[15] also suggests that he must have been exposed to examples of religious art similar to those seen by Marx in the collection made by d'Alton for Bonn, and copied by him for his students. In addition, it may be assumed too that Albert had been made aware in Bonn of the work of the Nazarene fresco-painter Jakob Goetzenberger

38. Ferdinand Olivier, *The Journey to Emmaus* (reproduced by gracious permission of Her Majesty the Queen)

who visited London with Cornelius shortly after the marriage of Albert to Victoria, in 1841, and who later returned to work in Britain for several of the years in which Albert reigned with Victoria as her Prince Consort and as patron of the English Pre-Raphaelites. As it was also these Nazarene artists who were specifically called upon to give advice on the painting of frescoes for Westminster to a committee presided over by Prince Albert in 1841 it is also quite possible that Albert's interest in them went back to his introduction to the frescoes which they had done for the Aula of the University at Bonn, and which Marx (though by contrast to Albert as unsympathetic to their religious art as he was to Westminster) must also have seen as a Bonn student.

In addition to the revival of Nazarene art which developed in London in the 1840s and 1850s with the help of the patronage given to both the Nazarenes and the English Pre-Raphaelites by Prince Albert, preparations took place in the London circle of German *émigrés* known to Marx for a grand 'Schiller-Feier', a celebration of Schiller's centenary, in 1859.

39. Sir Edwin Landseer, *Windsor Castle in Modern Times*, 1841–5 (reproduced by gracious permission of Her Majesty the Queen)

While he himself is not usually counted as a Pre-Raphaelite, Sir Edwin Landseer's 1841–5 portrayal of Queen Victoria, Prince Albert, and the Princess Royal in his *Windsor Castle in Modern Times* is typical of the romantic Pre-Raphaelite style favoured by the Prince Consort. It was begun at the time of a visit to London of the Nazarene artists Peter Cornelius and Jakob Goetzenberger, the designer and painter respectively of the frescoes which Albert had seen (two years after Marx) in Bonn in 1837–8.

The *Feier* was organised by some of the German exiles of the 1848 revolution then living in London. One of these, Marx's erstwhile friend, the poet Freiligrath, was actually berated by Marx for his planned participation in it. But this is more immediately the context not of the *Grundrisse* Introduction, but of the famous epistolary debate between Marx and Engels with Lassalle in 1859 on his historical drama *Franz von Sickingen*. Much discussed by critics concerned with Marx's and Engels' concept of the 'realistic' in literature, that debate is also interesting for Marx's criticism of Lassalle's tendency to 'Schillern'. Meaning 'to change colour', 'schillern' refers to the tendency of the work, in Marx's and Engels' eyes, to 'change colour' in the sense of avoiding the real material issues of the Revolution which was its subject. It is, however, also (of course) a pun on the name of Schiller, whose belief in the possibility of individual tragedy they accuse Lassalle of having taken as the model for his tragedy instead of Shakespeare.

Marx's and Engels' debate with Lassalle has unfortunately rarely, if ever, been discussed against the background of Marx's materialist reinterpretation of Schiller, two years earlier in the *Grundrisse* Introduction, as part, not of an aesthetic of Realism, but of artistic production. An analysis of the attitudes to art suggested there could, however, put its general aesthetic argument in a new light, as following from an aesthetic concerned as much with the role of art in materialist production as with the reflection of historical reality in art.[16]

Marx's *Grundrisse* Introduction of 1857 also represents, of course, not only a sophisticated reappraisal of the arguments for Hellenistic against Nazarene art with which he and Bauer and others had concerned themselves in the 1840s, but a more sophisticated attempt than had, for example, been made in the *Economic and Philosophic Manuscripts* of 1844 to integrate an analysis of artistic production and aesthetic perception into a general theory of economic production. This is particularly evident in Marx's indications that he will speak of the art work in terms of both its production and consumption, in order to explain how it is able both to produce an object of aesthetic value, and to create a subject for its object. He writes of how production is also consumption, and of how it creates its consumers by not only 'supplying the want with material, but the material with a want': 'The want for it [the object] which consumption experiences is created by its perception of the product. The object of art, as well as any other product, creates an artistic public, appreciative of beauty. Production thus produces not only an object for the subject, but also a subject for the object.'

One of the effects of the creation of a 'subject' by the art work, as described by Marx in this passage, is the creation of a public 'appreciative of beauty'. In that the creation of such a public seems also to imply an end to the alienation of the aesthetic senses of which he spoke in his 1844 *Economic and Philosophic Manuscripts*, one might further conclude that he had chosen to emphasise the avant-garde, reforming role to be played by art, rather than its alienation, in his *Grundrisse*. Even if this were to have been the case in that unfinished work, Marx's later writings, and notably those edited by Engels, such as *Capital* 1 to 3, and his *Theories of Surplus Value*, were, however, to return to the argument of his 1844 *Manuscripts* that art – like all other forms of production – was subject to alienation under the capitalist mode of production. This was of course to bind again his Saint-Simonist argument for an avant-garde, reforming role for art to both a critique of alienated production and to the proposition that art, together with other forms of production, would always be the victim of exploitation under industrial capitalism. Apart from the possible influence of Engels on these later works, it is clear that although synthesising Saint-Simonist and Hegelian ideas achieved some things for Marx (such as the translation of Feuerbach's theory of alienated consciousness into a theory of alienated production), it had also created an unresolved conflict of ideas in his work. The conflict discussed above was of course that between Saint-Simon's Utopian concept of an avant-garde of artistic and scientifically able producer–administrators and Feuerbach's less optimistic 'Hegelian' emphasis on the dominance of alienation in society. The continuing battle between productivist and determinist arguments in contemporary Marxism (and not only within its aesthetic debates) may furthermore reflect the unresolved character of Marx's synthesis of Hegelian and Saint-Simonist ideas in his early work.

It is perhaps also because of problems such as those just mentioned – as well as because of the increasing co-operation of the French Saint-Simonians with capitalist enterprises in the latter years of the nineteenth century – that the Saint-Simonist concept of an avant-garde of 'artistic producers' was to remain subsumed, though not entirely silent, in Marxist theory after Marx, beneath the more political and radically anti-feudal concept of an avant-garde of worker–producers suggested by Marx and Engels in their *Communist Manifesto* of 1848.[17] Following the 1917 revolution in Russia the Saint-Simonist concept of avant-garde which entered Russia in the early nineteenth century did, however, surface again in an avant-garde movement concerned both with uniting artistic and scientific talents and with joining the artistic avant-garde to the proletariat and its concerns. Because those avant-gardes were also less concerned with the problem of alienated or surplus labour which had concerned Marx in his criticisms of capitalism than with problems of insufficient or inefficient production, they were also to see nothing wrong in championing an avant-garde concept of artistic production as part of the new revolutionary ideology of their time. Only later, would, as will be seen, the Saint-Simonist concept of avant-garde again be silenced in Russia.

# PART TWO

# The Russian Saint-Simon: the artist as producer in Russia from the 1830s to the 1930s and beyond

# 6

*Saint-Simonists and Realists*

While in nineteenth-century France and Germany Saint-Simonism had by the 1850s begun to develop into what was to seem to Marx to be the very opposite of the programmes envisaged by Saint-Simon, Saint-Simon's ideas had remained alive but dormant and seemingly 'uncorrupted' in at least one strand of nineteenth-century Russian thought, that is, in the belief in the 'avant-garde' role to be played by the artist and intellectual in revolutionising Russia's still feudal and under-industrialised society. The history of the Saint-Simonian concept of the artist or intellectual as an 'avant-garde' producer in Russia is, however, complicated by at least two of the factors which helped to keep it dormant: by its censorship (together with the censorship of other Saint-Simonian and socialist ideas) under Nicholas I, and by the loss of interest in industrial development in the Russia into which it was introduced in the early nineteenth century. Despite these factors, even the briefest overview of the history of the survival, and suppression, of Saint-Simonian thought in Russia will nevertheless reveal its continuing presence there, from its introduction in the 1830s to the early years of the twentieth century.

Russian links with Saint-Simonian thought can in fact be traced back to Saint-Simon's own time. Not only had one young Russian intellectual, the Decembrist Michael Lunin, met Saint-Simon in Paris and heard him speak there of his belief that 'mankind could only reach its new destiny if sentiment, science and industry were joined together for the progress of society',[1] but, as Keith Taylor has written in the Introduction to his collection of the writings of Saint-Simon, Saint-Simonian thought had also entered Russia by 1829 by way of journals and books, as well as through the visit in that year of some French Saint-Simonians. Despite censorship, it was then taken up in the 1830s by such thinkers as the socialists Herzen and Ogarev.[2] Just as the July Revolution of 1830 in Paris was to increase interest in the theories of the

French Saint-Simonians, so, as Taylor also argues, the Polish Revolution of 1830–1 was to fire the interest of Russian thinkers in the Utopian socialism of Saint-Simon and his followers. Yet where the French in 1830 had had a context for the reception of Saint-Simonian thought, with both their industrialisation of industry and the reorganisation of their political and economic systems, early nineteenth-century Russia had not.

It was for this reason too, that, where Saint-Simonian ideas were spoken of in nineteenth-century Russia, they were frequently not those pertaining to Saint-Simon's arguments for the modernisation of industrial relations of production as much as the more mystical Saint-Simonian beliefs concerning the priest-like role to be played by the avant-garde artist or the coming of a new 'Third Testament'.[3] The theories of Saint-Simon which had to do with the need to reorganise labour and industry and to train engineers, scientists and artists to play the role of an avant-garde for the establishment of the new and better society of the future could find little actual application in early nineteenth-century Russia. Even though engineering had been established there in the eighteenth century as an academic scientific discipline in its higher technical colleges and military academies, interest in the practical development of industry and technology had waned after the time of Catherine the Great. When interest in the socialist philosophy which was the central part of Saint-Simon's theory was further actively discouraged by Nicholas I, the reaction to the Tsar's policies which developed came largely from a Populist movement little interested in Russia's industrial development. The particular union of art, technology, and social engineering envisaged by Saint-Simon for France (where many of his followers had attended the École Polytechnique to train to become, like the famed de Lesseps, engineers and architects) was really only to come to Russia in the revolutionary years after 1917. Similarly, only when Russia needed both machines and an avant-garde industrialised proletariat – in the revolutionary year of 1917 and after – was it to develop a 'machine aesthetic' which was not just an 'aestheticisation' of the machine (as it was, for example, for followers of the Italian Futurist, Marinetti) but a programme for the practical, economically productive, and socialism-orientated combination of art and technology.

Significantly enough, the Constructivist El Lissitzky also emphasised this point to members of the German Bauhaus on a visit there in 1923. Previously, in a lecture on new Russian art given in 1922, he had furthermore described the Constructivists' relationship with the machine as being one of mutual interdependence: 'It was the economy of the age which created the machine. The machine showed us movement, showed us circulation. It showed us life and how it vibrates and palpitates from the forces that flow through it.'[4]

With the point in mind that Russia was only to develop its own technology and its own 'machine aesthetic' in union with a socialist programme of reform in the first decades of the twentieth century, we are able to look back at the reception of Saint-Simonian thought in nineteenth-century Russia and consider it as an academic and partial reception which was yet to be fulfilled. Ironically, some conditions of its reception – such as the strict censorship of Saint-Simonian thought imposed by Nicholas I on Russian writers and artists[5] – were not dissimilar to those in which it was to disappear again in the twentieth century, under Stalinism. The existence of a strong censorship in nineteenth-century Russia was, however, not only to make the reception of the Saint-Simonian concept of the artist as leader of social reform difficult, but also to emphasise its desirability. In this sense at least, then, there was in nineteenth-century Russia a desire for the reception of Saint-Simon's concept of avant-garde which was to make its twentieth-century reappearance possible.

Because even the Hegelian aesthetic shared by the younger Belinsky,[6] with many others of his time, of art as a 'träumendes Spiegelbild' or 'dream-like mirror-reflection' of its society can be said to have been made difficult under a censor who in many cases objected to the truthful representation of reality,[7] it is not surprising to find Belinsky, Herzen, and others also turning to unite their Hegelian dialectic with elements of Saint-Simonian thought, as well as with the ideas for social reform of other 'Utopian socialists' such as Louis Blanc, Pierre Leroux, Proudhon, Fourier, Cabet, and Ledru-Rollin, to develop an aesthetic which would attribute to art the power of changing its social conditions. From this move to a 'productivist' aesthetic a debate arose between their older 'Hegelian' reflectionist theories of art and that of the Saint-Simonian concept of the artist as both producer and social administrator which was to surface again in the disputes of the 1920s and 1930s between Constructivists and Socialist Realists, and which still dominates many present-day debates on the Marxist concept of art.

Masaryk has quoted Saltykov on the influence of French socialism in Russia towards the end of the 1840s: 'From France, not of course from the France of Louis Philippe and Guizot, but from the France of Saint-Simon, Cabet, Fourier, Louis Blanc, and above all George Sand, we derived a faith in humanity; France irradiated to us the conviction that the golden age lies not in the past but in the future.'[8] This last phrase is in fact a partial quotation from Saint-Simon himself, who had written in full not merely that the golden age of humanity was still to come, but that this golden age lay in the perfection of the social order:

> L'âge d'or du genre humain n'est point derrière nous, il est au-devant, il est dans la perfection de l'ordre social . . .
>
> (The golden age of humanity lies not behind us, it is in front; it lies in the perfection of the social order . . .)[9]

The above passage (which ends with a reference to the avant-garde role of Saint-Simon's generation – 'nos pères ne l'ont point vu, nos enfants y arriveront un jour; c'est à nous de leur en frayer la route')/had also been quoted by Heinrich Heine in his 1830s critique of the Historical School of Ranke in the essay entitled 'Verschiedenartige Geschichtsauffassung' ('Various concepts of history'). As Heine's work (both poetry and prose) were widely read in Russia from the 1830s on, they were, in addition, yet another source of Saint-Simonian ideas there.[10] In fact not only was Heine frequently mentioned by Belinsky, Chernyshevsky, Plekhanov, Lunacharsky, and Lenin, but his writings were also known to the Constructivist El Lissitzky, whose father, as Sophie Lissitzky-Küppers has reported, had translated Heine.[11]

While Belinsky and other supporters of Saint-Simonian theory within Russia, such as Lavrov, were to take over from Saint-Simon the vision of a reconstructed social order led by a governing intelligentsia[12] – a concept revived in the 1920s but condemned as bourgeois in the 1930s – Belinsky is best remembered today not so much for his Saint-Simonian ideas but for his influence on others appropriated to the ranks of the theoreticians of Realism, such as Chernyshevsky and Plekhanov.

Hence while Belinsky's influence on Chernyshevsky's 1855 thesis on the aesthetic connection of art to reality has been emphasised, and he has been praised for establishing a critical social function for literature, as also for suggesting that literature could be a 'mirror' of real social relations, the fact that art was in fact more for Belinsky than this – as it had been for earlier Saint-Simonians – became to some extent lost to Russian history.[13] Like others of his kind (and including Chernyshevsky),[14] Belinsky was appropriated to a 'Realist' aesthetic in which art was seen above all to reflect rather than lead society. This appropriation could of course also be said to have been made easier by the fact that in Belinsky's time the practical implementation of Saint-Simon's concept of an avant-garde of artists, technocrats, and scientists was such a practical impossibility that the dispute between productivist and reflectionist theories of art, which it had helped engender, could only remain both theoretical and confused.[15]

Nevertheless, Hegelian theory was clearly antipathetic to the functionalist or productivist Saint-Simonist view of art, and Hegel himself (as Marx was aware) had been outspokenly antipathetic to the idea of an art whose ideal goal would be a union with technology and science. He had even argued against artists placing too much stress on the 'mechanical' or technical aspects of their work, as, for example, in this passage from the description of the Roman world in *The Philosophy of History:*

> Art too has its external side; when in art the mechanical side has been brought to perfection, Free Art can arise and display itself. But those must be pitied who knew nothing further; as also those who, when Art has arisen, still regard the Mechanical as the highest.[16]

The absence of interest in both the 'mechanical' and technological aspects of art in early and mid nineteenth-century Russia, which make Hegel's warnings sound irrelevant to her, also seem to be reflected in the way in which Chernyshevsky's thesis on the relationship between art and reality is said to have inspired the Realist painters of the 1860s – the 'Peredvishniki', or 'Wanderers' or 'Itinerants' – to take the Russian countryside and its newly emancipated peasantry as their subject-matter and Realism as their style. While they were later described by Socialist Realists of the 1930s as pioneers in the critical depiction of social reality, the nineteenth-century Wanderers can, however, be said to have been influenced as much by the religious paintings of the German Nazarenes in their early years as by any radical social theory. As we shall see, the Russian Wanderers of the 1860s had either been acquainted with the works of the German Nazarenes by teachers in the Academy of St Petersburg who had known the Nazarenes or their work, or had themselves seen examples of Nazarene art while travelling Europe or Russia itself, where several museums and churches had received gifts of Nazarene art through the Tsar's alliance with the Prussian monarchy.[17] Given our knowledge of what the Nazarenes had represented to Marx in his time, this connection between them and the Russian Social Realists of the 1860s and after must also place attempts to make Marx a precursor of Socialist Realism together with the Wanderers in an ironic, if not also a questionable, light.

Many Soviet histories of Socialist Realist art have none the less emphasised the role played by the Social Realists of the 1860s in the development of a Marxist form of Socialist Realism. Igor Golomshtok writes on the Soviet construction of an official history for Socialist Realist art:

> The whole history of world art was radically reviewed and official Soviet historians reinterpreted it in terms of a struggle between 'realistic' and 'anti-realistic' trends. Thus the greater part of the world's artistic culture was deemed 'anti-realistic' and consequently 'reactionary'. All the rich traditions of old Russian icon-painting, of the Western Middle Ages, of painters like Bosch, El Greco, Turner, not to mention the Impressionists and all who followed them, went out of circulation. The work of the Russian Wanderers – the direct precursors of Socialist Realism – was declared to be the 'supreme pre-socialist art, an art that scaled unprecedented heights unattained by the art of any other country either earlier or contemporaneously, and in all Soviet museums exhibitions of Russian art ended abruptly with their works.[18]

Ironically, it is perhaps the appropriation by defenders of Socialist Realism of Friedrich Engels' praise for the Düsseldorf artist Carl Hübner's 'socially realistic' painting of the Silesian weavers of 1844 as evidence of both his and Marx's preference for socially realistic art, which best reveals both the arbitrary nature of the appropriation of Marx to the canon of Socialist Realism and the links between Socialist Realism and the Nazarene school of painters who had in Marx's time represented the very antithesis of the type of art he would have praised.[19]

Although it was apparently begun before the weavers' riots in June 1844 Hübner's painting was seen by Engels after the event itself and described by him as a moving comment on the plight suffered by the weavers which had led to their riots:

> Let me on this occasion mention a painting by one of the best German painters, Hübner, which has made a more effectual Socialist agitation than a hundred pamphlets might have done. It represents some Silesian weavers bringing linen cloth to the manufacturer, and contrasts very strikingly cold-hearted wealth on one side, and despairing poverty on the other. The well-fed manufacturer is represented with a face as red and unfeeling as brass, rejecting a piece of cloth which belongs to a woman; the woman, seeing no chance of selling the cloth, is sinking down and fainting, surrounded by her two little children, and hardly kept up by an old man; a clerk is looking over a piece, the owners of which are with painful anxiety waiting for the result; a young man shows to his desponding mother the scanty wages he has received for his labour; an old man, a girl, and a boy, are sitting on a stone bench, and waiting for their turn; and two men, each with a piece of rejected cloth on his back, are just leaving the room, one of whom is clenching his fist in rage, whilst the other, putting his hand on his neighbour's arm, points up towards heaven, as if saying: be quiet, there is a judge to

40. Carl W. Hübner, *The Silesian Weavers*, 1844 (Kunstmuseum, Düsseldorf)

punish him. This whole scene is going on in a cold and unhomely-looking lobby, with a stone floor: only the manufacturer stands upon a piece of carpeting; whilst on the other side of the painting, behind a bar, a view is opened into a luxuriously furnished counting-house, with splendid curtains and looking-glasses, where some clerks are writing, undisturbed by what is passing behind them, and where the manufacturer's son, a young, dandy-like gentleman, is leaning over the bar, with a horsewhip in his hand, smoking a cigar, and coolly looking at the distressed weavers. The painting has been exhibited in several towns of Germany, and, of course, prepared a good many minds for Social ideas. At the same time, we have had the triumph of seeing the first historical painter of this country, Charles Lessing, become a convert to Socialism.[20]

While a close reading of that description of Hübner's *Silesian Weavers* will reveal that Engels has in fact made no explicit reference to the realism of the picture, but has praised it for having 'prepared a good many minds for Social ideas', it is generally assumed that he saw it as a work of Social Realism. Later commentators to Hübner have further described his *Weavers* as a socially realistic work which both mocks the figure of the industrialist in the manner of the satirical genre pictures of Hogarth and Wilkie, and parodies the sentimentality of the Nazarene school of painters then active in Düsseldorf. Some contemporary historians of the Düsseldorf School aware of Engels' appraisal of Hübner as well as of his friend Püttmann's earlier criticism of the sentimentality of the follower of Schadow, Christian Köhler, have even compared Hübner's central figure with Köhler's *Hagar and Ismael* of 1844, and implied that Hübner's is a parody of Köhler's.[21]

Apparently dismissing the fact that Hübner trained and continued in the same 'sentimental' Nazarenism as Köhler under Schadow between 1837 and 1841, critics have also described Hübner as a student of the 'less sentimental' faction of the Düsseldorf School associated with Lessing and Bendemann and praised by Püttmann in his critique of the Düsseldorf School in 1839. It was from this school that Hübner is also assumed to have developed the satirical style associated with the genre pictures of Hogarth and Wilkie. A closer look at Hübner's painting should, however, show that any similarity between his work and that of the British satirists mentioned is partial rather than general. Most importantly, although Hübner has painted a satirical portrait of the industrialist as 'Herrscher' or 'overlord' (the figure examining the cloth brought in by the weavers bears some similarity to portraits of Friedrich Wilhelm IV), he has given a sentimental portrait of the weavers themselves which could only be described as parodying the sen-

41. Christian Köhler, *Hagar and Ismael*, 1844 (Kunstmuseum, Düsseldorf)

As mentioned earlier, Köhler's allegorical *Poesie* of 1838 had been one of the winged figures criticised by Püttmann in 1839, and he was generally regarded as one of the more 'sentimental' painters of the Schadow School.

42. David Wilkie, *Reading the Will*, 1820 (Bayerische Staatsgemäldesammlung, Munich, Neue Pinakothek)

timentality of a Köhler or a Schadow at the expense of describing it – as Engels had done – as a sympathetic and non-ironic portrait of the weavers' plight.

The central tableau of Hübner's picture, towards which the observer is asked to look, and in which the plight suffered by the weavers is perhaps most strongly expressed, can moreover be compared to Renaissance *pietàs* or to that illustrated over by Annibale Caracci (a favourite of the early Nazarenes, as mentioned previously), as much as to Köhler's more contemporary *Hagar and Ismael*.

Yet here again, any interpretation of *Weavers* as a parody of its religious model would appear to turn the picture into an attack on the weavers themselves – who are clearly both the heroes of the piece and the vehicle of Hübner's use of Nazarene sentimentality, while they were in real life as religious as the pictures which their gestures evoke. Any suggestion that Hübner was parodying pictures such as Annibale Caracci's *pietà* would also have to explain how Hübner was not charged with blasphemy by the Prussian censor – the parody of a *pietà* figure in his picture entailing the interpretation of the weaver woman as an attack on the sentimentality of the Mary figure, as also the suggestion that the Christ figure has been replaced by the bolt of cloth, or the shroud of the Christ figure by its modern commercial equivalent. The main obstacle to interpreting Hübner's *Weavers* as a parody of Nazarene sentimentality rather than as an example of it, lies, however, in the fact that if the weavers themselves are to be described (as by Engels) as the heroes of the picture, then the sentimentality of which they are the vehicle cannot also be seen as parody. If *Weavers* is a parody rather than an example of Nazarene sentimentality then it must, that is, also be suspected of being a parody of subjects like the weavers themselves, and not the sympathetic portrayal of their social problems which Engels describes. If we cannot interpret the picture as both a sympathetic portrait of the weavers (as suggested by Engels) and as a satire on the sentimentality of the Nazarene School in which Hübner had been trained, we must moreover, conclude that the painting praised by Engels for its sympathetic depiction of the plight of the Silesian weavers, and later taken into the canon of Socialist Realist art on that account, is in part at least, an example of the sentimental and romantic Nazarene paintings of the type rejected by both Heine and the young Marx.[22]

As mentioned earlier, even Engels had not praised Hübner's *Weavers* as 'realistic'. When Marx was asked by Engels to help make known the work of one other painter representative of the 'critical realists' of the

43. Annibale Caracci, *Pietà*, 1603 (Kunsthistorisches Museum, Vienna)

Düsseldorf School – the painting entitled *The Workers before the Council, 1848* by J. P. Hasenclever (a friend of the poet and social activist Ferdinand Freiligrath)[23] – he too did not praise the 'realism' of the picture, but claimed it to be a *vital* and dramatic portrait. Marx wrote of the picture in the New York *Daily Tribune* of August 12, 1853:

> Those of your readers who, having read my letters on German revolution and counter-revolution, written for *The Tribune* some two years ago, desire to have an immediate intuition of it, will do well to inspect the picture by Mr *Hasenclever,* now being exhibited in the New York Crystal Palace, representing the presentation of a workingmen's petition to the magistrates of Düsseldorf in 1848. What the writer could only analyse, the eminent painter has reproduced in its dramatic vitality.

Given that one year previous to these comments Marx in his *Eighteenth Brumaire* of 1852 had mocked the imitation of the costumery and rhetoric of 1789 by the revolutionaries of 1848, and in part attributed their failure to that imitation, and given too the copying of the gestures of 1789 in Hasenclever's picture (in, for example, the echo of Horace Vernet's or Daumier's portrait of Camille Desmoulins in the figure of the orator in the background of the painting), it would also

44. J. P. Hasenclever, *The Workers before the Council, 1848* (Kunst-museum, Düsseldorf)

be hard to claim that Marx was entirely wholehearted in his support of Hasenclever.

Heine had already commented on the revival of the costumery of 1789 by Horace Vernet in his Desmoulins portrait in the review of the Salon of 1831 mentioned previously,[24] and complained in his *Lutezia* reports of 1841–43, in terms similar to those used by Marx at the beginning of his *Eighteenth Brumaire,* that the imitation of the costumery of the Roman Republic by artists of the French Revolution such as David had constituted a retrograde rather than a revolutionary development in the history of art. As Hasenclever was also regarded in his time as a German disciple of both Daumier and Vernet, the originality of his interpretation of the revolutionary events of 1848 must also have been questioned by Heine and Marx. Although not critical of Hasenclever, Marx's comments on his work must be taken for what they are – as the response to a request for support rather than as an unsolicited piece of praise.

Despite the absence of any evidence in the writings of Marx to show support for either the 'social realist' works of his time or for their Nazarene models (we have seen, on the contrary, that Marx may even have planned a criticism of the latter in 1842), Socialist Realist critics and apologists of the 1930s and after were not only to claim that their aesthetic was legitimated by Marx, but were also (as mentioned earlier) to claim as the direct precursors of Socialist Realism those Russian

45. Honoré Daumier, *Camille Desmoulins Making a Speech at the Palais-Royal* (private collection)

Social Realists of the 1860s and after, the Wanderers or Itinerants, who had, like Hübner and Hasenclever, been influenced by the German Nazarenes.

A brief survey of the work of some of the leading members of the Russian Wanderers, like I. E. Repin, the teacher of a Social Realist precursor of Socialist Realism, Isaak Brodsky, should illustrate the nature of their links with both the religious and socially critical painting of the German Nazarenes.

I. E. Repin (1844–1930), for example, had taken part in travelling exhibitions from 1874 on, and had become a member of the Society of Wanderers in 1878. Before that, as a student of the Academy of Arts in St Petersburg from 1864 to 1871, Repin completed several works on themes given him by his professors which had been derived from the Bible. Although the use of biblical themes was common in most academies of the time, several of Repin's professors had also been in contact with the German Nazarenes. While some of these German artists had visited Russia, Russian painters had also been able to see their work in Italy or Germany. One professor at the Academy of Arts in St Petersburg in Repin's time, the landscape artist A. P. Bogoliubov, had studied with the Düsseldorf School artist Andreas Achenbach in the 1850s. Contact with the German Nazarenes had furthermore been made earlier in the century by Alexander Ivanov (1806–58), who had

46. Alexander Ivanov, *Study of Christ Appearing Before the People,* 1837–57 (Tretyakov Gallery, Moscow)

become acquainted with the Nazarenes while working in Rome. Ivanov's famous *Study of Christ Appearing Before the People* of 1837–57 demonstrates particularly clearly the influence of the German Nazarenes on his work, as well as that of their early Renaissance Italian models.

Given the numerous connections between early nineteenth-century German and Russian artists, it is perhaps not surprising that several of the biblical themes assigned to Repin by his professors were ones which had been favoured by the German Nazarenes, and had been seen in Europe in the exhibitions of their work. The story of *Job and his Comforters* (painted by Repin in 1869), had, for example, already been painted by E. Wächter and by the Düsseldorf Nazarene, Julius Hübner.

The subject of *Christ Raising the Daughter of Jairus* – which won an Academy prize for Repin in 1871 – had also been painted by several Nazarene artists, including Overbeck, Gustav Richter, and E. von Gebhardt.

Later Repin turned to a more critical treatment of religious themes – as in, for example, his satirical depiction of participants in his *Religious Procession in the Kursk Province* of 1880–3 – while other Wanderers like I. N. Kramskoi and N. N. Gay continued to use biblical subjects and themes but to express their social concerns. Later still the tradition of religious painting popular in early nineteenth-century Russia was continued into the last years of the century by painters like the

47. I. E. Repin, *Christ Raising the Daughter of Jairus,* 1871 (The Russian Museum, Leningrad)

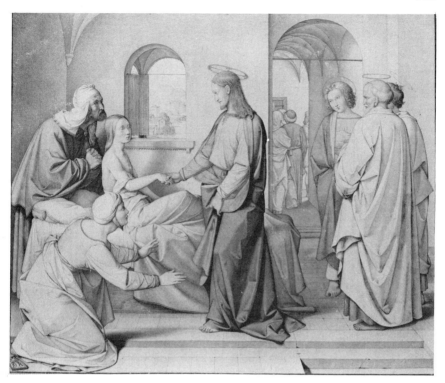

48. Friedrich Overbeck, *Christ Awaking the Daughter of Jairus*, 1815 (Kupferstichkabinett und Sammlung der Zeichnungen, East Berlin)

Wanderer S. V. Ivanov (1863–1910) and M. V. Nesterov (1862–1942), whose popular *Vision of the Young Bartholomew* (painted 1889–90), bears comparison with works of the English Pre-Raphaelites as well as with those of the earlier German Nazarenes. Nesterov studied at the Academy of Arts in St Petersburg from 1881–4 and began to show his work with the Wanderers in 1889. Despite the obviously religious character of his famous *Vision of the Young Bartholomew*, Nesterov's art is described in official Soviet texts as showing the 'inseparable ties between Russian Realist art and Soviet art'.

While many of the Russian artists of the late nineteenth century were influenced by the work of the German Nazarenes, Philipp Veit's romanticised *Allegory of Russia* also demonstrates an interest on the side of the German Nazarenes for Russia and its then role as an official ally of Prussia. The political alliance forged between Prussia and Russia after 1815 had (as mentioned previously) led to cultural exchanges taking place between the two powers, and to the exchange of artists as

49. M. V. Nesterov, *The Vision of the Young Bartholomew*, 1889–90

well as of works of art. So it was that Franz Krüger (the portraitist to the
Prussian Royal family) had gone to Russia to paint the Tsar and his
Court, while the friend of the Nazarene artist Wilhelm von Schadow,
Wilhelm Wach (1787–1845), had been asked by Friedrich Wilhelm III to
complete two altar-pieces – a *Resurrection* and a *Last Supper* – for the
Lutheran Church of St Peter and St Paul in Moscow in the 1820s as a gift
from the Prussian monarch to Moscow. (The works are mentioned by
Heine in his *Briefe aus Berlin*.) Later, in 1844, a favourite artist of
Friedrich Wilhelm IV, Ferdinand Theodor Hildebrandt (figs. 19 and 20),
also visited St Petersburg to paint the Court of Friedrich Wilhelm IV's
brother-in-law, Nicholas I. One year before this visit, in 1843,
Hildebrandt had completed a portrait of Vassily Andrejevich Zhukovsky (a painting owned by the Nationalgalerie, Berlin). Zhukovsky
had been tutor to the Tsar's family and the companion of the Imperial
Prince Alexander in Germany up to 1840, and had, during his time in
Germany, made the acquaintance of the Boisserée brothers, Caspar
David Friedrich, Goethe, and Immermann, as well as the Prussian
monarch Friedrich Wilhelm IV. Significantly, that same year 1843 had,
however, also seen Tsar Nicholas I put pressure on his Prussian relative
to ban Marx from Prussia and to strengthen the censorship of his

50. Philipp Veit, *Allegory of Russia* (Hermitage, Leningrad)

writings, which had, up to then, of course, been directed primarily against the use of State censorship and against the State patronage of those supportive (in Marx's view) of the ideas and icons of feudalism.

### Conclusion: Social Realism enters the twentieth century

Because of the radical causes taken up by the Russian Wanderers or Itinerants in the 1860s, the Russian Tsars of their time were not to be so tolerant towards them as they had been to the German Nazarenes who had been sent to visit Russia in the early part of the century. While the Tsars did not give the Social Realist painters of Russia the same kind of support given to the German Nazarenes by their allied Prussian monarchs, Friedrich Wilhelm III and Friedrich Wilhelm IV, the Society for Circulating Art Exhibitions in which the Social Realists of the 1860s and after had exhibited was later, however, to be encouraged by Lenin, and, in the 1920s, to join with the Association of Artists of Revolutionary Russia (Akh(R)R or AARR).

This association of 'revolutionary artists' was also to keep alive the tradition of Realist painting associated with the Social Realists throughout the 1920s when Constructivists and other avant-garde artists such as Tatlin, El Lissitzky, and Rodchenko were attacking the Realist painting of the nineteenth century and seeking to replace it with a new revolutionary synthesis of functional non-representational art, engineering, design, and architecture. When the Socialist Realists of the 1930s sought to re-establish the representational manner of painting of the Social Realists of the nineteenth century they sought too, however, to deny the revolutionary socialist character of the Constructivists of the 1920s, and to denounce abstract non-representational art as decadent. Rather than acknowledge the historical revolutionary character of both the Social Realism of the 1860s and the avant-garde experiments of the 1920s, Socialist Realism denied the revolutionary character of the latter and turned back to the nineteenth century for the authority it needed to prove the revolutionary character of its return to the Realist and representational style, which had been condemned as reactionary by the avant-gardistes of the 1920s.

One of the most influential but also most ambiguous theorists of Realism and critics of avant-garde art of the late nineteenth century chosen as an authority for Socialist Realism by apologists of the latter in the 1930s was the socialist and critic Plekhanov. While he had defended a reflectionist aesthetic in the 1880s and attacked the avant-garde of France as decadent in the early twentieth century, Plekhanov had also maintained a Saint-Simonian belief in the role to be played by art in the reconstruction of the material base of society.[25] This aspect of Plekhanov's thought was, however, largely overlooked in the 1930s, and his statements supporting Realist art emphasised in their stead. Ironically, although Plekhanov had followed Belinsky and Chernyshevsky in developing this Saint-Simonian concept of art as integral to social life and its reconstruction, his use of them to develop a theory of artistic Realism[26] in which modern twentieth-century abstract art was reviled as decadent (in part because of its French bourgeois origins) was also to help make possible their inclusion by later Soviet critics into the ranks of those writers who could be used to justify Socialist Realism.

Yet one problem with using Plekhanov as an authority for Socialist Realist theory (apart from the problem that he championed Saint-Simonian ideas later opposed by Socialist Realists) is that he did not leave a consistent theory of Realism behind him.[27] Criticising Chernyshevsky, Plekhanov was, in addition, to write ambiguously of the theory of Realism of his predecessor, claiming, for instance, to have derived his own Realist aesthetic from the theories put forward by Chernyshevsky, while also criticising him for too narrow a demand for a strict realism, exclusive of new revolutionary developments.[28] The ambiguous nature of Plekhanov's reading of Chernyshevsky can, however, be explained by the fact that Plekhanov had first of all taken an interest in him at a time when Chernyshevsky's theories were being put into practice by the Wanderers,[29] but had then developed (in part from his reading of Marx) a belief in the necessity of a revolutionised proletariat,[30] and, therefore, a brief for a proletarian, and not a 'Romanticised', peasant,[31] form of culture. To Plekhanov this pro-letarian culture of the future was also to have more in common with base than superstructure. Thus, although Plekhanov sometimes claimed that consciousness was generally determined by social existence, and 'reflected' in art, he (theoretically at least) also left a way clear for Constructivist and *Proletkult* artists of the 1920s to argue, in a Saint-Simonian manner, for a place for art in the economic base, and, hence, in the economic reconstruction and production of society. This vestigial 'avant-garde' Saint-Simonian element in Plekhanov's thought was, however, to be ignored by those Socialist Realists who used his theories to justify their aesthetic against the avant-garde of the 1920s in the 1930s.[32] Only recently, in fact, has Plekhanov's belief in an active role for art again been openly discussed by commentators on his work. V. Scherbina's Introduction to Plekhanov's *Selected Philosophical Works*[33] begins, for example, by emphasising Plekhanov's contribution to the defence of Realism, but later[34] makes the point that Plekhanov's explanations of the socially conditioned nature of art have been concentrated on by critics to the exclusion of any recognition of Plekhanov's belief in the 'active role of art'.[35]

If one other source of Saint-Simonian ideas in nineteenth-century Russia could be said to have been Feuerbach, then it is also interesting to see Plekhanov using him together with other nineteenth-century German Saint-Simonian writers as in, for example, his 1905 review of the Sixth Exhibition of Literature and the Arts in Venice. In an article on the proletarian movement and bourgeois art, in which he both quotes from Heine and relates Feuerbach's criticism of anthropomorphic Christianity to the religious art of Raphael, Plekhanov writes of a picture of a mother and child by Josef Israel, entitled *Madonna in a Hovel*, in a way which also recalls Marx's mention of Rembrandt's peasant madonna and Goethe's comparison of it with Raphael:

> she is an ordinary mother in an ordinary hovel. Why then is she a *Madonna*? Because she is also a mother like the most 'sublime' Madonnas of Raphael. The 'sublimity' of the latter lies precisely in their motherhood, but whereas in Raphael, as in Christian art in general, this purely human, and not only human, feature is made an attribute of the deity, in Israel's it *has been returned to man*. Earlier, to quote Feuerbach, man *devastated* himself by worshipping his own essence in the deity, but now he understands the vanity of this self-devastation and cherishes human features precisely because they belong to man.[36]

He adds:

> This is a revolution, which was extolled by Heine:

> 'Ein neues Lied, ein schönes Lied,
>     O Freunde, will ich euch dichten,
> Wir wollen hier, auf Erden schon,
>     Das Himmelreich errichten!'

> (A new song, a more beautiful song
>     will I compose for you, my friend:
> We wish to build on earth anon
>     Our own good version of Heaven!)

Despite the Saint-Simonian elements in his thought Plekhanov's personal taste in painting was, however, to remain in favour of Realism. In particular, the attack made on French Cubism by him in his *Art and Social Life* of 1912 (a tract based on a talk given in Paris, and at which Plekhanov clashed with Lenin's later Minister for Education, Lunacharsky), was to provide ammunition for the Socialist Realists of the 1930s in their attack on the Russian avant-garde followers of Cubism popular in the 1920s, because in that attack Plekhanov had equated abstract art with both cultural and political decadence. Whereas in fact Soviet Constructivism might have been seen by Plekhanov himself as fulfilling the aims of non-decadent art – as assisting, that is, in the 'development of man's consciousness, to improve the social system' – Socialist Realists, concerned to eradicate avant-gardes of the 1920s not sympathetic to their doctrines, identified Soviet Constructivism with the abstract French Cubism condemned by Plekhanov as decadent.

Though overlooking the political differences between French Cubists and Russian Constructivists, later critics of the latter were, however, correct in identifying stylistic similarities between the two schools of art. One 'manifesto' of Cubism, Albert Gleizes' and Jean Metzinger's *Du Cubisme*, specifically attacked by Plekhanov in 1912, had in fact had considerable influence on the art of the Russian Suprematists which preceded the development of the more design- and architecture-orientated art of the 1920s which was Constructivism. *Du Cubisme* had, however, only just appeared in France when Plekhanov gave his lecture there in 1912 on art and social life, in which he attacked it with particular vehemence as encouraging all that was for him most decadent in art. To Plekhanov *Du Cubisme* demonstrated the existence of a basically Idealist and subjectivist core to all Cubist art, while its attack on realistic representation and, in particular, Courbet,[37] represented to Plekhanov a subversion of his belief in the duty of art to reflect accurately social reality.

To Plekhanov Cubism was also the latest, most elite, and most absurd stage of the decadent 'art for art's sake' which he saw to have been favoured by the French bourgeoisie of the turn of the century, having been accompanied (in his eyes) by the degeneration of that 'l'art pour l'art' into an 'art for money's sake'. Challenged by Lunacharsky that his own principles of objective beauty (by which he was condemning the abstract art of the Cubists) were arbitrary, Plekhanov accused Lunacharsky of extreme subjectivism – of, that is, the very fault of which he had just accused French Cubism. Later, as Director of *Narkompros*, Lenin's Ministry for Education and the Arts, Lunacharsky was himself to condemn the decadence of 'art for art's sake', while also, however, defending the abstract works of Russian Constructivist artists as both truly proletarian and Soviet. Speaking on 19 December 1920 to the first Soviet Conference of the leaders of the Departments of Art under Narkompros, Lunacharsky concluded:

> The Proletariat must finally eradicate the sharp difference between life and art which has concerned the ruling class of the past. From now on art for art's sake does not exist. In the hands of the proletariat art will become a sharp weapon of communist propaganda and agitation. In the hands of the proletariat art is the tool, the means, and the product of Production.

In comparing Cubists and Constructivists on the basis of their non-representational abstract art, later adherents to Socialist Realism largely ignored the fact that, unlike the Cubists attacked by Plekhanov, but like their patron Lunacharsky, Constructivists like Rodchenko had sought to create a proletarian and activist form of art which was ideologically similar to the Saint-Simonist concept of avant-garde which had been partially taken up by Belinsky and Chernyshevsky, and utilised by Plekhanov in his attack on the decadence of French bourgeois art. Through the Constructivists of the 1920s Saint-Simon's original concept of a vanguard of artists and technocrats was, however, reintroduced into a Russia setting out on the roads of political and technological reform, and the concept of avant-garde repoliticised as a means towards linking art to technology and towards presenting art as a form of production integral to the economic and political development of its social context. How Constructivism was to represent the rebirth of this Utopian Saint-Simonian concept of the artist as producer will be looked at again in the following chapter.

# 7

## The Constructivists of the 1920s and the concept of avant-garde

As mentioned in the last chapter, Soviet Constructivist artists of the 1920s were concerned with developing a new kind of art which could, in conjunction with technology, develop revolutionary functional designs of practical use to their new society. It was this interest in developing the functional, useful side of their art for the purpose of producing technologically advanced and economically productive pieces of design art, architecture, and engineering which also helped unite Constructivist experiments in abstract painting and design to those socialist principles and goals which distinguish the art of Constructivism from that of pre-revolutionary Russian schools of abstract art.

The development of the functional side of art which became so closely associated with Constructivism was officially encouraged after 1917 through the foundation of institutions such as the *Vkhumetas* ('high-grade art-technical workshops') and Inkhuk, an 'Institute of Artistic Culture'. The latter had been formed in May 1920 to provide an impetus for the development of the arts, and had, by 1921, made a programme for the development of a functional 'productivist' form of art linked with industrial design, engineering and architecture. Indeed, most of the artists referred to in these pages as having revived the Saint-Simonist idea of the artist as avant-garde producer were involved in either engineering, architecture or design as well as in experimentation with new forms of art.

It is also because Constructivist artists like Tatlin, El Lissitzky and Rodchenko appear to embody or put into practice many of the theories of Saint-Simon on the need for art to be both technically avant-garde and economically productive that they (and not others) are discussed here in the context of a study of the history of the 'productivist' Saint-Simonist ideas found in Marx.

As much has recently been written on the 'avant-garde' artists of the 1920s from art-historical viewpoints, it is further not my intention here to present another art-historical survey of the period. As the aim of this part of the book is to consider the fate of Marx's 'productivist', Saint-Simonist ideas in twentieth-century Marxist aesthetic thinking and art practice, the avant-garde art of the 1920s will, like the Socialist Realism of the 1930s and after, be studied mainly in the context of what has been said in Part 1 about Marx's views on the visual arts of his time and about the Saint-Simonist ideas which have been found in some of those views. It is for this reason too that we shall be looking at a question not normally put in either art-historical studies of the Russian avant-garde of the 1920s or in theoretical discussions of the concept of avant-garde, that is, how the Constructivists' concept of the artist as belonging to a revolutionary group of *producteurs* concerned – together with technocrats and scientists – with the planning and production of new societies, may relate to the concept of avant-garde as put forward by Saint-Simon and his followers and as developed by Marx.

Although some critics have looked at the history of the concept of avant-garde, they have rarely connected it with both Marx and Saint-Simon as well as with the avant-garde Soviet artists of the 1920s. Hence while D. D. Egbert, for instance, in an essay on the idea of avant-garde,[1] acknowledges the debt to be paid to Saint-Simon by Marx for some of the latter's early ideas, he does not – in what is an otherwise exhaustive coverage of the history of the idea of avant-garde – explicitly connect either Marx's or Saint-Simon's concept of avant-garde to that of the Constructivists, or even speak explicitly of the latter.[2]

In another work explicitly dedicated to the idea of avant-garde, Renato Poggioli[3] has discussed modern avant-garde art but has, on the other hand, avoided mentioning the name of Saint-Simon in connection with the concept, giving its origins as coming from France, from 'a little-known Fourieriste, Gabriel-Désiré Laverdant', and his tract (published in Paris in only 1845), entitled 'De la mission de l'art et du rôle des artistes'. In the following passage quoted from that work, Poggioli also claims that Laverdant had stressed both the idea of the interdependence of art and society, and the doctrine of art as an instrument for social action and reform, as a means of 'revolutionary propaganda and agitation':

> Art, the expression of society, manifests, in its highest soaring, the most advanced social tendencies: it is the forerunner and the revealer. Therefore, to know whether art worthily fulfils its proper mission as initiator, whether the artist is truly of the avant-garde, one must know where Humanity is going, know what the destiny of the human race is . . .[4]

To Poggioli, Laverdant is one of the first users of the concept of avant-garde to stress its political character. Yet not only was Laverdant more typical of his time than exceptional in using the term in this sense (Saint-Simon and his followers had done so from at least the very beginning of the nineteenth century), but the history of the concept cannot be restricted to its 'political' or 'unpolitical' usage, as Poggioli would do here, as it can also be seen to involve (from Saint-Simon on) an economic argument for seeing the artist as a 'producer' of economic values.[5] This economic aspect of the term was, moreover, operative in the growth of the popularity of the concept of the avant-garde in nineteenth-century industrial Europe, as well as in its reappearance in the early years of the twentieth century in the newly industrialised Russia of the 1920s, and, in particular, in the programmes and practices of the avant-garde Constructivists of that time. It should, however, also be mentioned here (in the light of an earlier reference (in chapter 1) to Mercantilist arguments for supporting the arts as economically productive), that it was no doubt the connection of the Saint-Simonist concept of avant-garde with the ideas of both Marx and of the Russian socialist thinkers of the nineteenth century which was to make *it*, rather than any Mercantilist argument for the productivity of art, suitable for reception in Soviet Russia in the early years of its development.

The Constructivists Rodchenko, El Lissitzky, Tatlin, and the Vesnin brothers had all attempted in the 1920s, as Camilla Gray has written, to 'build a bridge between art and industry' in order to contribute to the economic development of the new Soviet society. Where El Lissitzky had been made Professor of Architecture in Vitebsk in 1918 and had used his talents as engineer, architect, designer and artist in such economically significant projects as the construction of the Russian exhibits for the world trade fairs participated in for the first time by the Soviets in the 1920s, other Constructivists were involved in such disparate concerns as stage design and the construction of a hydro-electric plant. Like the Saint-Simonian engineers of nineteenth-century France (whose achievements had been celebrated in the World Fair of 1889, and symbolised by its construction of the Eiffel Tower) the Constructivist engineers and architects of Soviet Russia regarded their constructions as monuments to their new society as much as contributions to its economic growth. In addition they were, like Saint-Simon and Marx, to aim for a new combination of theoretical and practical labour symbolic of their society's communist values. Marx had written of the need to overcome the alienation of mental from

51. Tatlin, Model for the 'Monument to the Third International', 1919–20

Tatlin's 'monument' had been planned as a Soviet counterpart to the Paris tower of the Saint-Simonian engineer Eiffel.

52. The Eiffel Tower had been built for the World Fair of 1889, the centenary of the French Revolution. Tatlin's 'Monument to the Third International' was of course dedicated to the celebration of the spirit of the Russian Revolution.

manual labour in works such as *The German Ideology*. Saint-Simon had written in the sixth letter of his *L'Industrie littéraire et scientifique liguée avec L'Industrie commerciale et manufacturière* of 1817:

> the unique goal to which all our thoughts and efforts should point is the most advantageous organisation for industry; for industry in the widest sense, embracing every kind of useful work, theoretical and practical, intellectual as well as manual.

Saint-Simon (who had himself attended the École Polytechnique a few years after its foundation in 1794) had of course also stressed the economic value of uniting intellectual and manual labour, and had written in one of his earlier works (published posthumously) that:

> Scientists, artists and industrialists are those who possess the highest and broadest abilities, the most positively useful in the light of the human mind

and that

> the work of scientists, artists and industrialists is that which, from the point of view of invention and of execution, contributes most to the nation's prosperity.[6]

In the very first years of the revolution, the Constructivists El Lissitzky and Rodchenko were also to echo Saint-Simon's encouragement of artists and engineers to co-operate in bringing to birth the new 'golden age' in their slogans, and to attempt to put the latter into practice in their monuments, engineering ventures, and new experimental designs for Soviet goods and propaganda. Rodchenko's 1921 claim that 'consciousness, experiment . . . construction, technology, and mathematics' were the 'brothers of the art of our age' might also be seen to have echoed Saint-Simon's call for mathematicians and artists to unite their talents, as well as the vagueness inherent in it.

Further to this Rodchenko was in 1921 to formulate with other Constructivists a programme of 'productivist' design art for Inkhuk, the Institute of Artistic Culture, which had the express aim of linking the applied to the fine arts and of making both economic in the sense also suggested by Saint-Simon in his description of his avant-garde. Here it must also be pointed out, however, that while 1921 was to see new economic problems arise, and new restrictions placed on the funding of the arts,[7] Rodchenko's call for art to become more functional and economically productive cannot simply be read as well-timed and astute reactions to these economic strictures, and to the threat they posed to the financing of those activities, such as the fine arts, which used rather than produced wealth. Although they were also necessary to the survival of the arts at that time in Russia, Rodchenko's programme for a productivist form of art was both summarising earlier 'Constructivist' manifestos and descriptions of 'productivism', and affirming an aim of a 'Committee of Applied Arts' formed in 1918 as an ancillary to the 'Scientific–Technical Department of the Supreme Council of the People's Economy'. This Committee had openly stated that 'by their

53. The Constructivist artist A. Rodchenko photographed in front of one of his three-dimensional constructions and dressed in a working overall designed by his wife, Varvara Stepanova

contribution to increasing exports, applied arts greatly promote the economic rise of the country',[8] and had thereby also given something like an 'official' Saint-Simonian policy to the Constructivists. The early years of the Bolshevik Revolution had in fact seen many of the unfulfilled Utopian socialist ideas of the nineteenth century (including those of Saint-Simon) put into policies such as the above, and the policy of the Committee of Applied Arts put forward in 1918 was but one of several 'Leninist' policies which would be seen by the Constructivists – at least in their earlier years – to be in harmony with their own aims.

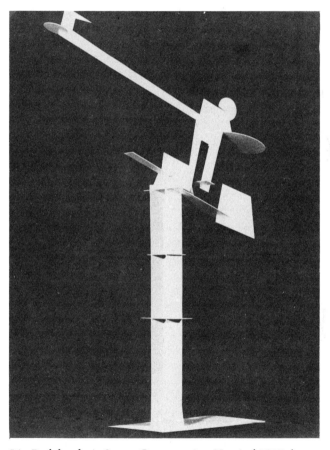

54. Rodchenko's *Space Construction No. 6* of 1918 demonstrates his early concern to turn the lines of Realist art into three-dimensional structures. Later, in 1920, Rodchenko wrote in his essay 'The line': 'The line has uncovered a new level of reality: to construct in a literal sense, and not to represent.'

Karginov also writes in his study of Rodchenko that in 1920 Rodchenko's art had not only reached the stage of 'laboratory experiments', but that his dreams had soared into the 'constructively organised future', in which life was to be organised directly by the 'artist–constructor', the 'artist–engineer'. The practical side of these Utopian visions was seen when, with his wife Varvara Stepanova, Rodchenko worked on the design of domestic and factory use objects for the new post-revolutionary society at Inkhuk to produce objects which could be successfully marketed and used.

As Karginov remarks further, Rodchenko had earlier been involved in a group formed towards the end of 1918 and calling itself 'Zhivskulp-tarkh' (a name made out of the words for painting, sculpture and architecture), whose goals were not unlike some of those later formulated by Rodchenko as those of Constructivism under the following slogans:

Construction is the arrangement of elements.
Construction is the outlook of our age.
Like every science, art is a branch of mathematics.
Construction is the modern prerequisite of organization and the utilitarian employment of material.
Art that is useless for life should be kept in museums of antiquities.
The time has come for art to be an organic part of life.
Constructively organized life is more than the enchanting and stifling art of magicians.
The future is not going to build monasteries for priests, or for the prophets and clowns of art.
Down with art as a showy gem in the dark, grimy lives of the poor!
Down with art as a means of escape for a senseless life!
The art of our age is conscious, organized life, capable of seeing and creating.
The artist of our age is the man able to organize his life, his work and himself.
One has to work for life, not for palaces, churches, cemeteries and museums.
Active work has to be done among the people, for the people, and with the people; down with monasteries, institutions, studios, studies and islands!
Consciousness, experiment ... function, construction, technology, mathematics – these are the brothers of the art of our age.

Rodchenko, 1921[9]

The Utopian element in Saint-Simon's vision of a new society built by artists, engineers, and scientists, expressed in these slogans, could also be said to have been echoed by the Constructivists in their vision of 'Futuria', a country where, as Karginov writes in the Introduction to his study of Rodchenko, life was 'to be governed by the laws of beauty and harmony'. Karginov continues, indicating the other more practical aspect of this link between the Constructivists and Saint-Simonism to be their wish to 'construct' this Utopia themselves by a union of technology, art, and industry:

> But they did more than daydream: when circumstances required it, they left the confined premises of their art 'laboratories' to do productive work in factories, printing offices, the building industry and elsewhere. They did so, not because they wanted to lower the standard of fine arts to the level of manual work, but because they wished to raise the qualitative standards of production, to breathe into it new life and sense, and to bring it into harmony with the requirements of a century of technical, social, and intellectual revolution . . .[10]

While taking over Saint-Simon's concept of an avant-garde of artist-producers, the Russian Constructivists of the 1920s appear, however, to have had nothing to do with the concept of the artist as priest which some French and Russian followers of Enfantin and Barrault had shared with the monkish German Nazarenes. In fact it is interesting to note that some Constructivists went out of their way to criticise that concept as if concerned that the similarity of their ideas to the Saint-Simonist concept of avant-garde art might also lead them to be associated with the more mystical aspects of Saint-Simonian thought.

Rodchenko's slogans had, for example, clearly stated that 'the future is not going to build monasteries for priests, or for the prophets and clowns of art'. Others had expressed similar sentiments. Nikolai Punin's address on the art of the proletarian revolution of 24 November 1918 had begun:

> The bourgeoisie conceived of art as something sacred with artists as its priests . . . The proletariat cannot have such an idea of art.[11]

Although later taking a more conservative approach to art policy, Punin had supported Constructivism, as it then existed, and had even defined some of its 'productivist' principles. He had, for example, said of the new proletarian art which was to be created: 'Bourgeois artists only designed ornamental pieces, leaving their realization to the craftsmen. The latter produce the objects themselves. They have a flair for seeing their inherent qualities. An entirely new era in art is sure to follow. The proletariat will create new houses, new streets, new objects of everyday life.' According to Karginov,[12] Punin was the first to define and distinguish 'decorative art' and 'productive' art, and, by 'emphasizing the object' became one of the precursors of the philosophy of 'Veschism' ('Objectism'). However, Punin's emphasis on the need for plain utilitarian objects 'of good quality and artistic execution' was, with its emphasis on the object, but an early stage in the development of the Constructivist and Productivist programmes proper which were to be instituted by Rodchenko at Inkhuk, and in opposition to Objectism. To Rodchenko and his fellow Constructivists the processes of production themselves were to be as important as the object produced.

The Constructivists' apparently 'Tayloristic' encouragement of the development of the technology involved in production was also symptomatic of the rejection by the avant-garde productivist artists of the 1920s of the fashion for traditional craft-work revived in Russia in the latter years of the nineteenth century by Populists, followers of the Wanderers, and artists interested in reviving Russia's national folk art. One commune which encouraged the revival of the traditional peasant crafts and arts, and which became home for a time for the Wanderer Repin, was that set up by the railway owner Mamontov on his estate at Abramtsevo outside Moscow in the 1880s. Where many of the craft artists working on these communes had (like some of William Morris' followers in England) turned away from the use of modern machinery in their work, Constructivist artists of the 1920s set out to apply their knowledge of technology and engineering to the refinement of the machinery which they saw to be necessary to their work and claimed that, rather than creating new divisions of labour antipathetic to both art and socialism, their new 'socialist machine-art' would serve to bring the artist closer to other social groups and professions.[13]

In addition, the Constructivists of the 1920s continued the rejection of the Realism of the Wanderers begun by Suprematists and abstract Cubists in the early years of the twentieth century by continuing the experiments with abstraction begun by forerunners such as Goncharova or Malevich, as well as by constructing art works of a functional or monumental nature which could not be shown in the traditional manner favoured by the nineteenth-century Realists as individual museum exhibits, but which were put outside in the street, or created their own space. The art of the Constructivists was also to demonstrate a new scientific and 'unsentimental' approach to Nature, by moving away from the sentimental imitation of Nature found in the works of the nineteenth-century Wanderers towards a scientific attempt to derive from it laws or tools which could be applied to the production of a new scientific and functional art.[14]

El Lissitzky both explained his aim in achieving a closer union of art and science in his Proun manifesto of 1920, and offered an attack on the Realist art of more conventional artists. He wrote:

> The artist is turning from an imitator into a constructor of the new world of objects. This world will not be built in competition with technology. The paths of art and science have not yet crossed.

El Lissitzky's so-called 'Proun' manifesto (in which 'Proun' stood for 'project for the affirmation of the new') had also begun with the anti-Romantic slogan: 'Not world visions, but – world reality'. In the manifesto El Lissitzky not only spoke of the necessity to reconstruct rather than simply imitate reality, but also advised the use of scientific methods of construction productive of aesthetic effect. One of the practical experiments in this dictum was the 'Proun rooms', three-dimensional geometrically designed realisations of El Lissitzky's concept of an 'interchange station between painting and architecture'.

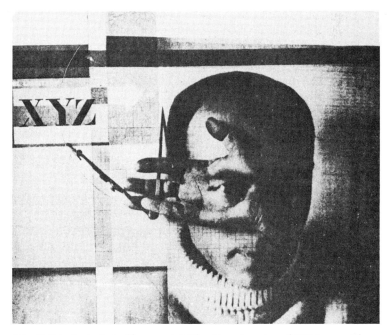

55. El Lissitzky's 'self-portrait' *The Constructor* of 1924, provides an example of his use of photographic montage, as also a statement of his Constructivist programme, in which the artist was encouraged to apply the skills of the engineer and the architect to art.

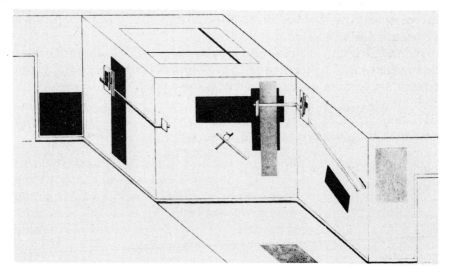

56. El Lissitzky, design for a 'Proun room' shown in 1923 in Berlin

The rooms, as first exhibited in 1923, were free-standing constructions, and were used while on exhibition to hang other works of Constructivist design art.

While Constructivist design engineers were attempting to free art and artistic design from the constraints of the representational style of the Realists of the nineteenth century, the experimental film-makers Vertov and Eisenstein were attempting to create both a new sense of space, and a new, revolutionary concept of time to suit the concept that they and their society had entered a new time with the revolution of 1917. Vertov's *Man with a Movie Camera* was, for instance, but one of the successful, and influential, experiments with the 'Machine Aesthetic' in film to come out of this period, and was also at least in part a product of the experiments executed by Constructivist artists and designers in the early 1920s. Vertov had in fact worked together with Rodchenko in the filming of the newsreel series *Kino-Pravda* from 1922 on, had constructed photomontage[15] posters for Eisenstein, and had befriended El Lissitzky at the time of making his *Man with a Movie Camera* in the mid 1920s. Richard Taylor writes of Vertov's programme: 'Founder and leader of the Cine-Eye group he had proclaimed the cinema's creation of a new reality: "I am the Cine-Eye, I create a man more perfect than Adam was created . . . through montage I create a new, perfect man".'[16] In this 'Promethean' sense too,[17] Constructivist art presented itself as a productivist as well as an optimistic[18] and Utopian programme.

As producers of goods of at least some economic value, as well as of Soviet film and trade propaganda, the individual Constructivists named in this book saw themselves as playing a role in the economic growth of their new Soviet State, as well as a leading intellectual role in its artistic development and in the creation of a new proletarian subject for their art objects. Having assumed these 'avant-garde' roles, many of these same Constructivists were, however, to come into conflict with that other vanguard of Soviet life, the Party, as well as with a revival of the Realist easel-painting which they had earlier condemned and rejected.

# 8

*Avant-garde vs. 'Agroculture':*
*problems of the avant-garde –*
*from Lenin to Stalin and after*

## Introduction

E. H. Carr has written in his essay 'A historical turning point: Marx,
Lenin, Stalin':[1]

> For the best part of a century, the Russian intelligentsia – a group
> without precise counterpart elsewhere – had provided the leadership
> and the inspiration for a series of revolutionary movements. Lenin's
> *What is to be done?*, published in 1902, was a plea for a party of
> professional revolutionaries under intellectual leadership to spearhead
> the proletarian revolution; and Trotsky, in a famous polemic two years
> later, accused the Bolshevik party of 'attempting to *substitute* itself for
> the working class'.
>
> When therefore the survival of the revolutionary regime was placed
> in jeopardy by the inadequacy, quantitative and qualitative, of the
> proletariat, the party, led and organized mainly by intellectuals,
> stepped into the gap . . .

Carr continues:

> The Russian Revolution was made and saved not by a class, but by a
> party proclaiming itself to be the representative and vanguard of a
> class . . .

To Carr, this assumption of the role of vanguard by the Party marked a
shift from Marx's concept of revolution made by a class using the force
of its mass strength to that of revolution made and maintained by a
political elite.

Apparently aware of the differences between his concept of the Party
as vanguard and of Marx's attribution of that role to the proletariat, as
also of the common origin of those two concepts in the earlier Utopian
socialist idea of avant-garde, Lenin had, however, linked his concept of a

136

vanguard of theoretically advanced Party members to both Marx and Engels and to the French Utopian socialists in his *What is to be Done?* of 1902. Speaking first of the Party as not merely a vanguard of the proletariat but as a harbinger of theory, Lenin also praised the role played by Herzen, Belinsky, and Chernyshevsky in developing socialist theory in Russia:

> At this point we wish to state only that the role of vanguard fighter can be fulfilled only by a party that is guided by the most advanced theory. To have a concrete understanding of what this means, let the reader recall such predecessors of Russian Social-Democracy as Herzen, Belinsky, Chernyshevsky, and the brilliant galaxy of revolutionaries of the seventies; let him ponder over the world significance which Russian literature is now acquiring; let him . . . but be that enough!

After naming Herzen, Belinsky, and Chernyshevsky as leaders of the Russian socialist intelligentsia, Lenin turned to Engels' comments on the need for a theoretically informed proletarian movement, and quoted amongst these Engels' remarks on the debt owed by German socialism to the Utopian socialism of Saint-Simon (the theoretician of avant-garde himself), to Fourier, and Owen. Later Lenin wrote in criticism of those afraid of theory: 'A "vanguard" which fears that consciousness will outstrip spontaneity, which fears to put forward a bold "plan" that would compel general recognition even among those who differ from us. Are they not confusing "vanguard" with "rearguard"?'[2]

While defending the concept of avant-garde when applied to his own party in 1902, Lenin was, after taking power in October 1917, to set about limiting the power of those other 'avant-garde' groups whom he saw as posing a threat to the avant-garde position of his party. Similarly, avant-garde artists and writers were displaced from positions of power in the Stalinist period which followed, and the intelligentsia maligned as a suspect group of intellectuals, who were to be recognised by the fact that they had benefited from the sale of their mental labour without being involved in manual work. Most definitions of the intelligentsia from this time were (despite the fact that this had been the most Russian of words), to see it, moreover, as a phenomenon produced under Western capitalism.

The 1959 edition of the *Fundamentals of Marxism-Leninism*, for example, offers the following description of the intelligentsia:

> The development of industry, technology and culture in capitalist society results in the formation of a broad stratum, the *intelligentsia*, consisting of persons engaged in mental work (technical personnel,

teachers, doctors, office employees, scientists, writers, etc.). The intelligentsia is not an independent class, but a special group which exists by selling its mental labour. It is recruited from various strata of society, chiefly from the well-to-do classes and only partly from the ranks of the working people . . .[3]

Defined in this way, the intelligentsia is seen as the expression of a division of labour between manual and mental labour and of leisured and proletarian classes produced by a capitalist mode of production.

If we were to see the Constructivists of the 1920s as a part of the 'intelligentsia' of that time, we should, however, have to distinguish their particular combination of mental and manual labour both from the post-Stalinist definition of the intelligentsia as consisting of a group of purely mental labourers, and from its relegation of the intelligentsia to non-working classes.

In that the Constructivists represented an intelligentsia which was involved in both productive manual labour and in social planning, they had of course also continued the Saint-Simonian tradition, developed by thinkers in the early nineteenth century and referred to by Lenin in 1902, of an avant-garde combining artists, scientists and engineers. In his somewhat eccentric book on the intelligentsia of Great Britain (which was researched and written in the late 1920s) D. S. Mirsky, while criticising the Comtean concepts of social engineering and scientism 'propagated' by H. G. Wells, praised the role played in Russia in the nineteenth century by the Saint-Simonists and George Sand in assisting the Russian intelligentsia in the fight they were then waging against the stagnation caused by (in Mirsky's words) 'a serf-owning nobility and a merchant class lost in asiatic and mediaeval murk'.[4] Mirsky had also defined the intelligentsia as an 'independent' group of intellectual thinkers of positive social value; yet the transformation of the concept of intelligentsia in the mid-1930s into a term of abuse in Soviet vocabularies, and the reinforcement of the idea of the Party as vanguard, saw the suppression of the Saint-Simonist tradition referred to by Mirsky, as well as the curtailment of the independence of its Soviet heirs, the avant-garde artists of the 1920s who had redeveloped and put into practice a new productivist aesthetic concerned with the artistic, technological, and economic development of their new society.

Moreover, at the same time as Stalin was engineering the end of the independent intelligentsias which had thrived in the early 1920s, he was, as will be seen, to organise his own party bureaucrats into taking over the roles of both the literary and technical intelligentsias, and into combining these roles with their own pre-given role of maintaining and controlling public order, where, previously, Saint-Simonism had separated the avant-garde from the bureaucratic maintenance of order.[5]

## Saving Electricity: Constructivism under Lenin

To the encouragement of the Russian avant-garde of the 1920s, Lunacharsky, the head of Narkompros, the 'Commissariat of Enlightenment' (or 'Education') from 1917–29, had in the early years of his Directorship (in the first few years in which Lenin was in power) supported the idea that the work of both scientists and artists should be carried out with the 'minimum' of outside interference and pressure', and that the State should also subsidise such work.[6] This policy had proved sympathetic to most avant-garde artists, as Lunacharsky had not only expressed his support for modernist abstract art in defending it against Plekhanov in Paris in 1912, before the Revolution, but had, after 1917, as head of Narkompros, continued in this role as a 'patron' of the avant-garde, until economic problems in the early 1920s had put increasing pressure on both himself and Narkompros to restrict the independence of the avant-garde, and to support only those less modernistic artists approved by Lenin and the Party as useful propagandists.[7]

Although Lenin had allowed Lunacharsky and the Constructivists to have their way for the most part of the three or four years following the revolution of 1917, he was, as mentioned previously, really much more of a follower of the Realist school inspired by Chernyshevsky than of the abstractionists of the avant-garde,[8] and was for this reason too, when economic cuts demanded tighter control over the activities of the avant-garde, to press Lunacharsky into criticising it. For this reason, however, Lunacharsky's later apparently critical remarks on modern art, such as his 1924 statement, quoted by Sheila Fitzpatrick in her study of Narkompros,[9] that 'Futurism was an offspring of the decay of capitalism', must be seen in context as having been determined by policies which were not necessarily of his own choosing.

Lunacharsky's condemnation of Futurism was furthermore ambiguous in that, although the term 'Futurism' had been used by some in Russia as a general descriptive term for abstract modern art, it may, in Lunacharsky's usage, have been meant to apply only to *some* modernist artists, and not necessarily to those known as Constructivists, who, by the time Lunacharsky was criticising Futurism, had developed a more useful and proletarian form of art than that represented earlier on by Russian modernist artists.

In fact, Lunacharsky was already giving his active patronage to Constructivist artists in 1919, at a time, that is, when he is said to have made his first attack on Futurism in Russia.[10] Soon after that, Lunacharsky further helped several Constructivists to positions within 'Izo', the Department of Visual Arts in Narkompros, having appointed, for example, Tatlin to the Committee under Shterenberg in Moscow, and Rodchenko to the museum department of the Petrograd branch of Izo. With such help from Lunacharsky Constructivism was able to establish itself as a movement, and was, by 1920, apparently in full accord with Lenin's own 'Saint-Simonian' policy of 'electrification plus the Soviets equals socialism'.[11] In fact, as Kenneth Frampton has written in his 'Notes on a lost avant-garde: architecture, U.S.S.R.,

57.  1922 photomontage by A. Rodchenko which juxtaposes the name for the Ministry of Arts, Narkompros, with the name of a play about Oliver Cromwell

1920–30',[12] the Productivists had even defined Constructivism as being based on concepts of 'tektonika' (a 'complex of societal and industrial techniques') and 'Faktura' (the so-called 'objectivity' involved in its realisation), which entailed the idea that communism and Constructivism would go together in the material construction of the new society.[13]

## Cutting supply to fund 'Agroculture'

Despite the economic value produced by Constructivist artists working under the Directorship of Lunacharsky after 1917, they were, as mentioned earlier, to see government funding for their work reduced after 1921 by the economic reforms instituted after the March 1921 uprising of the Kronstadt seamen who had helped the Bolsheviks to power in 1917. These economic reforms (known as NEP, the New Economic Policy) were introduced in order to allow more free trade (in part to encourage production by the disgruntled small producers on the land), but had at the same time cut government funding of areas such as the arts. Lenin's proud words (spoken in 1920), of how the revolution had freed the artist from 'the yoke' of the open market, ensuring that the work of the artist would be both protected and bought by the State, and that the artist would be left free 'to create freely according to his ideal, independent of anything else', were now to apply only to those works of art which were both *politically* and economically productive. Hence Lenin continued to support areas like the new film industry which had propaganda value,[14] but little else of the modernists if it did not have a clearly useful value to his own concerns.

Following the cutting of government funding for avant-garde artists, the reintroduction of the private art market in 1921 also led to the regrowth of the Realist art rejected by the avant-garde Constructivists in earlier years. Favoured by private art collectors to whom the avant-garde art of the Constructivists was still either a mystery or an aberration, the Realist art which had once been practised by the Social Realists of the 1860s (and which was to form the basis of Socialist Realist art) again became popular. Through the foundation of the Association of Artists of Revolutionary Russia (AKh(R)R) in 1922, and the revival of the Society of the Wanderers, Realism soon gained the organisational and political power which was to ensure its success over the avant-garde in the 1930s.[15] Although the cutting of government funding for their projects did not altogether eliminate Constructivist artists from the Soviet art scene, it did enable the Association of Russian Revolutionary Artists and the Society of the Wanderers to regain a

position of power over the avant-garde artists who had once attacked
their Realist paintings as retrograde easel-art, by, in particular, winning
power over the former avant-garde in the reorganization of the artists'
associations of 1932 which led to the establishment of the Union of
Soviet Artists, which was (in its turn) to provide a platform for Socialist
Realism in later years.

In retaliation against the cutting of funding to them by the
government after 1921 many Constructivists – including the leading
members of *Vkhumetas*, Brik, Rodchenko, and Stepanova – had (in the
mid 1920s)[16] openly attacked economic cuts affecting their work as well
as the new support (both public and private) given to the traditionalist
Realist painters against whom they had earlier revolted, and against
whose work most of their social and artistic experiments had been
directed. The fight of the avant-garde against the revival of traditional
representational painting was also maintained by 'OCTOBER', a group
made up of avant-garde artists (and including several of the original
Constructivists) which had been formed in the first half of 1928. Like
the *Vkhumetas* artists, the OCTOBER group was, however, disbanded
after 1930[17] and within a few years subjected to new guidelines

58 Klutsis, photomontage

59. Alexander Gerasimov, *Stalin and Voroshilov in the Grounds of the Kremlin*, 1938 (Tretyakov Gallery, Moscow)

It is interesting to note here that while believing with other apologists of Socialist Realism that art should give a 'truthful depiction of reality', Alexander Gerasimov has so composed his picture as to make the figure of Stalin taller than that of Voroshilov. (Although neither man was tall, Stalin was, in fact, the shorter of the two.)

formulated for the new official doctrine of Socialist Realism. In order to survive these developments the Constructivists El Lissitzky and Rodchenko turned away from their abstract art experiments towards the more functional and less controversial area of design, while others like the photomontage artist Klutsis continued to apply their art to State propaganda[18] but with new, officially approved content, as in, for example, his photomontage of a smiling Stalin juxtaposed on to a collection of apparently cheerful farm workers.

Later depictions of Stalin, such as those by his favoured artist Alexander Gerasimov (1881–1963), dispensed with the avant-garde techniques of the Constructivists and returned to a more traditional (and less ambiguous) representational style.

60. Alexander Gerasimov, *The Old Bridge, Florence*

Alexander Gerasimov was not only famous in Stalin's time for his portraits of Stalin and Lenin but was also noted for his landscapes. He had, moreover, studied with painters associated with the Wanderers such as A. E. Arkhipov and A. Serov. This water-colour can even be said to echo the Italianate landscapes of the German Nazarenes which had been favoured by many of the nineteenth-century Russian Wanderers. Compare Gerasimov's landscape with, for instance, those by Friedrich Olivier and Rehbenitz illustrated previously.

*Engineering the end: the victory of Socialist Realism over Constructivism*

Following Stalin's introduction of the doctrine of Socialist Realism at the Seventeenth Party Conference of the Soviet Communist Party in February 1932, Alexander Gerasimov and other Realist painters set about to formulate guidelines for the new Socialist Realist painting and sculpture. Gerasimov's collected speeches and articles on Socialist Realism from the Stalin era were published by the Academy of Arts in Moscow, in 1952, under the title *For Socialist Realism*, and he was later credited with having prevented Khrushchev from approving a more liberal policy towards modernism for the visual arts. It was, however, A. A. Zhdanov's speech to the Soviet Writers' Congress of 1934 which first proclaimed a philosophy of Socialist Realism for the arts in general. In that speech Zhdanov spoke continually – in what now looks to be a cynical parody of the Constructivists' description of the artist as engineer – of Stalin's call to writers to be the 'engineers of human souls'. Asking, with rhetorical redundancy, what this might mean, Zhdanov claimed:

> In the first place, it means knowing life so as to be able to depict it truthfully in works of art, not to depict it in a dead, scholastic way, not simply as 'objective reality', but to depict reality in its revolutionary development.[19]

The 'truthful depiction of reality' aimed at by Socialist Realism was to serve to replace the abstract, non-representational art favoured by the avant-garde, as well as the concept of the artist as engineer developed by the Constructivists of the 1920s. Where from the Saint-Simonians to the Constructivists the concept of engineering had meant the involvement of the artist in the production of new scientific knowledge or technological construction, engineering was now given the meaning of political manipulation. Zhdanov continued:

> In addition to this, the truthfulness and historical concreteness of the artistic portrayal should be combined with the ideological remoulding and education of the toiling people in the spirit of socialism. This method in *belles lettres* and literary criticism is what we call the method of socialist realism.

Such a method was also, in Zhdanov's words, to be 'proudly tendentious'. Later official definitions of Socialist Realism were also to stress the propagandistic function of art and literature. According to one such definition, Socialist Realism was to be understood as the 'reflection of historical reality in artistic images which express the perception of reality', and its task, the 'ideological conversion and education of the workers in the spirit of socialism'.[20]

The latter point – that the task of Socialist Realism was the 'ideological conversion and education of the workers in the spirit of socialism' – was also part of the broader programme for the creation of a 'New Socialist Man'. Whereas the Constructivists of the 1920s had thought to contribute to the development of a new Soviet proletariat by way of their encouragement of proletarian labour and their own contributions to economic development and productivity (like Rodchenko, many were involved in the design of workers' clubs as well as with commercially productive projects), the creation of a 'New Socialist Man' in Stalin's time was to see the artist used as propagandist. In this sense the concept of art creating a 'subject for its objects' (as described by

Marx in his *Grundrisse,* and as practised by the productivist artists of the 1920s) was also taken from the context of its productivist philosophy (where it had been given the task of developing a new functional form of art for a new type of avant-garde worker), and turned into the idea that the artist was to use his or her art to mould the worker in a manner already dictated by the State. Further to this, Socialist Realist artists were told that while educating the worker in the 'spirit of socialism' they must also 'reflect' historical reality in their art. The Socialist Realist concept of intervention was also in this regard one which was attributed not to the artist but to the State, and meant that artists themselves, as well as their subjects, would be moulded to the State's ideas. This was implied not only in the directions given by Zhdanov to Soviet artists and writers in 1934, but also by the setting up of new tighter State controls over the artist in the form both of unions and of censorship laws in the 1930s.

To achieve the 'ideological conversion' of its workers, Socialist Realist art was to present heroic, idealised pictures of them, as shown here, for example, by this monument by Vera Mukhina of a worker and collective farm girl – a pair representative of the union under the communist flag (with its hammer and sickle) of industry and agriculture.

Zhdanov's definition of the aims of Socialist Realism was clearly aimed both at encouraging a form of heroic art which would celebrate the new Soviet worker, and at mocking the claims of such avant-garde artists as the Constructivists for seeing their art as an important part in the growth of productivity and technology within Russia. Indeed Zhdanov asserted, in the next part of his speech,[21] that artistic production was lagging behind economic life, implying that artists like the Constructivists had not contributed to economic growth as they had claimed, and suggesting that in the future artists of all kinds would have to recognise their inferiority to the political side of the Party, as well as to be prepared to take directions from it. Ambiguously, the art of the future as described by Zhdanov would have both to acknowledge its limitations and be able to portray the heroes of the State in all their glory.

The tendency to ambiguity if not to contradiction in Zhdanov's concept of Socialist Realism is also to be found in his statements on Romanticism. Firstly, he proclaimed:

> To be an engineer of human souls means standing with both feet firmly planted on the basis of real life. And this in its turn denotes a rupture with romanticism of the old type, which depicted a non-existent life

61. Monument by Vera Mukhina

Although Mukhina experimented with modernistic designs before the 1920s, and even submitted a model for a modernistic representation of Revolution in 1923 (the *Flame of Revolution* of 1922–3), this monument (like others completed by her in the 1930s) has been seen to represent the spirit of Socialist Realist art. (Her portrait, painted by the Realist artist Mikhail Nesterov in 1940, hangs in the Tretyakov Gallery, Moscow.)

and non-existent heroes, leading the reader away from the antagonisms and oppression of real life into a world of the impossible, into a world of utopian dreams . . .[22]

Yet he continued:

Our literature, which stands with both feet firmly planted on a materialist basis, cannot be hostile to romanticism, but it must be a romanticism of a new type, revolutionary romanticism.[23]

Never clearly distinguished from the 'old romanticism' spoken of by Zhdanov, the new, recommended by him to artists and writers alike, was often expressed by Socialist Realist artists in terms still reminiscent of the old, from which it was supposed to differ.[24]

62. S. Riangina, *Ever Higher!*, 1934

While using the typically Romantic figure of the mountaineer, Riangina's tribute to the modern Soviet worker appears to reverse the technique of nineteenth-century Romantic artists such as C. D. Friedrich by using human figures to dwarf Nature, instead of Nature to dwarf the human figure. The effect of Riangina's dramatic exaggeration of scale in favour of the human figure achieves, however, an identification of the human subject with the heroic side of Nature, in which it appears to resemble Romantic art.

Discussion of contradictions within the new aesthetic put forward by Zhdanov were, however, to be as actively discouraged as the representation of conflict and contradiction within art. What was to be 'engineered' were not only the 'souls' of the workers but, as suggested earlier, the souls of the artists themselves, so that these so-called 'engineers' were ultimately put into the contradictory role of 'engineers' who were themselves the mere tools of a party political machine. It is even more ironic, then, to note that one of Stalin's first show trials was of a fictional party named the 'Industrialists',[25] and that attacks on the

63. Caspar David Friedrich, *Wanderer over the Sea of Cloud*, 1818 (Kunsthalle, Hamburg)

While C. D. Friedrich's *Monk by the Sea* depicts a Nature which shows the human figure dwarfed by its immensity, his *Wanderer over the Sea of Cloud* uses a scale closer to that of Riangina's picture. Unlike Riangina's worker-heroes the protagonists of Friedrich's paintings are often alone, though they are also often of the mountaineering type refunctioned by Riangina to illustrate the heroism of the modern worker.

avant-garde Constructivists and productivists coincided with the appropriation of their roles as both avant-garde artists and engineers by the ideologues of Socialist Realism.[26]

### The institutionalisation of Socialist Realism in the visual arts

Stalin's inauguration of the concept of Socialist Realism in February 1932, following the Seventeenth Party Conference of the Communist Party of the Soviet Union (which had made the decision to give a 'socialist economic basis and a classless society'[27] to the proletarian revolution of 1917 in the Second Five-Year Plan of 1933–7) led in April 1932 to the abolishment of the proletarian art organisations which had

64. The Akh(R)R had merged with the society for circulating art exhibitions (the society born of the Wanderers) in 1923, and was to preserve and encourage the Realism advocated by the latter. In this photograph of 1926 Isaak Brodsky is shown with his teacher, the Wanderer I. E. Repin, after the merging of the Wanderers with the Akh(R)R.

survived within Narkompros,[28] to the disbandment of all previous official artists' societies, and to the setting up of the Union of Soviet Artists to control the visual arts. This union had then given the Directorship of the newly revived Artists' Academy to Isaak Brodsky, the Realist painter known mainly for his portraits of Lenin, who had been a student of the Social Realist Repin.

The Union of Writers was formed after the Union of Artists, in 1934. These new developments had (as mentioned earlier) followed the show trials of 1928 against the engineers of the Shakty district, the so-called 'Industrialist' party in 1930, and the Mensheviks in 1932.[29] The Socialist Realism thus established in the wake of a terror against supporters of the old avant-garde was described as having for its basic principle 'the truthful, historically concrete depiction of reality in its

65. Isaak Brodsky, *Lenin in the Smolny Institute*, 1930 (Tretyakov Gallery, Moscow)

Isaak Brodsky painted several portraits of Lenin while a member of the Association of Russian Revolutionary Artists prior to being appointed to the Directorship of the Academy of Arts organised by the newly formed Union of Soviet Artists in 1932. Although Brodsky's photograph-like attention to detail distinguishes his work from the more Romantic style of later proponents of Socialist Realism such as Alexander Gerasimov, his influence can be found in the Realist art of, for instance, his student, Vladimir Serov.

66. Vladimir Serov, *Peasant Delegates Talking to Lenin*, 1950
(Tretyakov Gallery, Moscow)

This version of Lenin in the Smolny Institute at the time of the 1917
revolution is clearly a homage by Serov to his former teacher, Isaak
Brodsky. Serov, who was Chairman of the Union of Soviet Artists in the
war years 1941–5 and President of the USSR Academy of Arts from
1962 to his death in 1968, is also known for his painting *The Winter
Palace is Taken!* of 1954.

revolutionary development', and as its most important task 'the
communist education of the masses'.

Both Akh(R)R artists and Socialist Realists sought to replace the
Constructivists who had enjoyed the patronage of Narkompros in the
1920s, and who had previously rejected the Realist form of art favoured
by them. Not only were Constructivists gradually displaced from their

teaching positions and excluded from the exhibitions of the Academy and the Union of Soviet Artists in the 1930s, but they were also virtually eliminated from official Soviet art history. Hence, although there are detailed and illustrated articles on Realists such as the Wanderer Repin in the *Bol'shaia Sovetskaia Entsiklopediia* (The *Great Soviet Encyclopedia*) of 1950–8 (an edition prepared under Stalinist direction), there are no individual entries for Constructivists like Rodchenko or Tatlin, while the one mention of Constructivism (in volume 38) begins with a description of it as a bourgeois form of art antipathetic to Realism.

Those artists who are named as Constructivists are, moreover, not Russian, but French (Le Courbusier), and German (e.g. Gropius) – architects and designers who did not share the political beliefs of the Russian Constructivists, and who had previously been condemned by Marxists critical of the latter.[30] Only later editions of the *Encyclopaedia*[31] give proper acknowledgement to Russian Constructivists such as Rodchenko and the Vesnin brothers, and show us a more sympathetic account of the movement as a whole. So, for example, in the 1973–82 English translation of the *Encyclopedia*'s third edition, Constructivism is described as having advocated the 'construction of an environment that actively guided life's processes', and as having 'contrasted the simplicity and the underlying utilitarianism of the new forms, which personified to them democracy and the new relationships between people, with the ostentatious splendor of bourgeois life'. It is then further admitted, but with some obvious hesitation, that 'to a certain degree, the aesthetics of constructivism facilitated the establishment of Soviet artistic design'.[32]

The demise of the Constructivist 'aesthetic' (if it can be so called) in the 1930s had followed long battles between the avant-garde of the early twentieth century and Plekhanov, Lenin and the *Proletkult*,[33] and (after the death of Lenin) the avant-garde of the 1920s and those Realist artists who subscribed to the official doctrine of Socialist Realism. El Lissitzky's fears about the redevelopment of both Realist art and of State control over the artist had been made clear in letters written to his wife as early as August and September 1925. On 1 August he wrote:

> What's going on in the art-world? The powers that be are attempting to create a revolutionary art from above. The State has always had a David, who paints, as occasion demands, today *The Oath of the Horatii* and tomorrow the *Coronation of Napoleon*. Only at the moment we lack a David . . .[34]

Ironically, El Lissitzky was to be proved correct not only about the lack of great painters amongst those who would pay court to Stalin, but also about the way in which Stalin would also (like Napoleon I and Napoleon III) make and immortalise his *Eighteenth Brumaire* with the help of his 'Court' artists, 'from above'. In a letter of 8 September El Lissitzky wrote of the limitations of Realist art in general:

> It boils down to this – whether art is taking an active part or merely 'reflecting'. If it's the latter, then it's a game and nowadays people have plenty of other more exciting games . . .

The polarisation of reflectionist and productivist theories of art and of Realist and abstract art practices which was to occupy theorists and activists of the 1930s had begun in earnest. From now on Marx too would be called upon to take sides in the debate (and, most often, on the side of Realism), even though it had not been fought in all those terms in his time, and he himself had never clearly expressed any enthusiasm for the German Realism then popular, much of this having, of course, been produced by artists associated with the Romantic or Nazarene schools antipathetic to what he and his colleagues represented.

Obviously it is impossible to know what Marx would have thought of either the Soviet Socialist Realists or Constructivists of this century. Despite this fact, Constructivism, once the embodiment of the avant-garde in Soviet Russia, was condemned as decadent by many Marxists in the 1930s and after, while Marx's works were called upon to provide authority for Socialist Realism. Similarly, while Engels' praise for painters assumed to be Realists like Carl Hübner was attributed to Marx, Marx's praise for the realism of Balzac was taken as authority for the new programme of literary Socialist Realism, and little notice was taken of his point (as reported by both Kautsky and Lafargue), that Balzac was to him a good realist because he was able to describe the future as well as the present. Paul Lafargue, for example, had written in his *Reminiscences of Marx* of 1890, that he (Marx) 'admired Balzac so much that he wished to write a review of his great work *La Comédie humaine* as soon as he had finished his book on economics. He considered Balzac not only as the historian of his time, but as the prophetic creator of characters which were still in embryo in the days of Louis Philippe and did not fully develop until after his death under Napoleon III'.[35] Clearly, too, such Realism – though Marx himself appears never to have used the term – was not (for either Marx or Engels) to exclude a Saint-Simonian or 'productivist' belief in the avant-garde function of art, as it was to do later, under different historical circumstances, for Stalin.

As Donald D. Egbert writes in his article 'The idea of "avant-garde" in art and politics',[36] Balzac himself had, moreover, once been a Saint-Simonian, a point overlooked by most of those who call him a Realist, and particularly by those using him to prove Marx to be a Socialist Realist. Egbert writes: 'One famous figure, who, like Hugo, passed from the influence of the Saint-Simonians almost to becoming a Fourierist, was the great Romantic–Realist author, Honoré de Balzac, destined to become Marx's favourite novelist.' Although in both his 'Realism' and his Saint-Simonianism Balzac might be characterised as a 'Romantic', Egbert adds that Balzac was also 'deeply interested in the visual arts', and that his 1838 novel, *Un grand homme de province à Paris,* had not only led to the popular use of the word 'Bohemian' for artists and writers, but had also depicted the latter as an 'avant-garde group in opposition to the stuffy bourgeoisie'. Further to this (as Maximilian Rubel and Margaret Manale indicate in their *Marx without Myth*),[37] Marx had taken a certain pleasure in watching Balzac laugh at the exertions taken by the Raphaelite 'realist' artist in his *Le Chef d'oeuvre inconnu* of 1832 – the story of an artist 'so intent on producing on canvas with the greatest exactness the image he had in his head, that he reworked, retouched, and corrected his painting until finally nothing remained'.

Apart from its falsification of the historical Marx's attitude to both Realism in art and the concept of avant-garde art, the battle between productivist and reflectionist concepts of art in Soviet aesthetics was originally aimed at replacing an avant-garde concept of art as an innovative form of aesthetic or social production with a concept of art which, despite its advocacy of a 'revolutionary romanticism', saw the artist as having the task of representing that which was officially approved. Added to this, the montage art of Rodchenko and Klutsis was (as already seen) abandoned for the less contradictory and less critical forms of realist representation of the Social Realists. Where Constructivists had often aimed at an estrangement of the art object through a use of montage or design which directed the attention of their public on to the production process itself, Realism as practised by Stalin's 'Social Realists' was aimed at a unity of form and content which would not arouse the critical curiosity of the art lover for an understanding of the processes of artistic production themselves, but encourage the direct perception of the message expressed. One criterion of aesthetic merit in Soviet aesthetics thus also echoed Hegel's criticism of the mechanical in art:

> In genuine art, the 'technology' of the work itself is not visible.

Precision and clarity of purpose are distinctly expressed both in the work's structure (relationship of characters and elements of content) and in its architectonic composition (structural stability, unity and proportionality of all components).[38]

John Berger has written in his study of the sculptor Ernst Neizvestny[39] of how the elimination of criticism and of the representation of contradiction and dynamism was to undermine the effectiveness of Socialist Realism:

Works which are intended to have a long-term effect need to be far more complex and to embrace contradictions. It is the existence of these contradictions which may allow them to survive. They need to be concentrated, not upon the isolated exigencies of the moment, which can only be made total by social action submitting to and mastering them, but upon the new, now imaginable totality which reality represents.

He continues:

It is the great advantage of the Russians that they think of art as prophetic. It is their tragedy that under the autocracy of Stalin, the belief in the prophetic quality of art was subtly but disastrously transformed into the belief that art was a means of definitely deciding the future now.

Despite its suppression by Socialist Realism, the art of the avant-garde of the 1920s was, however – for better or worse[40] – to survive long enough into the future to influence the development of modern art in both East and West.

### Conclusion: the legacy of Constructivism in Soviet art

Not only has Constructivism had an enormous influence on European and American modernism, from the Bauhaus to American minimal art, geometric abstraction, and colour-field painting,[41] but it has, despite censorship, created a legacy within the Soviet Union itself, within the so-called 'unofficial' art produced there in the 1950s and 1960s. One such example was the programme for 'Kineticism' proclaimed by Victor Stepanov, in which art, science, and technology were all to be united for the purpose of a 'kinetic' interaction in which the alienation of the arts from technology – and of 'man from man' – might be overcome. The concept of 'alienation' has been added, but much else is familiar, and like Constructivist art of the 1920s much of this 'unofficial' art has both opposed Realist modes of artistic representation and stated its aim to be the creation of a 'dynamic estrangement' of the viewer from the realistic representation or perception of reality. In addition to this, the contemporary artist Vladimir Nemukhin writes that 'when you break up an object it acquires greater dynamism and tension', and that this 'stems from inner protest, disquiet, uncertainty about the morrow, unease'. He adds, 'For some this protest is associated with their personal fate, for others it is of a social nature.'

In the early experiments made with photomontage by Rodchenko and his fellow Constructivists, the use of alienation effects to make the art object strange had been aimed both at disrupting traditional techniques of representation, and the audience's expectations for the same, and at turning the eye of the viewer away from the immediate experience of the represented or montaged object towards the art process itself, and to the conditions in which it had been produced. Given that under a canon still supportive of Socialist Realism and still antipathetic to the alternative avant-gardism of productivist art such a use of montage and modernist alienation techniques was regarded as dangerously subversive, it is perhaps not surprising that much of the art which continued to use such techniques to represent the conditions of artistic production remained 'unofficial'.

Such 'unofficial' art was also almost always as concerned with illustrating the 'how' of artistic production as with showing or representing its objects. In doing this it further showed that although Realist art is often described as being able to represent objects 'as in a mirror', it has rarely been concerned with representing the mirror itself.

Some unofficial Soviet art has, however, not only acted in a 'subversive' manner in rejecting the Realist emphasis on 'showing that' for a modernist emphasis on 'showing how', but has also used 'Aesopian' or ironic language in commenting on how some modernist art has been subject to political controls.

One artist who became known for his use of a covert and often private form of satire is Oscar Rabin,[42] whose *Still Life with Fish and Pravda* of 1968 offers a part realistic, part cubistic depiction of a fish unwrapped from a page of *Pravda*, and lying across an ambiguously worded headline reading 'Beware art . . .', or 'Discreet art . . .'. Clearly, the headline can be read as pointing us to the character of Rabin's own art - seen as dangerous by the censor, and made discreet in its satire by his threats. It is a montage – ironically presented as a realistic depiction of a kitchen scene – which comments on the reaction of modernist artists to the warnings of *Pravda* and other Party journals to tame their satire, and to make it more 'discreet'. Here, as elsewhere, Rabin has offered an ironic –

67. Oscar Rabin, *Still Life with Fish and Pravda*, 1968 (Alexander Glezer and the Musée de l'Art Russe Contemporain, Montgeron)

68. David Shterenberg, *Agitator*, 1928

and discreet – challenge to official Soviet art and its doctrines: in this case by 'laying bare' its silencing effect on unofficial art itself. In fact, Rabin's use of the montage techniques of the Soviet modernist artists of the 1920s in his *Still Life with Fish and Pravda* is discreet not only in its general reference to the suppression of their montage and abstractionist techniques by Socialist Realism, but also in its apparent reference to, and quotation of, older avant-garde works such as Shterenberg's *Herrings* or his *Agitator* of 1928, a painting in which a copy of *Pravda* and a cubistic glass rest in the foreground of a scene depicting an agitator and his audience.

Quotation of works no longer in favour with Socialist Realism are common in Rabin's work, and seem to represent a type of 'samizdat' speech aware but also defiant of the censorship of art which will not conform to the official Soviet view of art. Even Rabin's depiction of a large chemise on a washing-line can – despite his public claims to have 'painted it from life'[43] – be seen as a 'discreet' 'hommage' to the Surrealist painter Magritte, whose 'Ceci n'est pas une pipe' drawings and other works, such as his *In memoriam Mack Sennett* of 1936–7 and *Philosophy in the boudoir* of 1947, had been part of a humorous attack on the pretensions of European Realism throughout the period in which Socialist Realism was consolidating its hold in Soviet Russia. Because

69. Oscar Rabin, *The Chemise*, 1975 (Alexander Glezer and the Musée de l'Art Russe Contemporain, Montgeron)

Magritte was also one of those artists who had signed a manifesto in 1935 protesting against the Soviet treatment of the Surrealists at the International Congress of Writers for the Defence of Culture in Paris of that year, he could not easily be included in the canon of artists acceptable to Socialist Realism. For such reasons, too, the quotation of his work by a Soviet artist would seem to go against official Soviet art policy. Moreover, if Rabin's works can be seen to contain oblique quotations from artists such as Magritte, then they must also be said to

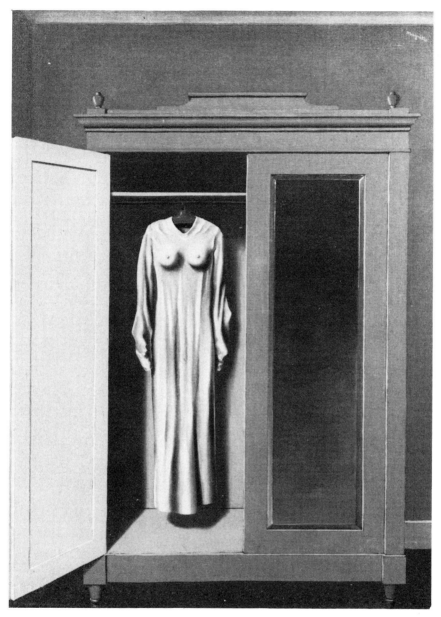

70. René Magritte, *In memoriam Mack Sennett*, 1936–7 (Musée Communal la Louvière)

have linked themselves to a programme of modernistic 'meta-art' in which the naive representation of objects is revealed as having perpetuated not truth but falsity. As in the work of the avant-gardistes of the 1920s, the emphasis here has been put on the processes of artistic

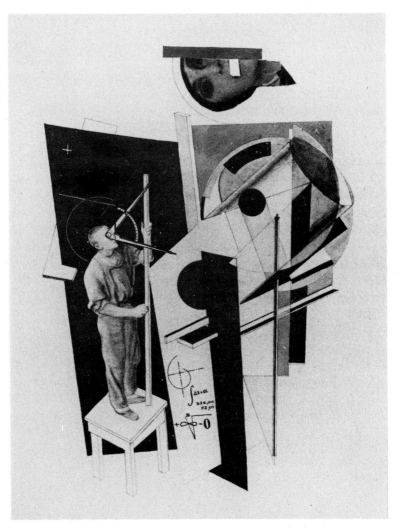

71. El Lissitzky, *Tatlin at Work*, illustration for Ehrenburg's *Six Tales with Easy Endings* (Collection Mr and Mrs Eric Estorick)

El Lissitzky's portrait of Tatlin at work on the construction of his 'Monument to the Third International' demonstrates the Constructivist belief in the need for art to show how the art work itself is constructed.

production themselves rather than on the art object, and is political not only in its implicit rejection of the representational function of art as defined by Socialist Realism, but also in its analysis of the processes of control behind artistic production. In short, while Socialist Realism was concerned – to use Gilbert Ryle's terms – to 'show that', Soviet Modernism can be seen to have been concerned to 'show how' the art work and its theories have worked.[44]

The question of to what extent Constructivists and Productivists of the 1920s were culpable in their failure to question the political road being taken by the Party under Stalin must, however, not be silenced by any recognition of the questioning, self-analytical character of their art. Together with their initial failure to assert their position as avant-garde over such ideologues for Socialist Realism as Zhdanov, their virtual disappearance from public view under Stalin may not only reflect an absence of any real union of the avant-garde as it then was with the political centre, and a failure of nerve in sometimes putting up with policies antipathetic to their own, but also – despite their progress in linking the arts to technology – a failure of the concept of avant-garde itself, as formulated by Saint-Simon, as a constructive force of any lasting economic and social power.[45] Indeed, the very emphasis put on the economic and social function of the avant-garde by Saint-Simon which has been consistently stressed in this study as indispensable to its proper definition may in fact be said to have been responsible, to at least some degree, for the political failure of the concept. Even when freed of the Hegelian concept of alienation by 'avant-gardistes' of the 1920s,[46] we may say that because the avant-garde was in fact never concerned with exercising actual political power, it was always to be a marginal – and a temporary – social force.

Whether it could, or should, ever be more than what it was – a disparate collection of experimental and often unconventional artists, architects, and engineers – is of course a question which can only be answered hypothetically and with some value judgement attached to its hypothesis. Even this fact, however, should alert us to one other main problem with the concept of avant-garde as formulated by Saint-Simon, and as taken up in practice by the Russian Constructivists of the 1920s – the problem, that is, that it was, and still is, an essentially Utopian idea.

# Conclusion

At the end of his very detailed study of Marx's knowledge of world literature, S. S. Prawer writes:

> Marx never uses the image of 'mirroring' or 'reflecting' when speaking about literature – though he does occasionally use it, when speaking about language and philosophy.[1]

Despite such evidence (and claims by other critics such as Demetz and Morawski[2] that Marx never used the word 'Realism'), it is still, as indicated previously, a widely held belief that Marx could be described not only as a 'Realist' (and at least as much a one as Engels),[3] but also as an authority, or apologist, for the Stalinist doctrine of Socialist Realism.

In the preceding chapters we have, in indicating the ahistorical character of seeing Marx as a defender of Socialist Realism, attempted to point to a much more pervasive (and much ignored) argument in Marx, for seeing art as a form of production, as well as to the importance of studying Marx's aesthetic arguments in their historical context, and, in particular, in the context of the theories and practices associated with the visual arts of his day.

The study of the visual arts in Marx's time which has been offered in the early chapters of this study has, moreover, shown Marx to have been involved in debates concerned not (as in the twentieth century) with the conflict between Realism and Modernism, but with the political patronage afforded the religious Romantic art made popular in the early nineteenth century by the German Nazarenes. Also associated with that issue was, as seen, Marx's use both of Saint-Simon's criticism of vestigial feudal elements in nineteenth-century industrial societies, and of the concept of avant-garde with which Saint-Simon had countered the feudal concepts of leadership and patronage operative in his time.

Ironically, the emphasis on the opposition between 'realism' and

164

'modernism' found in most modern discussions of Marx's aesthetic views (and based in the conflict between Socialist Realism and Modernism in Soviet history, as also in such debates as those between Lukács, Adorno, Brecht and Korsch)[4] has so led to the historical background to Marx's writings on art and art patronage being looked at as a closed book, that even recent works claiming to have reopened the productivist debate on the visual arts have avoided relating this to the historical Marx, or to the visual arts as they were actually practised in his time.[5] Further to this, the Althusserian silencing of studies of the young, supposedly 'Hegelian' Marx have (ironically) also led to the silencing of those 'unhegelian' Saint-Simonist elements in the young Marx's thought which might well have added fuel to the Althusserian attack on Lukácsian and other 'representationalist' interpretations of Marx's theories.

One further 'irony' which might be mentioned here is that of how the silencing of both the avant-garde 'productivist' artists of the 1920s and Marx's own productivist aesthetic by Socialist Realists of the 1930s has repeated the silencing experienced by Marx himself in Prussia in the 1840s. As that silencing or censorship can also be said to have contributed to Marx's criticisms of a system of State patronage of artists similar to that revived by the Soviets in 1917 and combined with a repressive censorship in the 1930s, as well as to his awareness of the contradictory factors affecting the processes of artistic production and consumption, the silencing of his own theories of artistic production (to which that awareness contributed) is not only ironic, but indicative of still unresolved contradictions within Marxist theory itself. While in this study several of these contradictions have been traced back to Marx, others may, of course, be seen to have derived from more recent expositions of his works and of the theories produced by them.

The purpose of this book has, however, not been to review contemporary theories of Marxist aesthetics in detail (for this is both the task most frequently taken up by others, and a temptation to move away again from the analysis of the historical Marx), but to open a new field of inquiry into the type of visual art given patronage in Marx's time and then to ask how it relates to the aesthetic debates in which Marx and his contemporaries have been involved in their own time and since. One further result of that investigation has of course been the suggestion that whether or not Socialist Realism has 'created' its own history or been created by it, its roots can be shown to be in a 'Populist' tradition related more to the school of Nazarene painters representative for Marx of the patronage of a feudal monarchy antipathetic to his beliefs and goals than to Marx's own views on art. If, however, such conclusions are seen to have implications for modern ideological debates despite their orientation towards a historical analysis of the context of Marx's thought, then these implications should not be allowed to lead us away again from the historical analysis of their origins. Rather they should bring us to further study of Marx's thought, and to the critical analysis of those questions and theories related to it (and to modern Marxism) which may since have disappeared from view.

# Notes

## Introduction

1 Although other Russian artists have been given the title 'avant-garde', the term will be applied here mainly to Constructivists of the early 1920s such as El Lissitzky, Tatlin and Rodchenko, who best represent the original Saint-Simonist concept of the avant-garde as consisting of a union of artists, scientists, and engineers able to pool their talents to produce artistic goods of technological as well as of economic value.

## 1 Hellenes vs. Nazarenes

1 See Heinz Monz's *Karl Marx und Trier* (Trier, 1964), and Boris Nicolaievsky and Otto Maenchen-Helfen's *Karl Marx: Man and Fighter* (1936; Harmondsworth, 1976), for further discussion of Marx's early life in Trier.

2 Georges Gurvitch, 'Saint-Simon et Karl Marx', *Revue Internationale de Philosophie*, 14 (1960), 399–416.

3 Heine was to meet Marx in Paris in 1843. Heine had arrived in Paris in 1831, had met and worked with some of the Saint-Simonians involved with the Saint-Simonian journal, *Le Globe*, and had sent articles on the French Saint-Simonians to Germany throughout the 1830s. He had also heard Hegel lecture in Berlin in 1821–2, and had been active in those same years in the Verein für Kultur und Wissenchaft der Juden (a society aimed at a comparative study of Jewish and European culture and history, of which Eduard Gans was also a member).

4 See John Plamenatz, *German Marxism and Russian Communism* (London, 1954), p. 308, for further discussion of similarities between the ideas of Marx and Saint-Simon.

5 Heinrich Heine, *Sämtliche Werke*, ed. Ernst Elster (7 vols., Leipzig, 1887–90), vol. 3, pp. 284–6.

6 Heine also contrasts the spiritualism of Cornelius with the sensualism of Rubens in this passage.

7 It has previously been claimed by critics tracing the concept of avant-garde back to Saint-Simon that this had first been used by him in 1825 to describe the advance or leading role which artists, technocrats and scientists were to

play in the establishment of the new social order outlined in his *Nouveau christianisme*. Still others have referred to his and Halévy's *Opinions littéraires philosophiques et industrielles* of the same year, in which an artist describes his group as serving society as its avant-garde by creating and spreading new ideas within it. Although, as Taylor mentions in his edition of selected works by Saint-Simon (*Henri Saint-Simon (1760–1825)*, translated and edited by Keith Taylor (London, 1975), p. 310), the *Opinions* are sometimes attributed not to Saint-Simon but to the Saint-Simonian Olinde Rodrigues, the evidence given for the latter's authorship has not yet been generally accepted as conclusive.

8  Translated by Taylor, p. 71.

9  Translated in *The Political Thought of Saint-Simon*, edited by Ghita Ionescu (Oxford, 1976), p. 132.

10  Taylor, p. 194.

11  *Ibid.*, p. 47. Taylor writes that after 1820 the term 'industrielle' was applied by Saint-Simon only to those doing practical work in farming or industry. While limiting the application of 'industrielle', Saint-Simon did, however, continue to use the term 'producteur' to describe artists and other members of the avant-garde. (Taylor also points out, on pp. 47–8, that Saint-Simon had seen history as the history of a struggle between idle and non-idle classes, and had included artists and scientists among the latter.)

12  As Bernard Smith writes in his *Place, Taste and Tradition* (1945; 2nd edn, Melbourne, 1979, p. 97), the commercial possibilities of art – especially when related to the improvement of the design of manufactured goods – had been promoted from the early eighteenth century on in Europe, and to some extent under the aegis of Mercantilism. He writes:

> The argument that art education would lead to an improvement of design and so promote commerce was not new. It had been used throughout the eighteenth century and was an aspect of the Mercantilist theory that maintained that it was the duty of the state to develop flourishing manufactures, so as to increase the export of commodities and thereby increase the import of gold. Arguments that an improved knowledge of art would foster commerce had been used at the re-organization of the Vienna Academy in 1725, at the foundation of the Munich Academy in 1770, and by the Dublin Society when they established a drawing class in that city. The programme of the British Institution was 'to improve and extend our manufactures by that degree of taste and elegance of design which are to be exclusively derived from the cultivation of the Fine Arts, and thereby to increase the general prosperity and resources of the Empire'. John Stuart Mill as late as 1867 gave voice to the utilitarian concept when he defined art as 'the endeavour after perfection in execution', i.e. as an aspect of the process of manufacture, albeit an idealized aspect.

13  See the Fourth Fragment of Saint-Simon's 'On Social Organization' in Ionescu (ed.), *The Political Thought of Saint-Simon*, p. 233.

14  Heine's continuing antipathy to the painters of the Nazarene School was also to be echoed in his 1833–6 studies of the Romantic School and of the philosophy and religion of Germany. In the latter work, for example, Heine not only gave praise to the philosophy of Saint-Simonism while attacking its critics, but also took as his ideal period in German history the Reformation

abhorred by the Romantics and Nazarenes as the period which had led to the disintegration of the Catholic Church in Germany.

15 George G. Iggers has written in his study of the political philosophy of the Saint-Simonians, *The Cult of Authority: The Political Philosophy of the Saint-Simonians* (The Hague, 1958), p. 49, that the concept of progress had been for them something absolute: progress was to affect all institutions 'simultaneously' (though possibly to different degrees), from the sciences and industry to the arts. Even the fall of one civilisation was to mark for them – as it had for Hegel – the rise of another: an idea also echoed by Marx in his *Eighteenth Brumaire* and by Heine in his essay 'Verschiedenartige Geschichtsauffassung'. There was, that is, to be no turning back in history, no repetitions, no farce. Hence Iggers writes on p. 57 that for the Saint-Simonians progress was also a 'continuous but not a constant progress', and that it was to be achieved through conflict and the progressive elimination of the inner contradictions in society. The alternation of organic and critical periods belonged to this process – critical periods serving to destroy older societies, and organic periods returning to a stability in which these gains could be made socially useful.

   To the Saint-Simonians there had been only two nascently organic sets of societies – those of Greece and Rome, and that of mediaeval Christian Europe. Each had ended with an intellectual revolution which (as in the case of Greece with Socrates, of Rome with Augustus, and of the Catholic world with the Reformation) had questioned their accepted beliefs and mores. To the Saint-Simonians, writing in their numerous journals and in the *Doctrine de Saint-Simon* of 1829, artists and *savants* had played a leading role in both critical and organic periods – in the first by challenging accepted beliefs, and in the second by making the new doctrines palatable and hence functional for the new society. These artists were also to play a leading role in the eventual 'total organisation' of men which would supersede all previous forms of organic society.

16 In his *Philosophy of History* (trans. J. Sibree, New York, 1956), p. 210, Hegel speaks, for example, of the World Spirit as represented in the oriental world in the figure of Osiris, 'the Egyptian Hermes'.

17 See Wilhelm Heinse's *Ardinghello* of 1787 (*Sämtliche Werke*, ed. Carl Schüddekopf, 5th edn (Leipzig, n. d.), vol. 4). Heine's view of Greek art as sensualistic art follows Heinse's *Ardinghello* rather than Wincklemann.

18 Hegel had praised the Greek sculptures of the Phryne in his *Ästhetik* (*Sämtliche Werke*, Jubilee edn (20 vols., Stuttgart, 1958), vol. 2, p. 377,) but had nevertheless described Romantic art as a higher development of Spirit than Greek art. Heine's opening description of Delacroix's Liberty as expressing the progress of a great 'Thought' or 'Idea' ('Gedanke') also echoes the language of Hegel's *Philosophy of History.*

19 Translated from Heine's *Französische Maler*, Heine, *Sämtliche Werke*, vol. 4, p. 37. See my article, 'The politicization of art criticism: Heine's portrayal of Delacroix's *Liberté* and its aftermath', *Monatshefte*, vol. 73, no. 4 (Winter 1981), 405–14, for further discussion of Heine's review of the Salon of 1831.

20 Heine's *Sämtliche Werke*, vol. 3, p. 395.

21 Immanuel Kant, *Critique of Judgement*, trans. J. H. Bernard (New York, 1964), p. 64.

22 See Nicos Hadjinicolaou, ' "La Liberté guidant le peuple" de Delacroix devant son premier public', *Actes de la Recherche en Sciences Sociales*, no. 28 (1979), 24.

23 Jane Clapp, *Art Censorship: a chronology of Proscribed and Prescribed Art* (New Jersey, 1972), p. 142. Ironically, the opening of art to the public in the Salons, which was begun in the mid eighteenth century, was also to see art made subject to stricter censorship in times of public unrest and dissent.

24 See the 1833 Postscript to Heine's *Französische Maler* of 1831 (*Sämtliche Werke*, vol. 4).

25 Daumier published a caricature of Louis Philippe balancing on a tightrope connecting Parliament to the issue of the *Forts détachés* or barricades in *Le Charivari* of 31 August 1833.


## 2 Feuerbach and the 'Nazarene' madonna

1 The Romantic writer and critic Friedrich Schlegel (the brother of August Wilhelm Schlegel) had frequently expressed his preference for the Nazarene School of painting over that of the Classicists of the time. Apart from favourably reviewing their work in 1819, he had, in essays later published in his *Ansichten und Ideen von der christlichen Kunst* (see *Kritische Friedrich Schlegel Ausgabe*, ed. Ernst Behler, vol. 4, ed. Hans Eichner (Zurich, 1959), pp. 5 and 237–62), praised the mediaeval art imitated and admired by the Nazarenes, and defined the original goal of art as the 'glorification of religion'. (A pencil sketch of Friedrich Schlegel by the Nazarene artist Ludwig Schnorr von Carolsfeld – the brother of Julius Schnorr von Carolsfeld, a painter of madonnas – can be seen in the Historisches Museum, Vienna.)

2 Reference will be made here to the Reclam edition of Feuerbach's *Das Wesen des Christentums* (Stuttgart, 1971), based on the third edition of 1849, and including its Forewords. The best known English translation is still George Eliot's *Essence of Christianity*.

3 *Das Wesen des Christentums*, p. 120.

4 *Ibid.*, pp. 8, 135ff. We shall see later that Feuerbach was not the first to make the point that the fetish character of Greek art could be applied to an analysis of Christian art. Apart from such critics as Debrosses and Grund, the writer Heinse, in his Ardinghello, *Sämtliche Werke*, ed. Carl Schüddekopf, 5th edn (Leipzig, n.d.), vol. 4, p. 191, had also suggested such a juxtaposition.

5 In his 1839 study of the Düsseldorf school of art, Püttmann echoes Feuerbach's 1833 criticisms of the false consciousness present in Christian art, but, unlike Feuerbach, ascribes the failings of the latter to a failed attempt to regain a union of art and religion enjoyed by the Greeks and since lost to history.

6 Translated from *Das Wesen des Christentums*, p. 71. It is also interesting to

compare Feuerbach's analysis of the way in which the mediaeval monk had created sensual images of the Madonna from his repression of his sexual desire for earthly women with the 'Young German' Thomas Mundt's novel *Madonna* of 1835. Mundt's novel had, moreover, been banned in 1835, together with Heine's 'De L'Allemagne' and the works of the Saint-Simonian School for its blasphemous, Saint-Simonian refunctioning of the New Testament into a 'Third Testament' vision of heaven brought down to earth.

7 The Nazarenes had lived as monks in their monastery near Rome, not only living apart from women, but, it is said, denying themselves the use of female models.

8 Goethe is said to have been one of the first to connect Wackenroder's *Herzensergiessungen eines kunstliebenden Klosterbruders* (Stuttgart, 1961) with the life-style and aesthetic beliefs of the German Nazarenes, though it is clear that they themselves had consciously modelled themselves on Wackenroder's Raphael-loving monk. Wackenroder's description (*Herzensergiessungen*, pp. 8f.) of the vision Raphael is said to have had of the Mother of God which lay behind the most inspired of his madonnas (which is, like many other passages in the *Herzensergiessungen*, built on Vasari's description of the lives of the great Renaissance artists) could also have provided Feuerbach with his idea that much of the religious madonna-art of Christianity was based in a false consciousness born of 'monkish' asceticism in that it had also been associated in the *Herzensergiessungen* with the monk's own dream visions. (See the *Herzensergiessungen*, p. 58 for Wackenroder's description of the monk's vision of Raphael and Dürer.) Given that the Nazarenes were at the time of Feuerbach's *Essence of Christianity* receiving even more of the patronage of the Royal Prussian House than before, while Feuerbach's career and publishing chances were coming more and more under threat from the Prussian censor, his choice of the 'Nazarene' monk for his attack on the alienating effect of the *Bildlichkeit* of the Christian religion may furthermore have had personal, if not also political grounds.

9 See Heine's *Stadt Lucca* of 1829–30, in his *Sämtliche Werke*, ed. Ernst Elster (7 vols., Leipzig, 1887–90), vol. 3, p. 386.

10 *Ibid.*, p. 395.

11 *Ibid.*, p. 397.

12 *Ibid.*, p. 417. Ludwig Feuerbach's nephew, Anselm Feuerbach (1829–80), was to become a painter in years in which the influence of the Nazarenes was still being felt in teaching academies throughout Germany, and particularly in Düsseldorf, where he was to study. Anselm Feuerbach was, however, to be influenced by both the new Realism of Courbet in Paris and by the Greek and Roman themes of the neo-classical schools. (See, for example, his *Gastmahl des Plato* of 1873, owned by the Karlsruhe State Art Museum.)

13 It has been suggested in the text that if Feuerbach's critique of anthropomorphic religion could be taken as a critique of the religion of his time (as Heine's *Atta Troll* and other contemporary works suggest it was), then his

criticism of the use by that religion of images and pictures to alienate the sensuality of the human subject to a divine, mythical figure might also relate to the art and cultural politics of the day (such as the official support given the Nazarene School and the Romantics). To my knowledge, no study has however yet been made of the possible reference to these artists in Feuerbach's work, important as it may also be to an understanding of the political significance of his critique of Christianity.

14  See Karl Grün's edition of Feuerbach's *Briefwechsel* for Henning's letter to Feuerbach of 17 April 1835, and Marx to Feuerbach, Kreuznach, 3 October 1843, *MEW* (1956–68), vol. 27 (*Briefe Feb. 1842–Dec. 1851*), pp. 419–21. It is in this letter that Marx requests Feuerbach's assistance with his 'französis-che-deutsche Jahrbucher' – addressing Feuerbach as 'one of the first German writers to speak of the need for a French–German alliance' in philosophy, and requesting him to contribute a critique of Schelling, for the embarrassment of the same and of the Prussian government supporting him. Here Marx not only mocks the acceptance by Pierre Leroux and other contemporary French thinkers of Schelling as a materialist after their own hearts, but names Feuerbach the 'umgekehrte' (reverse) Schelling, who does in fact represent what Schelling is supposed to represent but does not. What is interesting here is Marx's implicit connection of Feuerbach with the French materialism of those like the Saint-Simonians whom he quotes, through his use of Leroux's description of Schelling, as having realised their ideal 'union of the flesh and the idea', and as having 'clothed the abstract idea with flesh and blood' (*MEW*, vol. 27, p. 420). (French and German Saint-Simonians had often used these last two phrases to describe their own aims. Two such German 'Saint-Simonians' already mentioned in connec-tion with Feuerbach in these notes are Heine and Mundt. Heine had even spoken of Delacroix as having given the July Revolution its true 'physiognomy': Heine, *Sämtliche Werke*, vol. 4, p. 38.)

15  Feuerbach, *Das Wesen des Christentums*, p. 63.

16  Using Heine's distinction between the Nazarene and the Hellene, the editor of Feuerbach's correspondence, Karl Grün, wrote in 1874 on Feuerbach's 1842 criticisms in his *Vorläufige Thesen zur Reform der Philosophie* of the old 'mésalliance' between theology and philosophy, and advice to philosophy to join with the natural sciences:

> Da kann man sagen: *In hoc signo vinces*, in diesem Zeichen wird der Nazarener besiegt. (Here one can say: *In hoc signo vinces*, in this sign is the Nazarene conquered.) *Ludwig Feuerbach in seinem Briefwechsel und Nachlass*, ed. Karl Grün (Leipzig and Heidelberg, 1874), p. 112.)

17  In his *Introduction to a Critique of Hegel's Philosophy of Right* of 1843–4 Marx had also spoken of how Feuerbach's criticism of religion would be turned into a criticism of politics.

18  Wilhelm von Schadow's *The Holy Family beneath the Portico* of 1818 (fig. 10) was, for instance, originally completed for the Crown Prince of Bavaria and then repeated, by request of the Prussian monarch Friedrich Wilhelm III, for the royal Prussian collection.

### 3 *Marx's lost aesthetic: the early years under Friedrich Wilhelm IV*

1 Marx's daughters had given Marx a 'questionnaire' to fill out on his favourite authors, heroes, virtues, etc. in 1865. S. S. Prawer quotes it in his *Karl Marx and World Literature* (Oxford, 1976), p. 390. Although we may take Marx's answer that Diderot was his favourite prose writer to be correct, the irony and even levity with which he answered some of the other questions may allow us to think that Marxist Aesthetics has been fortunate that Marx was never asked to name his favourite artist.

2 Marx's 'certificate of release' from the Friedrich Wilhelm University at Bonn in 1836 records his attendance at lectures there in the Winter Semester of 1835–6 and Summer Semester of 1836, and notes that Marx had been 'diligent and attentive' in his attendance at the History of Modern Art lectures given by Professor d'Alton in the Winter Semester of 1835–6.

3 See H. Schrörs, *Die Bonner Universitätsaula und ihre Wandgemälde* (Bonn, 1906), p. 11:

> Zu dem Bonner Kreise, der wohlwollend und schützend über das Spiel der Musen in der Aula wachte gehört auch Eduard d'Alton, der Professor der neuern Kunstgeschichte. Der in den Kunstheiligtümern Italiens aufgewachsene Gelehrte, der selbst den Grabstichel führte, besass eine auserlesene Sammlung von Gemälden, Kupferstichen und Radierungen, mit der er einen Mittelpunkt der damaligen künstlerischen Interessen der Stadt bildete. Er unterhielt sehr lebhafte und intime Beziehungen zu dem Alten von Weimar, und so gelang es ihm, auch dessen Aufmerksamkeit auf die im Entstehen begriffenen Wandgemälde zu lenken. Goethe in seinem abgeklärten Klassizismus war zwar ein abgesagter Gegner der stilistischen Art des Cornelius, der die Bilder als echte Kinder entsprossen waren, aber er gestattete, dass ihm eine Zeichnung der 'Theologie' durch Ernst Förster, einen der an ihr tätigen Maler, im Jahre 1825 vorgelegt wurde. Das Blatt fesselte ihn; dreimal liess er es sich zeigen und sich jedesmal zu längeren Gesprächen anregen. Obgleich er mancherlei Bedenken äusserte, lautete doch sein Spruch: 'Ein rühmliches Unternehmen und mit Eifer und ernstem Studium angefasst'.

Here Schrörs describes how d'Alton managed to draw Goethe's attention to the frescoes for the Bonn Aula, and how, despite Goethe's dislike of Nazarene art, he gave some praise to a sketch of the *Theology* fresco. Although Goethe's appreciation of Raphael also differed from that of the Nazarenes in several respects, he had (as d'Alton may have been aware) given his unconditional approval to the *Disputà* and *School of Athens* in his *Italienische Reise* of 1786. Goetzenberger's depiction of Goethe in his *Philosophy* fresco (1829–33) followed Goethe's approval of the sketch of Hermann's fresco.

4 Marx moved to Trier from Berlin in April 1841 and from there to Bonn in July, visiting Trier again from January to March 1842 and returning to Bonn to stay there until October of that year.

5 The predominantly Catholic Rhineland had (as mentioned previously) been under the administration of Protestant Prussia since 1815.

6 Jakob Goetzenberger had also painted the frescoes for Jurisprudence and Medicine (not illustrated), and had planned a fifth fresco for the Bonn Aula to

depict the 'protection of the arts and sciences through the Prussian Crown'. It was to show 'Borussia' seated in a cart and drawn by allegorical representations of the Prussian provinces. (See Schrörs, p. 95.) That Marx had shown as little respect for the disciplines of Jurisprudence and Medicine as he had for Philosophy and Theology while a student at Bonn can be seen from the satirical epigrams on medical students in the collection of poems which he presented to his father in 1837, and from his satirical comments on his law subjects in his unfinished comic novel, *Skorpion und Felix*. (I have discussed these further in *Reading the Young Marx and Engels* (London and New Jersey, 1978).)

7  In his February 1842 criticism of the new censorship instruction's protection of the Christian religion, Marx described religion as irrational, and as therefore being in contradiction to the spirit of the Rational State as espoused by Friedrich Wilhelm IV in his attempts to imitate Frederick the Great, and added that there had been no real unity within Christianity, but a collection of factional Churches. The latter argument was in direct contradiction to the ultramontanist argument of the Prussian monarch that a union of Catholic and Protestant interests would be a reunion of interests separated by the Reformation but joined in the days of the Holy Roman Empire. The argument that Germany should seek to restore the unity lost with the Holy Roman Empire and the decline of the Catholic Church in Germany had also been put by the Romantic poet and essayist Novalis in a tract intended for Friedrich Wilhelm III entitled *Die Christenheit oder Europa*. Marx was thereby implicitly rejecting an idea which had clearly been marked as romantic even before the ascendancy of Friedrich Wilhelm IV to the Prussian throne, while also explicitly condemning the Prussian monarch's 1841 censorship of criticism of the Christian religion as 'tendentious romanticism'.

Earlier Marx's Young Hegelian friend Karl Friedrich Köppen had also criticised Friedrich Wilhelm IV's imitation of Frederick the Great in a book on the latter monarch which was dedicated to Marx. Contemporary cartoons further satirised Friedrich Wilhelm IV's attempts to follow in the footsteps of his great predecessor. One example of these, of *circa* 1843, is reproduced by Remigius Brückmann in his article ' "Es ginge wohl, aber es geht nicht", – König Wilhelm IV. von Preussen und die politische Karikatur der Jahr 1840–1849', *Berlin zwischen 1789 und 1848: Facetten einer Epoche* (Akademie der Künste, Berlin, 1981).

8  In his book *Friedrich Wilhelm IV von Preussen: ein Baukünstler der Romantik* (ed. Hans-Herbert Möller (Munich, 1961)), Ludwig Dehio has described Friedrich Wilhelm IV not only as 'ein Nazarener der Baukunst' ('a Nazarene of architecture') but also as a monarch who had used the revival of interest in the Gothic to further both the idea of the development by Prussia of a national German art and his own pietistic leanings. In another study of Friedrich Wilhelm IV (*Friedrich Wilhelm IV.: das Schicksal eines Geistes* (Berlin, 1938)), Ernst Lewalter wrote that the Prussian King had even thought Hegel too rationalistic, so strong was his tendency towards the more mystical thought of pietism.

9  As later notes and references in the text will explain further, von Rumohr

shared Hegel's admiration for the great religious painters of the Italian Middle Ages and Renaissance admired by the German Nazarenes, while also differing from Hegel in his reasons for this admiration. According to Hegel in his *Lectures on Aesthetics* (in chapter 1 of Part 1), for instance, Rumohr had admired the art of such as Raphael for its talent in finding its forms in Nature rather than by way of an Ideal. For others like Marx, Rumohr's praise for Raphael would, however, have been comparable to that of Hegel in being for the author of a religious form of art supported by the romantic Prussian monarchy of his day.

10 Despite his criticism of Rumohr's emphasis on the need for art to find its forms in Nature in the first of his *Lectures on Aesthetics*, Hegel refers to and supports Rumohr's praise for Raphael and his school in the section on Italian painting in section 3 of Part 3 of the *Lectures*.

11 As Lifshitz and others have argued, Marx had most probably first read Hegel's *Ästhetik* in the Summer of 1837 in Berlin, together with works such as Winckelmann's *History of Ancient Art* and Lessing's *Laokoon*. In November 1837 Marx wrote to his father of his 'conversion' to Hegel through the Berlin *Doktorenklub* and of how he had then obtained the help of some of its members (namely Bauer and Rutenberg) for a plan to publish some of his own work.

12 This description of Hegel as Hellene was that which Heine (in 1844) was to claim had been suggested to the Young Hegelians by his 'Saint-Simonian' readings of Hegel. In addition to this, Heine was also to publish his 'Börne Book' in 1841, in which he again defended the Hellene over the Nazarene, and in political terms, as representing the superiority of a revolution concerned with material and social progress over that of the abstract political idea.

13 See Mikhail Lifshitz, *The Philosophy of Art of Karl Marx* (London, 1973), p. 34.

14 Bruno Bauer, *Hegels Lehre von der Religion und Kunst* (Leipzig, 1842), pp. 115f.

15 *Ibid.*, p. 117.

16 Parodying the pietists, Bauer compares the Greek Phryne to the Whore of Babylon of the Apocalypse. See also Chapter 1, n. 18 on Hegel's praise for the Greek Phryne.

17 Hegel's lectures on aesthetics were given at Heidelberg in 1818 and at Berlin in 1820, 1823, 1826, and 1828. They were published as the *Lectures on Aesthetics* by Hotho in 1835. Although in the context of his whole philosophical system, art was understood as belonging to the development of 'Absolute Spirit', and the State to 'Objective Spirit', the preference shown by Hegel for the Romantic Christian art favoured by the Prussian monarchy of his time in his *Lectures on Aesthetics* had allowed some to interpret him as having defended the subjugation of art to the cultural policies and patronage system of the then Prussian State. In opposition to the interpretation of Hegel's philosophy as a defence of the existing Prussian State, Bruno Bauer set out in his 1842 treatise on Hegel's attitudes to Christian art and religion to present him and his aesthetic as Hellenistic rather than Christian and Romantic, and as radical rather than conservative.

18 See letter to Ruge of 20 March 1842.

19 Engels' 'Friedrich Wilhelm IV.: König von Preussen' was first published in the *Einundzwanzig Bogen aus der Schweiz* of 1843.

20 Heine had written an attack on the Historical School in his essay 'Verschiedenartige Geschichtsauffassung' and had contrasted it there with the Saint-Simonian view of history. The leading members of the Historical School, Ranke and Savigny, were also known to be close friends of Friedrich Wilhelm IV.

21 Marx and Engels, *Gesamtausgabe (New MEGA)*, vol. 4/1 *(Exzerpte und Notizen bis 1842)* (Berlin, 1976). Lifshitz's 1933 study, *The Philosophy of Art of Karl Marx* was particularly valuable in its time in giving an account of these then unpublished excerpts. Lifshitz did not, however, offer any further description or analysis of the works from which Marx had excerpted his notes, and was also apparently uninterested in discussing the visual arts to which they – and Marx's planned treatise of 1842 – related. Although Lifshitz gives signs of having been sympathetic to an interpretation of Marx's aesthetic views free from the theories of Socialist Realism which had been officially approved in 1932 (his book concludes with an echo of the Constructivist slogan, 'Art is dead! Long live the art of the machine!'), he also fails to connect Marx's concept of artistic production with the Saint-Simonist concept of the artist as avant-garde producer with which Marx was clearly concerned in his early work, and without justification assumes Marx's praise for Greek art to be praise for Realism in a general or modern sense.

22 Where Feuerbach saw the fetishistic images of Christianity as having both enslaved and alienated its devotees, Hegel had described the fetishes of certain pagan religions as not having entailed any enslavement of the subject to the fetish. Writing in the Introduction to his *Philosophy of History* (trans. J. Sibree, New York, 1956, p. 94) on the 'fetiches' of certain Negro tribes, Hegel claimed that although the subject had objectified itself in these images, it had remained master of them. See n. 26 for Böttiger.

23 See Lifshitz, p. 37.

24 Marx and Engels, vol. 4/1, pp. 300ff.

25 Heine too had criticised Rumohr. Writing in his *Französische Maler* of 1831 (*Sämtliche Werke*, ed. Ernst Elster (7 vols., Leipzig, 1887–90), vol. 4 Heine claimed (in the middle of a discussion on the state of contemporary art criticism and aesthetics in a review of the art of Decamps), that he was in matters of art a 'supernaturalist' rather than a believer in the function of art as mere imitation of Nature, and added:

> A new aesthetician, the author of *Italienische Forschungen*, has attempted to make the old principle of the imitation of Nature palatable again by maintaining that the visual artist must find all of his types in Nature. This aesthetician has, in putting up the above basic rule for the visual arts, ignored one of the earliest of these arts, namely architecture, whose types one now sees with hindsight in wooded glades and rocky grottoes, but which one surely did not find in the first place. For they lay not in external Nature, but in the human soul.

This could also be compared with Marx on architect and bee in *Capital* Vol. 1 (*Werke (MEW)*, vol. 23, p. 193).

Ironically, criticism of Rumohr's emphasis on the need for art to imitate Nature had of course been made by Hegel in the lectures on aesthetics which he had given in the 1820s, and which were to be published by Hotho after the publication of Heine's reports on the Salons of 1831 and 1833, in 1835. (See n. 10 for the relevant section in the published *Lectures*.) In his critique of Rumohr, Hegel however had been concerned with rescuing a Kantian concept of an 'Ideal Beauty', rather than the individualistic and autonomous poetic imagination defended by the Saint-Simonian Heine in the above-quoted passage. Again unlike Heine, Hegel had also sought to develop a compromise position between Rumohr's desire for the artist to find his forms in Nature and his own emphasis on the need for art to represent an Ideal, by describing some examples of great art as having represented the 'Ideal in Nature'.

In the sense that Rumohr's praise for Raphael might also be seen as related to his argument that great art was that which had found its forms in Nature, it should of course be differentiated from Hegel's. While Marx may have intended to exploit Rumohr's emphasis on the 'natural' bases of great art for his radical reinterpretation of Hegel's *Aesthetics*, it would, however, seem (from, for example, his *German Ideology* of 1845–6) that he was as antipathetic to Rumohr's support for Raphael (as an artist favoured by Friedrich Wilhelm IV and his supporters) as he was to Hegel's.

Unlike some modern Marxist aestheticians Marx was not so concerned with the debate over the Realism of art as with the issue of the patronage of Romantic religious artists by the Prussian monarch and his State. As pointed out elsewhere in this study, 'Realism' in Marx's time was, furthermore, as much connected with those Romantic artists as with social criticism, and Rumohr's defence of an art which could find its forms in Nature was as much associated with the modern Romantic Nazarene art which he could be seen to have supported as with a reaction against Hegel's Idealist aesthetics. (In the section of chapter 3 of Part 1 entitled 'The relation of the Ideal to Nature', Hegel himself implies that Rumohr's reaction against art that only sought to represent an abstract Ideal was being matched by a 'freshening of interest' in the use of colour by the older Italian and German schools – the schools, that is, that were then being imitated by the Romantic German Nazarenes. Clearly a full analysis of Hegel's debate with Rumohr, and of the aesthetic ideas of both, cannot be given in this review of Marx's reception of them. It is to be hoped that a later study will, however, be able to reveal more about the German aestheticians read by Marx who are discussed here only in relation to that reading.)

26 See Marx and Engels, *New MEGA* vol. 4/1, p. 333 for Marx's excerpt from Böttiger on the Greek anthropomorphisation of their gods. Böttiger's comparison of the Greeks with the Christian art of painters such as Raphael occurs on p. 174 of the second edition of Parts 1 and 2 of Böttiger's *Ideen zur Kunst-Mythologie* (2nd edn, 2 vols., Leipzig, 1850):

Auch die neuere Kunstblüthe, die in der Malerei ihre Vollendung erhält, so wie die der Alten in der Plastik, konnte nur durch das Ideal der reinen Menschenfigur in der Gottheit gedeihen. So erscheint sie uns in ihrer höchsten Verklärung bei Rafael.

Rafaels Gott der Vater in Florenz schwebt auf den vier symbolischen Thieren nach Ezechiels Vision im ersten und zehnten Capitel. Dort im Ezechiel offenbart sich der wahre Orientalismus in seiner allegorischen Wunderfülle. Der Unanschaubare schwebt auf einer mystisch-komponirten Thiergestalt, die viel ähnliches mit dem Jupiterideal des Phidias haben muss, veranschaulicht, und er erscheint thronend, auf der Thierwelt, die hier nur dienende Trägerin wird. So herrscht auch in der neuen Kunst stets der rein menschliche Hellenismus und unterwirft sich die allegorischen Thier-Hieroglyphen des Orients, da wo die Kunst nicht in die Hände der Skizzisten, Nebulisten und Phantasten verfällt.'

Rumohr (pp. 565–6 of his *Italienische Forschungen*, ed. Julius Schlosser (Frankfurt on Main, 1920)) reminds his readers that Vasari had described Raphael's depiction of Ezekiel's vision of God as 'un Cristo a uso di Giove', as a 'Christ in the manner of Jupiter'. As stated earlier, Rumohr's search for 'natural forms' in Christian art (to which reference is also made in the preceding note) did not lead him – any more than it did Böttiger – to a critique of Christian *Bildlichkeit* in the manner of Feuerbach's criticism of it in *The Essence of Christianity*.

27 Heine's *Elementargeister* also provides an example of his interest in the idea, formulated by Gibbon and others, that Christian culture had been built from the ruins of paganism and still contained many of the latter's traits.

28 On p. 211 of his tract *Hegels Lehre von der Religion und Kunst* (Leipzig, 1842), Bauer ascribes to the pietist pastor Friedrich W. Krummacher (an enemy of Saint-Simonism and disliked by both Heine and Engels) the opinion that 'art is the magic of the devil' ('Die Kunst ist die Magie des Satan'). Bauer concludes this attack with a parody of pietism and the claim that it would like to see a form of art which was solely concerned with painting the wounds of Christ. (See Bauer, pp. 220f.)

29 The articles on censorship written by Marx for the *Rheinische Zeitung* in 1842 referred to previously give numerous examples of the way in which he was to relate his studies of Christian art and religion to contemporary political issues.

30 The *Rheinische Zeitung* was a paper which had represented the views of liberal industrialists and free-traders opposed to the conservative 'feudal' character of Friedrich Wilhelm IV's economic policies. After being banned for his refusal to let the *Rheinische Zeitung* be censored in 1843, Marx turned towards the study of political economy. In exile in Paris (after October 1843), he also met up with Moses Hess and Heine – two of the writers from whom he had earlier learnt of the ideas of Saint-Simon.

### 4 Marx's 'Economic and Philosophic Manuscripts' and the development of a 'productivist' aesthetic

1 Marx's 1844 *Economic and Philosophic Manuscripts* are not only unfinished, but consist in part of notes similar to those which Marx was used to making while reading other works. Despite their fragmentary nature, the 1844 *Manuscripts* nevertheless contain many arguments not to be found in Marx's early writings which are important for an understanding of the development of some of his later theories.

2 See Marx's *Economic and Philosophic Manuscripts,* Third Manuscript, section entitled 'Private property and communism'.

3 Heine, *Sämtliche Werke,* ed. Ernst Elster (7 vols., Leipzig, 1887–90), vol. 6, pp. 391–7.

4 See Marx, *Capital,* vol. 3, section 7. The original German begins:

> Das Reich der Freiheit beginnt in der Tat erst da, wo das Arbeiten, das durch Not und äussere Zweckmassigkeit bestimmt ist, aufhört . . .

5 David McLellan, *Marx before Marxism* (Harmondsworth, 1972), pp. 243ff. The reference to Schiller's *Briefe* is to his *Briefe über die ästhetische Erziehung des Menschen.* McLellan then quotes from the edition by W. Henckmann (Munich, 1967), p. 92:

> Enjoyment was separated from labour, the means from the end, exertion from recompense . . . The aesthetic formative impulse establishes . . . a joyous empire wherein it releases man from all the fetters of circumstance, and frees him, both physically and morally, from all that can be called restraint.

6 Kant, *Critique of Judgement* (New York, 1964), p. 180. We may use the term 'aesthetic' when speaking of Marx's concept of a liberation of the senses in his 1844 *Manuscripts,* because the term still had the function in the nineteenth century of describing the science of the 'conditions of sensuous perception'. (See also Raymond Williams, *Keywords* (Glasgow, 1977), p. 27.)

7 Marx's earliest piece of philosophical writing, his thesis on Epicurus, was completed in April 1842, just prior to his departure from Berlin for Bonn.

8 Kant, *Critique of Judgement,* p. 27.

9 *Ibid.,* p. 44.

10 *Ibid.,* pp. 146–7. Not all eighteenth-century art historians, however, had criticised useful art. Donald D. Egbert notes in his article 'The Idea of "Avant-Garde" ', *The American Historical Review,* 73, no. 2 (December 1967), 342, n. 6, that Johann Georg Sulzer's *Allgemeine Theorie der schönen Kunst* (4 vols., Leipzig, 1771–4) – a work possibly known to Marx – had described the period of Greek and Etruscan art as one in which art still had utility, or, as Marx might have said, 'use value'. According to Egbert, the French Republican painter David had also shared this view of ancient art, while (as Egbert also notes) none other than 'Marx's favourite prose writer', Diderot, had defended the concept of the 'useful' arts in the article 'Art' of the first volume of the *Encyclopedia* of 1751.

11 The word 'disinterested' describes here a 'lack of interest, self-interest, or purpose', but also designates a type of art which is above the servicing of natural needs. One modern Marxist who has argued against such a view of art is Adolfo Sánchez Vázquez, who suggests (in his *Art and Society: Essays in Marxist Aesthetics* (London, 1963), p. 63) that art and use objects are alike in essence because both satisfy certain needs – art satisfying in particular the need to *humanise* work.

12 Herbert Marcuse, *Eros and Civilisation* (2nd edn, London, 1969), chapter 9, 'The aesthetic dimension', pp. 143–60.

13 Herbert Marcuse, 'Art and revolution', in *Counter Revolution and Revolt*

(Boston, 1972), p. 97. See also Marcuse, *The Aesthetic Dimension* (Boston, 1977).

14  Marx was later to condemn Bruno Bauer for having stayed a 'Romantic' in economic matters and being an enthusiast for the eighteenth-century Physiocrats. Marx wrote to Engels on 18 January 1856:

> Bruno verschiedene Male wiedergesehen. Die Romantik stellt sich mehr und mehr als die 'Voraussetzung' der kritischen Kritik heraus. In der Ökonomie schwärmt er für die Physiokraten, die er missversteht, und glaubt an die spezifischen Gnadenwirkungen des Grundeigentums. Ausserdem schätzt er hoch Adam Müllers, des deutschen Romantikers, ökonomische Träumereien . . .

### 5 Towards an outline of artistic production, or the 'charm' of a materialist aesthetic

1  See Marx and Engels, *The German Ideology*, ed. S. Ryazanskaya (Moscow, 1968), pp. 441–2; ed. C. J. Arthur (New York, 1970), pp. 108–9.

2  Reference has been made (in chapter 3) to Marx's mention of Rembrandt's portrait of the Mother of God as a Dutch peasant-woman in his article on the 'Debates on freedom of the press' of 19 May 1842, and to Goethe's remarks on the same painting in his commentary on Falconet (*Schriften zur bildenden Kunst* (Stuttgart, 1952), pp. 53ff.). It is also interesting to note that apart from the comparison made between Raphael and Dutch artists by both Marx and Heine, comparisons of the kind were also exercising the minds of artists of the time such as Delacroix, who was, for example, to compare Rembrandt with Raphael (in favour of the former) in his *Journal* for 6 June 1851.

3  Although Marx writes that Vernet is not a representative of the belief that artistic labour has a 'unique' character and can be done only by 'unique' individuals, but rather of the idea that an artist's work can be shared by many, he is not entirely uncritical of the results achieved by the modern division of labour used by Vernet in his workshops. Heine had also suggested a criticism of Vernet in the conclusion to his review of Vernet's exhibits in the Salon of 1831 in summing him up as a 'many-sided painter who paints everything, Holy pictures, battles, still-lifes, animals, landscapes, portraits, and all "in haste"'. He had, further, in a *Lutezia* report of 7 May 1843, described a contemporary French caricature of Vernet painting a historical scene alone and on a galloping horse, which he may even have brought to the notice of Marx when meeting with him in Paris that year.

4  Marx spent several pages of the *German Ideology* of 1845–6 attacking the distortion of Saint-Simon's doctrines by his French followers and by German 'bowdlerisers' of Saint-Simon such as Karl Grün. Earlier, in November 1843, in his article 'On the progress of social reform on the Continent' for no. 1 of the Chartists' journal, the *New Moral World*, Engels had attacked the French Saint-Simonians as having become a laughing-stock in France on account of their neo-religious leanings. Prior to that article, in a letter of 15 June 1839 to his friend Friedrich Graeber, Engels had caricatured such Saint-Simonian slogans as their call for the 'emancipation of the flesh' in a marginal sketch to his letter.

5 Marx, *Grundrisse*, trans. Martin Nicolaus (Harmondsworth, 1979), pp. 110–11.

6 John Hoffman, 'Marx on art', *Artery*, 13, 9–12.

7 *Ibid.*, 10.

8 Marx, *Grundrisse*, p. 110.

9 As in his *German Ideology* of 1845–6, Marx would appear to be maintaining here a distinction between Saint-Simon and his followers – in this case the bankers and engineers (like Enfantin and De Lesseps) who have (in the terms used by Heine in his 1855 commentary to the second edition of his Saint-Simonian histories of the Romantic School and of German philosophy and religion) turned Saint-Simon's vision of a 'golden age' (his 'l'âge d'or') into an age of material enrichment, or 'l'âge de l'argent'.

10 See also Marx, *Grundrisse*, p. 109.

11 Marx, *Grundrisse*, p. 111. Compare with Schiller's 'On naive and sentimental poetry', *Friedrich von Schiller Sämmtliche Werke* (Stuttgart and Tübingen, 1818), vol. 8, Part 2, pp. 49ff.

12 *Ibid.*, p. 46.

13 Marx was, as mentioned previously, also studying works such as E. Müller's history of ancient Greek aesthetics at this time.

14 To Frederick Antal (*Hogarth and his place in European Art* (London, 1962), pp. 192ff.), nineteenth-century English art was in general more radical than the French or German art of that time because of the 'stronger social position' held by the English middle class after 1832. The English Pre-Raphaelites are hence also seen by Antal to have been more radical than the German Nazarenes. While the example of Ford Madox Brown would seem to bear out this hypothesis, not all Pre-Raphaelites could, however, be said to have been more politically or artistically radical than their German counterparts, and if Francis D. Klingender's interpretation of Ford Madox Brown as an early Social Realist painter in his *Art and the Industrial Revolution* (1947; ed. Arthur Elton (London, 1972)) has encouraged the idea amongst Marxist art critics that Ford Madox Brown can be seen as a progressive socialist painter, it should not be forgotten that that artist had also been inspired by the German Nazarenes and had, for a time at least, painted in their style.

15 K. Th. Gaedertz writes in his account of d'Alton in his reminiscences, *Bei Goethe zu Gast* (Leipzig, 1900), p. 157 of Prince Albert's attendance at d'Alton's lectures in 1837–8:

Keiner der erlauchten Fürstensöhne welche die Universität Bonn damals zu ihren akademischen Mitbürgern zu zählen das Glück hatte, unter ihnen Prinz Albert, Gemahl der Königin von England, versäumte d'Alton's Vorlesungen; durch ihn wurden sie, wie Schlegel neidlos gesteht, in das Heiligtum gebildeter Geister eingeführt.

Although they do not discuss Albert's time with d'Alton, further details of his support for the German Nazarenes and English Pre-Raphaelites can be found in Keith Andrews' *The Nazarenes: a brotherhood of German Painters in Rome* (Oxford, 1964), and William Vaughan's *German Romanticism and English Art* (New Haven and London), 1979. See also Frank Eyck's *The*

*Prince Consort: a Political Biography* (London, 1959), for details of Albert's political dealings with Friedrich Wilhelm IV.

16  Here it is also important to note that 'modern' (Romantic) art is described by Marx at the beginning of his *Grundrisse* Introduction as inferior both to Greek art and to Shakespeare, the writer suggested by him to Lassalle in 1859 as a better model for historical and political drama than the Idealist Schiller. For this reason too the debate between Marx and Engels and Lassalle, which has usually been taken to support the view of Marx and Engels as defenders of Realism, can also be seen as continuing Marx's unfinished Introduction to his *Grundrisse*. Rather than outlining a Realist aesthetic, his Preface to 'A contribution to the critique of political economy' of 1859 was of course also to suggest that aesthetics was itself an area in which men were able to 'fight out' the social conflicts of their time.

17  Although they do not actually use the term 'avant-garde', Marx and Engels attribute such a role to the proletariat in passages like the following from the section 'Proletarians and Communists' of the *Manifesto*. Translating Saint-Simon's concept of an avant-garde of scientists and artists into that of an avant-garde proletariat party, they wrote:

> The Communists, therefore, are on the one hand, practically, the most advanced and resolute section of the working-class parties of every country, that section which pushes forward all others . . .
>
> (Marx and Engels, *Manifesto of the Communist Party* (Moscow, 1966, pp. 60f.)

Other Saint-Simonian ideas to be found in the *Manifesto* include the suggestions that the 'means of production and exchange', on whose foundations the bourgeoisie had 'built itself up', were generated in feudal society; that workers may be compared to the slaves or serfs of such a system; and that workers could be organised into trade unions.

## 6  Saint-Simonists and Realists

1  See Frank E. Manuel, *The New World of Henri Saint-Simon* (Cambridge, Mass., 1956), pp. 190f.

2  Keith Taylor (ed.), *Henri Saint-Simon (1760–1825)* (London, 1975), pp. 52ff. D. S. Mirsky writes on Herzen in his *History of Russian Literature* of 1926 (ed. Francis J. Whitfield (London, 1964), pp. 130 and 210), that Herzen had not only 'pioneered the positivist and scientific mentality of nineteenth-century Europe and of socialism in Russia', but had mixed materialist and scientific ideas with the Romantic and had been inspired not only by the socialism of Saint-Simon but by his 'gospel of the flesh' as a repudiation of traditional religion. As Mirsky goes on to write on pp. 210–11, Herzen had also, however, translated Saint-Simon's programme for a new technologically advanced society into one for a socialist agrarian Russia, a translation which may in Herzen's time have been born of necessity rather than invention. Mirsky's *History of Russian Literature* had been begun in the 1920s, and its first section completed by 1925. At this time Mirsky also began work on his *Intelligentsia of Great Britain*, a work which reflects his

own belief in the necessity for a successful proletarian revolution of finding a competent intelligentsia to help guide it. After returning to Stalinist Russia, publishing *Intelligentsia*, and working with the Union of Soviet Writers in the 1930s, Prince Mirsky disappeared.

3 It was also for such reasons that Saint-Simonian sympathisers such as Chernyshevsky were later to turn against Saint-Simonism.

4 Sophie Lissitzky-Küppers, *El Lissitzky* (London, 1980), p. 337.

5 A deputation of Saint-Simonians led by Barrault had been refused entry into Russia in the 1830s after an earlier expedition had succeeded in gaining entry. Despite this, Barrault's treatise on the artist as priest had considerable influence in Russia.

6 In 1839 Belinsky was the literary critic of St Petersburg's *National Times*. It was at this time that he moved from a Hegelian aesthetic to a more historical study of culture and literature, but also towards an interest in French socialist thought, in Saint-Simon, Louis Blanc, Pierre Leroux and Proudhon. See T. G. Masaryk, *The Spirit of Russia* (2 vols., 1919; 2nd edn, trans. Eden and Cedar Paul, London, 1955), vol. 1, pp. 362f.

7 Andrzej Walicki suggests in his *History of Russian Thought, from the Enlightenment to Marxism* (trans. Hilda Andreas-Rusiecka (California, 1979), p. 116) that in nineteenth-century Russia Hegelian philosophy had been welcomed as an 'antidote to Romanticism' (such as, for example, the 'introspective day-dreaming and attitudes of Romantic revolt inspired by Byron and Schiller'), and was largely interpreted as a philosophy of 'reconciliation with reality'. Whether it could, as Walicki suggests, also have inspired a philosophy of 'rational and conscious action' without the influence of French socialist thought, or the Left Hegelianism related to it, seems questionable. Walicki does, however, show Belinsky to be one case in which the two areas of thought did combine to form a philosophy of action (see Walicki, p. 125). He also points out (p. 126), that Belinsky was acquainted with some of the works of Marx and Engels: for example, Engels' 'Schelling und die Offenbarung', Marx's 'On the Jewish question', and Engels' article in the *Deutsch–Französische Jahrbucher* of 1844, his 'Contribution to a critique of political economy'.

8 Masaryk, vol. 1, pp. 123–4.

9 Saint-Simon, 'De la réorganisation de la société européenne' (1814), *Oeuvres de Saint-Simon et d'Enfantin* (Meisenheim on Glan, 1964), vol. 15, pp. 247–8.

10 A further source of Saint-Simonian ideas in Russia in the early years of the twentieth century was of course the commentaries to his work which had been allowed to be published. Examples of these include S. Shteinberg's history of Saint-Simonism, published in St Petersburg in 1900, and Ivan Ivanovitch Ivanov's *Saint-Simon and Saint-Simonism*, published in Moscow in 1901.

11 See Lissitzky-Küppers, p. 15 and the bibliographies of A. I. Gordon (*Geine v Rossii: 1830–1860* (Dusaube, 1973) and *Geine v Rossii: 1870–1917* (Dusaube, 1979)) and A. I. Metallov (ed.) (*Geinrich Geine: Bibliographia* (Moscow, 1958)) of Russian translations and discussions of Heine. Although

admired by many for his poetry, Heine was also read in Russia for his essays and other prose works. Many of his poems also present the arguments of his prose works in poetic form. (I have discussed the way in which Saint-Simonian ideas are presented in Heine's verse in *Die Parodie: eine Funktion der biblischen Sprache in Heines Lyrik* (Meisenheim on Glan, 1976).) Clara Hollosi mentions in her article 'Views on Heine in Russia in the beginning of the twentieth century', *Heine Jahrbuch*, 17 (1978), 180f., that Lunacharsky had also made use of Heine's opposition between the Nazarene and the Hellene. One of the monuments erected in Petrograd in 1918 was, moreover, to Heine, and was (like several others) designed in the form of a Greek herm, with a sculptured head on top of a plain pedestal.

It is also interesting to note again here that several of the paintings praised by Heine in the Salon exhibition of 1831 (such as, for example, Delaroche's *Cromwell Gazing into the Coffin of Charles I* and works by Vernet) were to find their way to the St Petersburg Academy in either their original form or in copies, and were exhibited in the Hermitage after the revolution. They are mentioned by Sir Martin Conway in the record of his visit to Soviet Russia in 1924 in his *Art Treasures in Soviet Russia* (London, 1925).

12  Belinsky and Lavrov gave expression to the Saint-Simonian idea that culture was (through its leading minds) a 'leading motive power in the history of progressive peoples'. Given this, there would seem to be a good case for arguing that the Russian concept of a ruling intelligentsia did have at least some of its roots in Russian Saint-Simonian thought. (An obelisk erected in the Alexander Gardens of the Kremlin in 1918 includes the names of Belinsky, Lavrov and Saint-Simon in a list of the fathers of the Revolution which begins with Marx and Engels and ends with Plekhanov.)

13  See, for example, Klaus Städtke, *Ästhetisches Denken in Russland* (Berlin and Weimar, 1978).

14  Chernyshevsky is described by Walicki (p. 186) as having been an avid reader of Saint-Simon. Later, as Plekhanov's 1908 article, 'The ideology of our present-day philistine' claims (Georgi Plekhanov, *Selected Philosophical Works*, ed. V. Scherbina (5 vols., Moscow, 1981), vol. 5, p. 527), Chernyshevsky was also to express criticism of the Utopian element in Saint-Simonism. In the early years of the Bolshevik Revolution Chernyshevsky was, however, to be prized for his own optimistic and avant-garde beliefs. Umanskij, for example, reports in his book on the art of revolutionary Russia at that time (*Neue Kunst in Russland, 1914–1919* (Potsdam and Munich, 1920), p. 35) that amongst those 'revolutionary' sayings to be found on the pillars of the Moscow Royal Theatre after 1917 were lines ascribed to Chernyshevsky:

Strive for the future, wait for her, believe in her, bring as much out of her into the present as you can.

15  Plekhanov was to write in 1908 in defence of Belinsky's hesitation between Hegelianism and Utopian socialism, and of his ultimate choice of the latter, that 'the terrible undeveloped state of Russian social relations, which were

the only ones that Belinsky could know and observe' had prevented Belinsky from finding a practical solution to the theoretical problems which were also to confront Marx and Engels, and, in Plekhanov's view, to be solved by them. (See Plekhanov's 'Ideology of our present-day philistine', *Selected Philosophical Works*, vol. 5, p. 511.)

16 Hegel, *Philosophy of History*, trans. J. Sibree (New York, 1969), p. 289.

17 Prussia, Russia and Austria had formed their alliance in 1815 and the then Prussian monarch, Friedrich Wilhelm III, had sought to cement the new ties with Russia through cultural exchanges involving the presentation of German art works to Russian museums and churches and the visits of German artists to Russia. (Friedrich Wilhelm III had also sought to strengthen the bonds between Prussia and Russia by marrying his daughter Princess Charlotte to the Imperial Prince Nicholas in 1817.) Although Camilla Gray writes in *Russian Experiment in Art, 1863–1922* (New York, 1970; London 1971), p. 9, that the Russian Realist painters of the 1860s were later to react against Academicians inspired by the German Nazarenes, it cannot be denied that many had been influenced by German Nazarene art in their early years, and that their early work demonstrates that influence.

18 Igor Golomshtok and Alexander Glezer, *Soviet Art in Exile* (London, 1977), p. 85. To Golomshtok the Russian Wanderers were the 'direct precursors of Socialist Realism'. Others, such as Elizabeth Valkenier, have emphasised the fact that the Wanderers were 'appropriated' to the Socialist Realist 'tradition'. (See her *Russian Realist Art* (Michigan, 1977).)

19 Some Socialist Realist genre pictures such as Boris Ioganson's *At an Old Urals Mill* of 1937 (Tretyakov Gallery) might be compared to Hübner's *Silesian Weavers*, and Donald Drew Egbert has written in his book, *Social Radicalism and the Arts* (New York, 1970; London, 1972), p. 78 that Hübner's *Weavers* 'was regarded in communist East Germany after World War II as an important forerunner of the socialist realism developed in the Soviet Union under Stalin and his successors'. Of course Engels' admiration for the painting was to influence this interpretation, but its links with both Nazarene and Social Realist art of the nineteenth century were also to contribute to its inclusion in the 'canon' of Socialist Realism and thus to any actual influence it might have had on Socialist Realist art.

Here one might add that Engels' identification of Realism with materialism (which Egbert discusses in his *Social Radicalism and the Arts*, p. 82) may have contributed not only to the belief that Marx's materialism entailed a defence of Realism in all its forms, but also to the 'silencing' of Saint-Simon's materialist concept of artistic production in modern Marxist theory. (As suggested earlier (with reference to Marx's 1857 *Grundrisse* Introduction), while Marx may have thought of describing his materialist method of history as 'Realist', he would have known that to call his aesthetic 'Realist' would not only have understated its productivist character, but associated it with aesthetics which were in fact 'Idealist'.)

Engels' other, actual, remarks on Realism, made in his letters to Miss Harkness in the late 1880s, have of course also been used to argue that Marx and Engels together supported in general a 'Realist' aesthetic (applicable to both the literary and the visual arts) even though they were written down after Marx's death.

20  Engels made his comments on Hübner's *Weavers* in an article for the journal *New Moral World* of 13 December 1844. (See *Karl Marx, Frederick Engels, Collected Works*, vol. 4, *Marx and Engels, 1844–1845* (London, 1975), pp. 230–1.)

Following his description of Hübner's painting Engels lists both Püttmann and Heine amongst the 'most active literary characters among the German Socialists', and ends by quoting Heine's 'Song of the Silesian Weavers'. Whereas Marx and Engels were to quote Heine again in their *Deutsche Ideologie (The German Ideology)* of 1845–6, they were (as mentioned previously) to mock both Püttmann and Karl Grün as 'True Socialists'. It should be mentioned here that as Püttmann's *Die Düsseldorfer Malerschule und ihre Leistungen . . .* contained no reference to Carl Hübner, it cannot be said that Engels had been influenced by Püttmann in his assessment of Hübner, although his reference to Karl Lessing's 'conversion' to Socialism is a reference to an artist praised by Püttmann as one of the least sentimental of the Düsseldorf Nazarenes. Engels makes no explicit connection, however, between Lessing and Hübner, and no comment on Hübner himself of the kind he makes of Lessing. Ironically, it would, moreover, seem that the 'True Socialist' Karl Grün was closer to seeing Hübner's *Weavers* as a work of 'social realism' than Engels. Writing of the Cologne Exhibition of 1844 in which he had seen Hübner's painting, Grün praised the *Weavers* as a sober, prosaic and simple representation of its subject. (See Karl Grün, *Anekdota* (n. p., 1845), pp. 56–7.)

21  Rolf Andree writes in the Catalogue to the 1979 exhibition in the Düsseldorf Kunstmuseum of the 'Düsseldorfer Malerschule' (*Die Düsseldorfer Malerschule*, ed. Wend von Kalnein (Mainz on Rhine, 1979), pp. 344ff.), that Hübner's *Weavers* would not have been possible without some familiarity with the satirical genre paintings of artists such as David Wilkie, and that the painting caricatures several types and gestures popular in the 'Düsseldorfer Malerschule' at the time, from the *Herrscherporträt* to the fainting woman, as painted by Köhler in his *Hagar and Ismael* of the same year. Without stressing the parodic character of Hübner's imitation of the gestures then popular in the 'Düsseldorfer Malerschule', Irene Markowitz also speaks of Hübner as having imitated the gesture of paintings such as Köhler's *Hagar and Ismael* in his *Weavers*, in her essay 'Rheinische Maler im 19. Jahrhundert', *Kunst des 19. Jahrhunderts*, ed. Trier and Weyres (Düsseldorf, 1979), p. 109.

22  Marx also makes ironic reference to Kaulbach's Nazarene *Hunnenschlacht* in his *Great Men of Exile* of 1852. Its target, Gottfried Kinkel, had published a history of Christian art in 1845, and was later condemned with Freiligrath by Marx for involvement in the 1859 'Schiller-Feier'.

23  It was Freiligrath who took Hasenclever's *Workers before the Council* of 1848 to London on his flight there in 1851, and encouraged both Marx and Engels to view and discuss it.

24 See Heine, *Sämtliche Werke*, ed. Ernst Elster (7 vols., Leipzig, 1887–90), vol. 4, p. 35.

25 Despite these subtleties in Plekhanov's arguments, and the criticism of his Socialist Democrat politics by Lenin in 1917, Plekhanov was, with Lenin, to be taken as an authority by Socialist Realists for their defence of a Realist and reflectionist theory of art. (See, for example, the *Great Soviet Encyclopedia* (30 vols. and index, London and New York, 1973–82), vol. 10 (1976), p. 9 and vol. 20 (1979), p. 221.) Plekhanov's defence of Realist art, and criticism of modern abstract art, do not, it is argued here, however, necessarily exclude sympathy for the 'productivist' idea that art can become a part of the economic and social base.

26 As the opening pages of Plekhanov's 1897 tract on Belinsky's literary views show (*Selected Philosophical Works*, vol. 5, pp. 178ff), Belinsky had previously been accused by some of having supported art 'for art's sake', rather than an 'art for society's sake' aesthetic. Plekhanov's interpretation of Belinsky as a Hegelian who had believed the function of art to be the reflection of social reality was thereby intended to disprove the view that he was an aesthete interested only in a 'l'art pour l'art' aesthetic, rather than to deny the French socialist elements in his thought. Indeed, it would even seem to be because of those socialist elements that Belinsky was able to develop a form of 'Hegelian aesthetic' concerned with the reflection of social life in art rather than with the reflection of the 'Ideal'.

27 As Andrzej Walicki has suggested (pp. 425f.), Plekhanov was inconsistent in many of the views he expressed, and not least in his apparently contradictory support for both an 'objective', anti-normative and anti-prescriptive materialist aesthetic and his own 'prescriptive' definition of a Realist aesthetic.

The latter was referred to by Plekhanov as Belinsky's aesthetic code (although, as Walicki also remarks, it had had little real basis in Belinsky), and set out five requirements for the work of art. These were that the work of art must:

1 represent life as it is with the help of images, not syllogisms,
2 portray the truth without embellishments or distortions,
3 express a concrete idea that encompasses the whole subject in its unity,
4 have a form appropriate to its content, and
5 show unity of form, that is, the harmonious coordination of all its parts.

(As summarised by Walicki, p. 426.) For the full text see Plekhanov, *Selected Philosophical Works*, vol. 5, pp. 196–7, where, moreover, point 4 is translated as demanding a harmonisation of form and thought: an ideal later also espoused by Lukács in his defence of a 'Realist' form of art against abstract modernism.

28 See Plekhanov's 1897 essay on Chernyshevsky's aesthetic theory, *Selected Philosophical Works*, vol. 5, p. 260.

29 As remarked already the Peredvizhniki or Wanderers had taken Chernyshevsky's concept of art as contributing to social reform through its 'truthful explanation to reality' as their aesthetic. In taking the Russian peasantry as their subject-matter, the Wanderers were also much closer to

Populism than to Plekhanov's later Marxist belief in the proletariat as vanguard of revolution.

30  Plekhanov had argued at the International Socialist Congress of 1889 that change could only come with the development of a new revolutionary proletarian class.

31  Plekhanov criticised the Populists as Romantics in his 1897 essay on Belinsky (*Selected Philosophical Works*, vol. 5, p. 210).

32  See also n. 25. In his *Art and Social Life* of 1912 Plekhanov criticised Belinsky and Chernyshevsky for their lack of interest in the class nature of art while at the same time praising the Saint-Simonians for their recognition of the needs of the working classes of their time, suggesting that his occasional criticisms of the Russian Saint-Simonian Belinsky had not so much been a rejection of his Saint-Simonism, as a correction of its faults. They were, moreover, those faults which had in large part been determined by the pre-industrial character of the class structure of Belinsky's day. This timely correction of the Russian Saint-Simonian tradition was, however, to pass almost unnoticed in Plekhanov's work, so that, again, the fulfilment of Saint-Simonian theory in Russia with the proletarian machine aesthetic of Constructivists such as Rodchenko was to be read by the Socialist Realists of later years not as a Russian, but as an imported, Western theory.

Here it should also be mentioned that Plekhanov had in 1912 also criticised those Saint-Simonians who had 'addressed only the rich' and had made themselves an avant-garde in which the proletariat could have no leading active part. It is significant perhaps also not only that Plekhanov was then addressing a French audience who would have known many of those later French Saint-Simonians accused by Plekhanov of forming an elite addressed only to the rich, but that he was, in criticising this 'decadent' stage in Saint-Simonism, echoing sentiments expressed by both Heine and Marx, who had criticised the mystical and the corrupt amongst the Saint-Simonians of their time, while continuing to take seriously the work of their mentor, Saint-Simon. (See also chapter 5, n. 9.)

33  Plekhanov, *Selected Philosophical Works*, vol. 5. V. Scherbina is the author of other works diverging from the strictly Socialist Realist norms of the 1940s and early 1950s. One of these is his essay 'Of Socialist Realism' of 1957, which speaks of a new concept of Realist art which would not dictate any compulsory method of representation, style, or form, would enable reality to be presented in a number of ways, and play down the antagonisms usually set up between realist and non-realist forms of art. (Published in *Voprosy Literatury* (1957, no. 4), and referred to in the report of the Cultural Theory Panel attached to the Central Committee of the Hungarian Socialist Workers' Party, in *Radical Perspectives in the Arts*, ed. Lee Baxandall (Harmondsworth, 1972), p. 256.)

34  Plekhanov, *Selected Philosophical Works*, vol. 5, pp. 13f.

35  *Ibid.*, p. 14. Scherbina continued in what might also appear to be an attack on Socialist Realist dogma, but which he claims to be a criticism of the 'enemies of Marxism' and 'decadent Naturalists':

His [Plekhanov's] statements on the cognitive importance of art, its role in the transformation of reality, are most valuable for elucidating the active influence of art on life. In this respect Plekhanov's aesthetics is opposed to many theories of art of the past and present which limit the function of art to the *passive reflection of life* . . .

Plekhanov's concept of an art which reflected social life while also interacting with it must, of course, also be distinguished from the earlier Russian 'Hegelian' concept of art as a 'mirror of its age'. Even if that too could be seen as having been influenced by French socialist ideas (see n. 26), it had not previously been used to describe art as playing an active role in the development of the economic base of society.

36 Plekhanov, *Selected Philosophical Works*, vol. 5, pp. 398–417. This passage also shows that Plekhanov did not fully follow Hegel's aesthetic views. Although, as Henri Arvon remarks on pp. 5–6 of his *Marxist Aesthetics* (Ithaca and London, 1973), Plekhanov was impressed by Hegel's comments on how the art of the Dutch reflected their social life, his criticism here of the 'other-worldliness' of Raphael's madonnas shows that like Marx he did not share Hegel's preference for them.

37 In *Du Cubisme*, Gleizes and Metzinger reject the so-called 'avant-garde' Realism of Courbet as not having gone far enough beyond the Realism popular in his time. Although acknowledging Courbet's radicalism, they accuse him of being 'enslaved' to an indiscriminate representation of Nature. To many modern Western critics Courbet has of course continued to represent the idea of the radical 'avant-garde' artist. Because this concept of avant-garde has, however, little to do with the Saint-Simonian concept of an avant-garde of artist–producers being investigated here, but emphasises the individual radicalism or bohemianism of the artist, it is not one which is pursued in the course of this study. It should also be pointed out that within Russia Courbet has above all been linked to the 'Peredvishniki' or Wanderers – and hence also to Socialist Realism – rather than to the avant-garde of the 1920s. Igor Golomshtok has written in his essay on unofficial Soviet art in his *Soviet Art in Exile* (p. 82) that the Social Realists of the 1880s had, by following Courbet's Realism, even then marked a 'backwardness' in Russian art, because by the 1880s the avant-garde in France was represented not so much by Courbet as by Cézanne and the Post-Impressionists.

It is difficult to say what Marx knew or thought of Courbet. There are, it would seem, no specific references to him in Marx's published writings, and it is unlikely that Marx would have taken note of his work while in Paris in 1843, for Courbet had arrived there himself only in 1840. If Marx had seen any of Courbet's early Paris work, he would, moreover, have most probably seen portraits or Romantic genre-pieces. (T. J. Clark mentions in his *Image of the People: Gustave Courbet and the 1848 Revolution* (London, 1973), p. 36, that one of the few pieces sold by Courbet in his early years in Paris was an altar-piece to the church at Saules.) Clearly Courbet's early Romantic and religious pieces would not have impressed the young Marx in 1843, just one year after he had given up work on his treatise against Christian and Romantic art. Whether he would have praised the later Courbet if he had seen those early works may also be questionable. In the absence of specific comment in Marx's writings on either the early or late Courbet, we may have to remain satisfied with questions rather than answers.

### 7 *The Constructivists of the 1920s and the concept of avant-garde*

1 Donald Drew Egbert, 'The idea of "avant-garde" in art and politics', *The American Historical Review*, vol. 73, no. 2 (December 1967), 351ff.
2 The closest Egbert comes to making these connections is in his description of the politics of the avant-garde in the 1920s, where he discusses the contradiction between Lenin's concept of the Party as avant-garde and Socialist Realism.
3 Renato Poggioli, *The Theory of the Avant-Garde* (1962) (Cambridge, Mass., 1968), pp. 8ff.
4 *Ibid.*, p. 9.
5 Further criticisms of Poggioli's and Egbert's definitions of 'avant-garde' are made by Nicos Hadjinicolaou in an article of 1978 translated in *Praxis*, 6 (1982), 39–70, as 'On the ideology of avant-gardism'. Despite his differences with Egbert and Poggioli, Hadjinicolaou can however also be said to have concentrated his attention on the political and 'elitist' connotations of the concept of avant-garde, rather than on the economic and social functions mentioned here in connection with Saint-Simonist theory and Russian Constructivist art practice.
6 See *The Political Thought of Saint-Simon*, ed. Ghita Ionescu (Oxford, 1976), pp. 225f.
7 In 1918 Lenin had approved a programme for the construction of monuments to heroes of the new Soviet State such as Marx and Engels, as also to artists and writers such as Cézanne and Heine. The cuts of 1921 saw restrictions placed on programmes of this kind.
8 When Saint-Simon's argument for uniting the arts with technology was made again by the Russian Constructivists in the early 1920s, it was made in a situation where capitalism – such as it had existed in Russia – and its alienated or surplus labour were assumed to have been abolished. Hence the principal aim of the Committee of Applied Arts, to which Rodchenko and others had belonged, could be defined as that of 'developing and supporting the artistic creativity of the people . . .', but also (as here) 'by the contribution to increasing exports of the applied arts', that of 'greatly promoting the economic rise of the country' (see German Karginov's *Rodchenko* (London, 1979), p. 8).
9 *Ibid.*, p. 90.
10 *Ibid.*, p. 7.
11 *Ibid.*, p. 88.
12 *Ibid.*
13 Like the Saint-Simonians of the 1830s, the Constructivists were led by their belief in the role of the artist as social engineer and *producteur* to formulate programmes for collective work. Where, however, Enfantin's Saint-Simonians had moved further away from society through following the idea

(developed in 1830 by Barrault) of the artist as priest, the Constructivists maintained a practical working order, in which the individual artist was above all part of a working team. Just as the machine was to help them eliminate divisions between artistic labour and other forms of production, so it was – in their view – also to help them eliminate the elitism and isolation of the artist.

14 See Robert C. Williams, *Artists in Revolution: Portraits of the Russian Avant-Garde, 1905–1925* (London, 1978), p. 161.

15 The word 'montage' came from the language of engineering, and was regarded by Rodchenko and other Constructivists as being one of the most 'avant-garde' methods available to the 'artist–engineer' for reconstructing images of reality.

16 Richard Taylor, *Film Propaganda: Soviet Russia and Nazi Germany* (London, 1979), p. 103.

17 Herbert Marcuse was of course to use the term 'Promethean' in his *Eros and Civilization* to contrast the 'performance' principle to what was for him the more positive, less alienating aesthetic female principle. Believing in the positive social and artistic value of technology, the Constructivists had made no such distinction. At the same time – and in the best Saint-Simonian tradition – many of the Russian avant-garde artists of the 1920s concerned with the development of a 'machine aesthetic' were women, and included Goncharova, Alexandra Exter, Lioubov Popova, Nadesha Udaltsova, Nina Kogan, and Sonia Delaunay.

18 In an interview used by Robert Hughes in his BBC programme, *The Shock of the New*, the *émigré* Constructivist artist and engineer Naum Gabo explains that the word 'Constructivism' had itself reflected the optimism of the artists of the time. Although associated with the Russian Constructivists before 1920 (as well as being an important artist in his own right), Gabo is not discussed in this study at any length because of his rejection of the trend of Soviet Constructivism after 1920 towards a more functionalist or, in our terms, productivist and Saint-Simonist programme for the arts.

*8 Avant-garde vs. 'Agroculture': problems of the avant-garde – from Lenin to Stalin and after*

1 E. H. Carr, 'A historical turning point: Marx, Lenin, Stalin', in *Revolutionary Russia*, ed. Richard Pipes (Cambridge, Mass., 1968), p. 289.

2 Lenin, *What is to be Done?* (Moscow, 1978), p. 84 (previous quote from p. 26). Lenin's *What is to be Done?* was first published in 1902. Its title is taken from Chernyshevsky's *What is to be Done?*, a work written during the author's two-year period of imprisonment in St Petersburg in the early 1860s for revolutionary and subversive activities, which has as its hero Rakhmetov, an idealistic, radical Populist.

3 *Fundamentals of Marxism-Leninism* (Moscow, 1961) (translated from the 1959 Russian edition), pp. 190–1, quoted in Lloyd G. Churchward, *The Soviet Intelligentsia* (London, 1973), p. 3.

4 D. S. Mirsky, *The Intelligentsia of Great Britain* (London, 1935), p. 50.

5  See *The Political Thought of Saint-Simon*, ed. Ghita Ionescu (Oxford, 1976), p. 229.

6  See Sheila Fitzpatrick, *The Commissariat of Enlightenment* (Cambridge, 1970), p. xv. (Lunacharsky died in 1933 after two or three years of declining political power. Publication of his works was only recommended after 1953, according to Fitzpatrick, *The Commissariat of Enlightenment*, p. 310.)

7  See for example Igor Golomshtok's essay, 'Unofficial art in the Soviet Union', *Soviet Art in Exile* (London, 1977), p. 83. Golomshtok claims that after 1922 Lunacharsky was even to support the slogan, preferred by Lenin, of 'back to the Wanderers'.

8  See C. Vaughan James, *Soviet Socialist Realism: Origins and Theory* (London, 1973), pp. 20ff.

   Apart from his personal preference for realist, reflectionist art Lenin was also attributed a concept of 'Reflectionism' in Soviet theory which emphasised the centrality of reflection to human behaviour and to the physical world in general. A recent description of the concept of 'Reflection' in the *Great Soviet Encyclopedia* (30 vols. and index, London and New York, 1973–82), vol. 19 (1978), p. 662, however, claims that Lenin had a dialectical concept of reflection which – *contra* 'revisionist' critics such as Garaudy and Petrović – did *not* deny the 'creative activity of consciousness'. The concept of reflection which was attacked by critics such as Garaudy as in opposition to a dialectical concept of reflection and a creative consciousness able to intervene in material reality (in the avant-garde Saint-Simonian sense discussed in this study) was, nevertheless, one which had been propounded in Lenin's name in Stalinist times.

9  Fitzpatrick, *The Commissariat of Enlightenment*, p. 126.

10  *Ibid.*, p. 127. The name 'Futurism' was also associated with the *Proletkult* against which Lenin led an attack in 1920. Later Lenin ordered Narkompros to take charge of the *Proletkult*.

11  Writing of Lenin's concept of productivity as 'electrification plus the Soviets', E. H. Carr has written in 'A historical turning point', *Revolutionary Russia*, ed. Pipes, p. 282:

> One thing that had not changed – or, rather, that had been greatly intensified – was the emphasis on productivity. Marx stood on the shoulders of the Enlightenment thinkers and of the classical economists in treating production as the essential economic activity, to which all other categories were subsidiary: and he was in essence right when he saw the key to the future in the hand of the industrial worker and treated the individual peasant cultivator of the soil as an obsolescent unit of production. The Russian Revolution for the first time explicitly proclaimed the goal of increased production and identified it with socialism: Lenin's remark that socialism meant electrification plus the Soviets was the first primitive formulation of this idea . . .

Lenin's programme for 'electrification' was, of course, also Saint-Simonian in its belief in the need for the avant-garde of the revolution to constitute a new technical intelligentsia, able to develop industry and technology.

   Carr also suggests (pp. 283ff.) that Lenin's programme of 'electrification' for the 'pre-industrial' Russia taken over by the Bolsheviks in 1917 was not only aimed at making pre-industrial Russia more productive than the capitalist West, but at creating an industrialised proletariat which could carry out the communist revolution described by Marx as being the task of the industrialised proletariat of his time.

In other matters, as in, for example, his concept of a centrally directed administration, and plans for a State bank, Lenin's name has also been linked with Saint-Simonism. See, for example, Martin Krygier's essay, 'Weber, Lenin and the reality of Socialism', in *Bureaucracy*, ed. Eugene Kamenka and Martin Krygier (Melbourne, 1979), p. 78.

More cynically, Alec Nove tells the story in his *Economic History of the U.S.S.R.* (1969; Harmondsworth, 1980), pp. 70f. of how Lenin's plans for electrification were considered Utopian on their introduction because the map on which the electrification of Russia was shown itself used up almost all of the electricity then available for the city of Moscow.

12 Kenneth Frampton, 'Notes on a lost avant-garde: architecture, U.S.S.R., 1920–30', *Avant-Garde Art*, ed. Thomas B. Hess and John Ashbery (New York and London, 1968), p. 110.

13 The agreement of Soviet Constructivist artists with Lenin's electrification programme was also expressed by Rodchenko in a pseudo-mathematical formula (similar to those favoured by Lenin) in the Constructivist journal, *Kino-Fot* in 1922. The slogan was set out in the following manner:

> LENIN    AND    EDISON
> Communism   and   Technology

14 See Richard Taylor, *Film Propaganda: Soviet Russia and Nazi Germany* (London, 1979).

15 The declaration of the Akh(R)R of May 1922 specifically attacked the Constructivists in its claim that its artists wanted 'to give a real picture of events, not abstract constructions, which have discredited our revolution in the eyes of the international proletariat'.

16 See the August–September 1924 edition of *LEF* (the journal of 'Left Artists and Writers'), in which Rodchenko, Brik, and other members of *Vkhumetas* attack the funding of Realist artists in preference to themselves.

17 In 1931 the OCTOBER group had argued with the successor of the old Akh(R)R, RAPkh (The Revolutionary Association of Proletarian Artists, which supported Realist artists in the time it was active, between 1931 and 1932). In 1932 the Party distanced itself from RAPkh, however, and set up the Union in which Socialist Realism was to develop as the official Soviet aesthetic.

18 Other photomontage and poster artists such as Natalia Pinus were obliged in the 1930s to leave the avant-garde group OCTOBER and to join the officially approved society of poster artists if they wished to obtain work in their profession. While such artists continued to use the photomontage characteristic of earlier Constructivist design art in the early 1930s, later formulations of the methods to be used by Socialist Realist artists were to discourage its use.

19 A. A. Zhdanov, 'Soviet literature – the richest in ideas: the most advanced literature', in *Soviet Writers' Congress 1934* (London, 1977), p. 21.

20  See the entry 'Art' in *Marxism, Communism, and Western Society*, ed. C. D. Kernig (8 vols., West Germany and New York, 1972–3), vol. 1 (1972), p. 186. The authors refer also to Camilla Gray's *The Great Experiment: Russian Art, 1863–1922* (London, 1969; New York, 1972).

21  Zhdanov, p. 23.

22  *Ibid.*, p. 21.

23  *Ibid.*

24  In its use of both a heroic subject-matter and an often almost allegorical style such Socialist Realism was not only to give visual expression to Zhdanov's programme for Soviet art, but was also to hark back to the allegorical paintings of the early Social Realists, and to echo those of the Nazarenes before them. In this Soviet art was also to move back away from the Saint-Simonian productivist aesthetic of Constructivists such as El Lissitzky and Rodchenko towards the earlier Russian Hegelian idea (shared by some German Romantic artists), that art should not merely reflect and imitate Nature, but should also depict the as yet unrealised Ideal concealed within it.

25  See Sheila Fitzpatrick, 'Cultural revolution as class war', *Cultural Revolution in Russia, 1928–1931* (Indiana, 1978), pp. 9–12, on the 1930 show trials of the so-called 'Industrialist' party, and the March 1928 trial of mining engineers and technicians from Shakhty. Fitzpatrick writes that this was a 'turning point in Soviet policy toward the bourgeois specialist. From this time the technical intelligentsia ceased to be seen as the Party's natural ally in industrialisation, and became a potentially treacherous group whose real allegiance was to the dispossessed capitalists and their foreign supporters.' Here it should also be added that these show trials, in which the technical intelligentsia were purged, were to precede Stalin's own appropriation of their role in his 'Stakhanovite' programme of the mid 1930s. Hence in his speech to the first Conference of the Stakhanovites of Industry and Transport of the Soviet Union, in November 1935, we find him encouraging the increase of industrialisation and technology which would boost Soviet production, while also laying the foundations for a new, Stalinised technical intelligentsia to replace that purged in 1930.

26  See Zhdanov.

27  See Fitzpatrick's 'Cultural revolution as class war', in *Cultural Revolution*, for an analysis of the way in which Stalin was to eliminate the old technocrat and intellectual class in order to establish his own Party men in these classes.

28  See Fitzpatrick's *The Commissariat of Enlightenment*, pp. 89ff. See also John E. Bowlt, *Russian Art of the Avant-Garde: Theory and Criticism 1902–1934* (New York, 1976), pp. 288ff. for a brief documentation of how the Decree on the Reconstruction of Literary and Artistic Organisations of 23 April 1932 from the Central Committee of the All-Union Communist Party led to the disbanding of all previous official artists' societies and prepared the way for Zhdanov's proclamation of Socialist Realist art in 1934.

29  It is thought that Riazanov, the editor of Marx's juvenilia, was one of those convicted at the Menshevik trials of 1932.

30 Max Raphael was one Marxist art historian to criticise Le Courbusier's 'Constructivism' as egocentric while refraining from publicly criticising the Russian Constructivists. Raphael himself has also been credited with developing a 'productivist' aesthetic in the 1930s, although, somewhat like Walter Benjamin, he was also worried about the appropriation by capitalism of similar concepts. See Norbert Schneider's Postscript to Max Raphael's *Arbeiter, Kunst und Künstler* (Frankfurt on Main, 1975) for a discussion of Raphael's 'productivist' ideas.

31 See the English translation of the 3rd edn of the *Great Soviet Encyclopedia* (30 vols. and index, London and New York, 1973–82), vol. 13 (1976), p. 101.

32 *Ibid.*, vol. 1 (1973) p. 519. The avant-garde, on the other hand, is described as being in general an elitist and bourgeois movement, found in the art of the West of the 1920s. The only other entry under 'Avant-garde' is for a Ukrainian athletics team bearing the name 'AVAN-GARD'.

33 See C. Vaughan James, *Soviet Socialist Realism*, pp. 112ff. for an account of Lenin's attack on the *Proletkult*.

34 Sophie Lissitzky-Küppers, *El Lissitzky* (London, 1980), p. 65.

35 Quoted by Morawski, *Marx and Engels on Literature and Art*, ed. Lee Baxandall and Stefan Morawski (St Louis, 1973), p. 150.

36 Donald Drew Egbert, 'The Idea of "avant-garde" in art and politics', *The American Historical Review*, vol. 73, no. 2 (December 1967), 348.

37 Maximilian Rubel and Margaret Manale, *Marx without Myth* (Oxford, 1975), p. 222.

38 See Part 2 of the entry 'Art' in *Marxism, Communism, and Western Society*, ed. Kernig, vol. 1.

39 John Berger, *Art and Revolution* (London, 1969), p. 55. Berger also claims Socialist Realism to be Socialist Naturalism in practice. Neither, however, is explicitly justified by Marx.

40 As Tom Wolfe has recently argued in his *From Bauhaus to Our House*, many of the most Utopian Bauhaus and Constructivist ideas – such as their plans for vast skyscraper housing blocks and villages – have become the reality of today's slums. The reasons for this are, however, numerous, while it should also be remembered that the Constructivists who first planned these then revolutionary 'high-rise' villages had consciously planned them specifically for their proletarian society and as cost-saving as well as space-saving developments.

41 The influence of Constructivism on modern Western art begins not just with the German Bauhaus but with Berlin Dada. Even before the German Dadaists and 'Neue Sachlichkeit' artists of the 1920s came to experience the Russian Constructivist artists at first hand, books and pamphlets had made Constructivism known in Germany. One Soviet arts administrator and diplomat, Konstantin Umanskij, even contributed to this publicity through his book *Neue Kunst in Russland, 1914–1919* of 1920. Indeed it may well have been Umanskij's translation into German of the Constructivist slogan, referred to previously with reference to the conclusion of Lifshitz's study of Marx's philosophy of art, that inspired the Berlin Dadaists in 1920 to open their 'Dada-Messe' ('Dada-Fair') with the slogan, 'Die Kunst ist tot! Es lebe

die Maschinenkunst Tatlins!' After condemning the Wanderers and praising Tatlin, Umanskij wrote (p. 19):

Die Kunst ist tot – es lebe die Kunst, die Kunst der Maschine mit ihrer Konstruktion und Logik, ihrem Rhythmus, ihrem Bestandteile, ihrem Material, ihrem metaphysischen Geist – die Kunst des Kontereliefs.

Because (as John Willett has pointed out in his *The New Sobriety: Art and Politics in the Weimar Period 1917–1933* (London, 1978), p. 75), the Berlin Dadaists could not have seen Tatlin's new 'machine-art' by 1920 (an exhibition of modern Russian art was shown in Berlin only in 1921) it is likely that they had borrowed their phrase from some such contemporary description of Tatlin's art.

42  See Igor Golomshtok and Alexander Glezer, *Soviet Art in Exile* (London, 1977), pp. 154f.

43  *Ibid.*, p. 155.

44  Peter Bürger suggests in his *Theorie der Avantgarde* of 1974 (2nd edn, Frankfurt on Main, 1981), that avant-garde art not only has the function of spotlighting the characteristics of art in general (p. 24), but, as Marx suggested was the function of bourgeois economics in his *Grundrisse*, also provides us with an understanding of its historical context. (Marx is quoted as saying in his *Grundrisse*, that bourgeois economy only came to its understanding of feudal, ancient, and oriental economy after the self-criticism of bourgeois economy had begun: in saying this, he was also probably thinking of his own contributions to this 'self-criticism'.)

45  Iggers and other critics of Saint-Simonism have pointed to those 'contradictions' within Saint-Simonist theory which were to enable it to be used by both socialism and Fascism. Above all, the Saint-Simonian belief in a centralised technocracy (a Utopian concept, the dystopian possibilities of which were to be unwittingly demonstrated in Bellamy's *Looking Backwards*, to which William Morris was to reply with his *News from Nowhere* of 1890, and which were to be consciously made grotesque by Zamiatin with reference to the Soviet State in *We* of 1920), has led some critics to suggest that it has played a part in the development of modern totalitarian theories of the State. In the sense that there is, however, no direct political application of the theory to be judged, its consequences cannot be assessed accurately or defined so certainly. Often the practices and theories of the Constructivists of the 1920s were, moreover, to come into conflict with Stalinist policies only to be taken over by them. So it was, for example, that the advocacy by the Constructivists of the 1920s of an avant-garde of artists and technocrats was, in Stalin's time, seen as both a threat to the bureacracy then being centralised by him, and as a source of a new concept of a 'vanguard' class of Party artists and writers subject to the Party, which was to be used, from 1931 on, through the Union of Soviet Artists and Union of Soviet Writers, both to control the old avant-garde which had arisen in Lenin's time, and to take over its functions. (Lenin's mention in his *State and Revolution* of 1917 of the socialist principle being 'He who does not work, neither shall he eat' also gives some indication of

how loosely Saint-Simon's dictum 'to each according to his works . . .' – as taken up later into the Soviet constitution – was to be interpreted within the reality of Soviet politics.)

46 As mentioned briefly earlier, not only was Marx's theory of alienation less well known in the 1920s than his later, but related, theory of surplus labour, but the 'post-revolutionary' situation in which the Constructivists of the 1920s worked was one to which, theoretically at least, the criticism of alienation was thought to be less relevant than the actual task of making the new socialist society industrialised and economically self-sufficient.

*Conclusion*

1 S. S. Prawer, *Karl Marx and World Literature* (Oxford, 1976), p. 409.
2 Peter Demetz, *Marx, Engels und die Dichter* (Frankfurt on Main, 1969), p. 127, and Stefan Morawski, Introduction to *Marx and Engels on Literature and Art*, ed. Lee Baxandall and Stefan Morawski (St Louis, 1973), p. 30.
3 Morawski, *Marx and Engels on Literature and Art*, p. 4, refers to how critics such as Demetz (*Marx, Engels und die Dichter*) have distinguished between Engels' support of Realism and Marx's indifference to it. Despite this, he himself chooses to speak of Marx as sharing the conception of Realism described by Engels in his letter to Miss Harkness, even though that was, as mentioned in n. 19 to chapter 6, written after Marx's death. In contrast to those who would identify Marx with Engels' views (and especially with those stated by Engels in the late 1880s), I have aimed at suggesting that Marx's views be analysed in their own historical context.
4 See the collection *Aesthetics and Politics* (New Left Books, London, 1978), for extracts from the debates between Lukács and Adorno. Although Brecht and Korsch were aligned against Lukács as supporters of an activist, even 'productivist' theory of literature and philosophy, Brecht also wrote in support of Socialist Realism in the visual arts, and, despite his attacks on reflectionist literary theory, cannot easily be brought into the debate between Socialist Realist and avant-garde art as a defender of the latter.

For a critical analysis of the relationship between Lukács' 'Critical realism' and Zhdanov's 'Socialist Realism', see Isaac Deutscher's essay, 'Georg Lukács and "critical realism"', *Marxism in our Time*, ed. Tamara Deutscher (London, 1972), pp. 283–94.
5 There are numerous examples of such works. One of the most recent is Janet Wolff's *The Social Production of Art* (London, 1981), which calls for more works of the nature of Hadjinicolaou's avowedly Althusserian attempt at describing the study of 'visual ideologies' in his *Art History and Class Struggle*. One other example is Terry Lovell's *Pictures of Reality: Aesthetics, Politics, Pleasure* (London, 1980). While Lovell is, in contrast to Wolff, critical of Althusserian writings on questions to do with the arts, and attempts to develop a new 'realist' Marxist aesthetic, which, it is claimed,

will take note of historical factors, *Pictures of Reality* also avoids either establishing any historical links between Marx and the visual arts of his own time or now, or critically evaluating Marxist art theory against a historical background which encompasses art practice.

# Select Bibliography

Encyclopedias

*Allgemeines Lexikon der bildenden Künstler*, ed. Ulrich Thieme and Felix Becker. 37 vols., Leipzig, 1907–50.
*Bol'shaia Sovetskaia Entsiklopediia*. 1st edn, 66 vols., Moscow, 1926–47; 2nd edn, 51 vols., Moscow, 1950–8; 3rd edn, 30 vols. and index, Moscow, 1967–78.
*Great Soviet Encyclopedia*. 30 vols. and index, London and New York, 1973–82.
*Marxism, Communism, and Western Society*, ed. C. D. Kernig. 8 vols., West Germany and New York, 1972–3.

Collected Works, Critical Literature, Catalogues

Ades, Dawn. *Photomontage*. London, 1976.
Adorno, Theodor W. and Horkheimer, Max. *Dialektik der Aufklärung* (1947). Frankfurt on Main, 1969.
*Aesthetics and Politics*. New Left Books, London, 1978.
Althusser, Louis. *For Marx*, trans. Ben Brewster. Harmondsworth, 1969.
*Reading Capital*, trans. Ben Brewster. London, 1970.
*Lenin and Philosophy*, trans. Ben Brewster, London, 1971.
*Essays in Self-Criticism*, trans. Grahame Lock. London, 1976.
Ames, Winslow. *Prince Albert and Victorian Taste*. London, 1968
Andreas, Bert and Mönke, Wolfgang. *Neue Daten zur 'Deutschen Ideologie'*. Hanover, 1968.
Andrews, Keith. *The Nazarenes: a Brotherhood of German Painters in Rome*. Oxford, 1964.
Antal, Friedrich. *Hogarth and his Place in European Art*. London, 1962.
*Raffael zwischen Klassizismus und Manierismus*. Giessen, 1980.
*Art in the Soviet Union, from 1917 to the 1970's*. Leningrad, 1977.
Arvon, Henri. *Marxist Aesthetics*. Ithaca and London, 1973.
Avineri, Shlomo. *The Social and Political Thought of Karl Marx*. Cambridge, 1968.
*Hegel's Theory of the Modern State*. Cambridge, 1972.
Bachleitner, Helmut. *Die Nazarener*. Munich, 1976.
Barrett, Michele *et al.* (eds.) *Ideology and Cultural Production*. London, 1979.

199

Baudrillard, Jean. *Le Système des objets: la consommation des signes*. Paris, 1968.

*Mirror of Production*. St Louis, 1975.

Bauer, Bruno. *Die letzte Posaune über Hegel*. 1841.

*Hegels Lehre von der Religion und Kunst*. Leipzig, 1842.

*Allgemeine Literaturzeitung, 1843–4*. 2nd edn, Charlottenberg, 1847.

Baxandall, Lee (ed.) *Radical Perspectives in the Arts*. Harmondsworth, 1972.

Belinskii, V. G. *Selected Philosophical Works*. Moscow, 1948.

Bellamy, Edward. *Looking Backward, 2000–1887*, ed. John L. Thomas. Cambridge, Mass., 1976.

Benjamin, Walter. 'The work of art in the age of mechanical reproduction', *Illuminations*, ed. H. Arendt. New York, 1968.

Berger, John. *Art and Revolution*. London, 1969.

*Ways of Seeing*. Harmondsworth, 1972.

'In defence of art', *New Society*, 28 September 1979.

Berlin, Isaiah. *Karl Marx*. London, 1972.

Börsch-Supan, Helmut. *Die Kunst in Brandenburg–Preussen*. Berlin, 1980.

Böttiger, C. A. *Ideen zur Kunst-Mythologie*. 2nd edn, 2 vols., Leipzig, 1850.

Bouglé, C. and Halevy, E. *Doctrine de Saint-Simon: exposition*. Paris, 1829.

Bowlt, John E. *Russian Art of the Avant-Garde: Theory and Criticism 1902–1934*. New York, 1976.

Brückmann, Remigius. ' "Es ginge wohl, aber es geht nicht", – König Wilhelm IV von Preussen und die politische Karikatur der Jahre 1840–1849', *Berlin zwischen 1789 und 1848: Facetten einer Epoche*. Akademie der Künste, Berlin, 1981.

Brüggemann, Heinz. *Literarische Technik und soziale Revolution*. Hamburg, 1972.

Bürger, Peter. *Theorie der Avantgarde* (1974). 2nd edn, Frankfurt on Main, 1981.

Butler, Elizabeth M. *The Saint-Simonian Religion in Germany*. Cambridge, 1926.

Carr, E. H. *The Bolshevik Revolution*. 3 vols., Harmondsworth, 1966.

'A historical turning point: Marx, Lenin, Stalin', *Revolutionary Russia*, ed. Richard Pipes. Cambridge, Mass., 1968.

Churchward, Lloyd G. *Contemporary Soviet Government*. London, 1968.

Clapp, Jane. *Art Censorship: a Chronology of Proscribed and Prescribed Art*. New Jersey, 1972.

Clark, T. J. *The Absolute Bourgeois: Artist and Politics in France 1848 to 1951*. London, 1973. *Image of the People: Gustav Courbet and the 1848 Revolution*. London, 1973.

Compton, Susan. *The World Backwards: Russian Futurist Books 1912–1916*. London, 1978.

Conway, Sir Martin. *Art Treasures in Soviet Russia*. London, 1925.

D'Alton, Joseph Wilhelm Eduard. *Das Riesen-Faulthier. Die Skelete der Pachydermata, und andere Werke*. Bonn, 1821–31.

Dehio, Ludwig. *Friedrich Wilhelm IV von Preussen: ein Baukünstler der Romantik*, ed. Hans-Herbert Möller. Munich, 1961.

De Laura, David J, *Hebrew and Hellene in Victorian England.* Austin, Texas, 1969.

Demetz, Peter. *Marx, Engels und die Dichter.* Frankfurt on Main, 1969.

Deutscher, Isaac. *Marxism in our Time,* ed. Tamara Deutscher. London, 1972.

Drengenberg, Hans-Jürgen. *Die sowjetische Politik auf dem Gebiet der bildenden Kunst von 1917 bis 1934.* Berlin, 1972.

Durkheim, Émile. *Socialism and Saint-Simon,* ed. Alvin J. Gouldner. London, 1958.

Easthope, Anthony. 'Marx, Macherey, and Greek Art', *Red Letters,* no. 6.

Eaton, Henry. 'Marx and the Russians', *Journal of the History of Ideas,* vol. 51, no. 1, January–March 1980.

Egbert, Donald Drew. 'The idea of "avant-garde" in art and politics', *The American Historical Review,* vol. 73, no. 2, December 1967.

   *Social Radicalism and the Arts.* New York, 1970; London, 1972.

Engels, Friedrich. *Ludwig Feuerbach and the End of Classical Philosophy,* ed. C. P. Dutt. New York, 1967. *See also* Marx, Karl and Engels, Friedrich.

Eyck, Frank. *The Prince Consort: a Political Biography.* London, 1959.

Feuerbach, Ludwig. *Sämtliche Werke,* ed. Bolin and Jodl., 10 vols., Stuttgart, 1903–11.

   *Das Wesen des Christentums.* Stuttgart, 1971.

Fitzpatrick, Sheila. *The Commissariat of Enlightenment.* Cambridge, 1970.

   'Cultural revolution as class war', *Cultural Revolution in Russia, 1928–1931.* Bloomington, Indiana, 1978.

Foucault, Michel. *The Order of Things* (1966). London, 1970.

Fry, Edward F. (ed.) *The Documents of 20th-Century Art: Functions of Painting by Fernand Léger.* London, 1973.

Fuller, Peter. 'Fine art after modernism', *New Left Review,* 119, January–February 1980.

   *Seeing Berger: a Revaluation.* London, 1980.

Gaedertz, K. Th. *Bei Goethe zu Gast.* Leipzig, 1900.

Gall, Ludwig. *Beleuchtung der Förster'schen sogenannten Kritik der gerühmtesten Dellirgeraethe.* Trier, 1835.

Gallwitz, Klaus (ed.) *Die Nazarener in Rom.* Munich, 1981.

Gans, Eduard. *Rückblicke auf Personen und Zustände.* Berlin, 1836.

Gassner, H. and Gillen, E. *Zwischen Revolutionskunst und sozialistischem Realismus: Dokumente und Kommentare. Kunstdebatten in der Sowjetunion von 1917 bis 1934.* Cologne, 1979.

Gaunt, William. *Victorian Olympus.* London, 1952.

Gay, Peter. *The Enlightenment: an Interpretation. The Rise of Modern Paganism.* London, 1966.

Géllert, Hugo. *Karl Marx: Capital in Pictures.* New York, 1933.

Gerasimov, A. M. *Za sotsialistichesky realizm: Sbornik statei i dokladov (For Socialist Realism: Collection of Articles and Speeches).* Moscow, Academy of Arts, 1952.

Gleizes, Albert and Metzinger, Jean. *Du Cubisme.* Paris, 1912; trans. as *Cubism.* London, 1913.

*Le Globe.* Paris, 1826–32.

Goethe, Joh. W. von. *Schriften zur bildenden Kunst.* Stuttgart, 1952.

*Italienische Reise.* Munich, 1961.

Golomshtok, Igor and Glezer, Alexander. *Soviet Art in Exile.* London, 1977.

Gordon, A. I. *Geine v Rossii: 1830–1860.* Dusaube, 1973.

*Geine v Rossii: 1870–1917.* Dusaube, 1979.

Grabar, I. *et al.* (eds.) *Istoriia russkoga iskusstva.* 13 vols., Moscow, 1953–69.

Gray, Camilla. *The Great Experiment: Russian Art, 1863–1922.* London, 1969; New York, 1972.

*The Russian Experiment in Art, 1863–1922.* New York, 1970; London, 1971.

Grün, Karl. *Anekdota.* N.p., 1845.

*Ludwig Feuerbach in seinem Briefwechsel und Nachlass.* Leipzig and Heidelberg, 1874.

Grund, Johann Jakob. *Die Malerey der Griechen.* Dresden, 1810.

Guerman, Mikhail (ed.) *Art of the October Revolution.* New York, 1979.

Gurvitch, Georges. 'Saint-Simon et Karl Marx', *Revue Internationale de Philosophie*, 14, 1960.

Hadjinicolaou, Nicos. *Art History and Class Struggle* (1973). London, 1978.

' "La Liberté guidant le peuple" de Delacroix devant son premier public', *Actes de la Recherche en Sciences Sociales*, no. 28, 1979.

'On the ideology of avant-gardism', *Praxis*, 6, 1982.

Hahn, Manfred. *Präsozialismus: Claude-Henri de Saint-Simon.* Stuttgart, 1970.

Hauser, Arnold. *The Social History of Art.* 2 vols., London and New York, 1951.

Hegel, G. W. Fr. *Sämtliche Werke.* Jubilee edn, 20 vols., Stuttgart, 1958.

*Philosophy of History*, trans. J. Sibree. New York, 1956.

Heine, Heinrich. *Sämtliche Werke*, ed. Ernst Elster. 7 vols., Leipzig, 1887–90.

*Historisch–kritische Ausgabe der Werke*, ed. M. Windfuhr. Düsseldorf, 1974–.

Heinse, Wilhelm. *Ardinghello* (1787). *Sämtliche Werke*, ed. Carl Schüddekopf, 5th edn (Leipzig, n.d.), vol. 4.

Heller, Agnes. *The Theory of Needs in Marx.* London, 1976.

Hermand, Jost. *Orte Irgendwo. Formen utopischen Denkens.* Königstein/Ts., 1981.

Hess, Thomas B. and Ashbery, John. *Avant-Garde Art.* New York and London, 1968.

Hessel, C. R. H. *Heines Verhältnis zur bildenden Kunst.* Marburg, 1931.

Hoffman, John. 'Marx on art', *Artery*, 13.

Hollosi, Clara. 'Views on Heine in Russia in the beginning of the 20th century', *Heine Jahrbuch*, 17, 1978.

Hughes, Robert. *The Shock of the New.* London, 1980.

Iggers, George G. *The Cult of Authority: the Political Philosophy of the Saint-Simonians.* The Hague, 1958.

Ionescu, Ghita (ed.) *The Political Thought of Saint-Simon.* Oxford, 1976.

James, C. Vaughan. *Soviet Socialist Realism: Origins and Theory.* London, 1973.

John, Erhard. *Einführung in der Ästhetik.* Leipzig, 1978.

Kalnein, Wend von (ed.) *Die Düsseldorfer Malerschule.* Mainz on Rhine, 1979.

Kamenka, Eugene. *The Philosophy of Ludwig Feuerbach.* London, 1970.

Kamenka, Eugene and Krygier, Martin (eds.) *Bureaucracy.* Melbourne, 1979.

Kant, Immanuel. *Gesammelte Schriften,* G. ed. Reimer. Berlin, 1910–?
*Critique of Judgement.* New York, 1964.

Kapov, Geeta. 'Realism and modernism: a polemic for present-day art', *Social Scientist,* nos. 89–90, December 1979–January 1980.

Karginov, German. *Rodchenko.* London, 1979.

Kertesz, George. 'The view from the middle class: the German moderate liberals and socialism', *Intellectuals and Revolution: Socialism and the Experience of 1848,* ed. Eugene Kamenka and F. B. Smith. London, 1979.

Klessmann, Eckart. *Die deutsche Romantik.* Cologne, 1979.

Klingender, Francis D. *Marxism and Modern Art: an Approach to Social Realism* (1943). London, 1977.
*Art and the Industrial Revolution* (1947), ed. Arthur Elton. London, 1972.

Koch, Hans (ed.) *Zur Theorie des sozialistischen Realismus.* Berlin, 1974.

*Kunst in die Produktion: Sowjetische Kunst, 1927–1933.* Catalogue. Berlin, 1977.

*Künstlerinnen der russischen Avantgarde. 1910–1930.* Catalogue of the Gmurzynska Gallery, Cologne. Cologne, 1979.

Laing, Dave. *The Marxist Theory of Art.* Hassocks, Sussex, 1978.

Leith, J. A. *The Idea of Art as Propaganda in France, 1750–1799.* Toronto, 1965.

Lenin, Vladimir Ilich.
*Collected Works.* 45 vols., Moscow, 1960–70.
*On Literature and Art.* Moscow, 1967.
*What is to be Done?* Moscow, 1978.

Lewalter, Ernst. *Friedrich Wilhelm IV.: das Schicksal eines Geistes.* Berlin, 1938.

Lifshitz, Mikhail. *The Philosophy of Art of Karl Marx* (1933). London, 1973.

Lissitzky-Küppers, Sophie. *El Lissitzky.* London, 1980.

Livergood, Norman D. *Activity in Marx's Philosophy.* The Hague, 1967.

Lovell, Terry. *Pictures of Reality: Aesthetics, Politics, Pleasure.* London, 1980.

Lukács, Georg. *Werke.* Neuwied, 1969.

Lunacharsky, A. V. *On Literature and Art.* Moscow, 1965.

Maas, Jeremy. *Victorian Painters.* London, 1974.

Macherey, Pierre. *Pour une théorie de la production littéraire.* Paris, 1970.

McLellan, David. *The Young Hegelians and Karl Marx.* London, 1969.
*Marx before Marxism.* Harmondsworth, 1972.
*Marx's Grundrisse* (ed.). St Albans. 1973.

Manuel, Frank E. *The New World of Henri Saint-Simon.* Cambridge, Mass., 1956.

Marcuse, Herbert. *Eros and Civilization* (1955). London, 1969.
*Soviet Marxism: a Critical Analysis.* London, 1958.
*Counter Revolution and Revolt.* Boston, 1972.
*The Aesthetic Dimension.* Boston, 1977.

Marx, Karl. *Theories of Surplus Value*, trans. R. Simpson. London, 1969.
  *Capital*. Moscow, 1974.
  *Grundrisse*, trans. Martin Nicolaus. Harmondsworth, 1979.
Marx, Karl and Engels, Friedrich. *Gesamtausgabe (MEGA)*, ed. Marx–Engels
  Institute Moscow. Frankfurt on Main, 1927–35.
  *Werke (MEW)*. Berlin, 1956–68.
  *Manifesto of the Communist Party*. Moscow, 1966.
  *The German Ideology*, ed. S. Ryazanskaya. Moscow, 1968; ed. C. J. Arthur,
  New York, 1970.
  *Collected Works*. London, 1975–.
  *Gesamtausgabe (New MEGA)*, ed. Institut fur Marxismus-Leninismus.
  Berlin, 1975–.
Masaryk, T. G. *The Spirit of Russia* (2 vols., 1919). 2nd edn, trans. Eden and
  Cedar Paul. London, 1955.
Mayer, Gustav. *Marx und der zweite Teil der Posaune*. n.p., 1916.
Mead, Igor and Sjeklocha, Paul. *Unofficial Art in the Soviet Union*. Berkeley and
  Los Angeles, 1967.
Mehring, Franz. *Karl Marx: the Story of his Life*. London, 1966.
Meszaros, Istvan. *Marx's Theory of Alienation*. London, 1970.
Metallov, A. I. (ed.) *Geinrich Geine: Bibliographia* (Bibliography of Russian
  translations and critical literature in the Russian language of the works of
  Heine). Moscow, 1958.
Metscher, Thomas. 'Literature and art as ideological form', *New Literary
  History*, vol. 11, no. 1, Autumn 1979.
Micha, René. 'Les femmes dans l'avant garde Russe (1910–1930)', *Art Forum*,
  May 1980.
Miller, Robert, F. 'The new science of administration in the USSR',
  *Administrative Science Quarterly*, September 1971.
Milner, John. *Russian Revolutionary Art*. London, 1979.
Mirsky, D. S. *The Intelligentsia of Great Britain*. London, 1935.
  *History of Russian Literature* (1926), ed. Francis J. Whitfield. London,
  1964.
Monz, Heinz. *Karl Marx und Trier*. Trier, 1964.
Morawski, Stefan. 'Mimesis – Lukács' universal principle', *Science and Society*,
  1, Winter 1968, 26–38.
  'The aesthetic views of Marx and Engels', *Journal of Aesthetics and Art
  Criticism*, no. 28, 1969.
  Introduction to *Marx and Engels on Literature and Art*, ed. Lee Baxandall and
  Stefan Morawski. St Louis, 1973.
Nash, J. M. *Cubism, Futurism, and Constructivism*. London, 1975.
Naumann, Manfred (ed.) *Gesellschaft, Literatur, Lesen*. Berlin and Weimar,
  1973.
*Die Nazarener*. Städelsches Kunstinstitut, Frankfurt on Main, 1977.
Nicolaievsky, Boris and Maenchen-Helfen, Otto. *Karl Marx: Man and Fighter*
  (1936), trans. G. David and E. Mosbacher. Harmondsworth, 1976.
Nochlin, Linda. *Realism*. Harmondsworth, 1977.

'Women artists in the twentieth century'. *Studio International*, vol. 193, no. 987.

Novalis. *Schriften*, ed. P. Kluckhohn, R. Samuel, H.–J. Mähl, G. Schulz, D. Schroeder and von Ritter, Stuttgart, 1960–.

Nove, Alec. *An Economic History of the U.S.S.R.* (1969). Harmondsworth, 1980.

Pankhurst, Richard. *The Saint-Simonians, Mill and Carlyle*. London, 1958.

Paramonov, A. *Peredvizhniki*. Moscow, 1971.

*Paris–Moscou 1900–1930*. Centre Georges Pompidou. Paris, 1979.

Pipes, Richard (ed.) *Revolutionary Russia*. Cambridge, Mass., 1968.

Plamenatz, John. *German Marxism and Russian Communism*. London, 1954.

Plekhanov, Georgi. *Selected Philosophical Works*, ed. V. Scherbina. 5 vols., Moscow, 1981.

Poggioli, Renato. *The Theory of the Avant-Garde* (1962). Cambridge, Mass., 1968.

Prawer, S. S. *Karl Marx and World Literature*. Oxford, 1976.

Punin, Nikolai Nikolaevich. *Russkoe i sovetskoe iskusstvo*. Moscow, 1976.

Püttmann, Hermann. *Die Düsseldorfer Malerschule und ihre Leistungen seit der Errichtung des Kunstvereines im Jahre 1829*. Leipzig, 1839.

Raphael, Max. *Proudhon, Marx, Picasso* (1932). New Jersey and London, 1980.
   *La Théorie Marxiste de la connaissance (Erkenntnistheorie der konkreten Dialektik* (1934)). Paris, 1937.
   *Arbeiter, Kunst und Künstler* (1938). Frankfurt on Main, 1975.
   *The Demands of Art* (1947). Princeton, 1968.

*Repin*, ed. G. Sternin. Leningrad, 1974.

Reumont, Alfred von. *Aus König Friedrich Wilhelm IV. gesunden und kranken Tagen*. Leipzig, 1885.

Rose, Margaret A. *Die Parodie: eine Funktion der biblischen Sprache in Heines Lyrik*. Meisenheim on Glan, 1976.
   *Reading the Young Marx and Engels*. London and New Jersey, 1978.
   *Parody/Meta-Fiction*. London, 1979.
   'The politicization of art criticism: Heine's portrayal of Delacroix's *Liberté* and its aftermath', *Monatshefte*, vol. 73, no. 4 (Winter, 1981), 405–14.

Rosen, Zwi. *Bruno Bauer and Karl Marx*. The Hague, 1977.

Rubel, Maximilian and Manale, Margaret. *Marx without Myth*. Oxford, 1975.

Rumohr, Carl Friedrich von. *Italienische Forschungen* (Berlin, 1827–31), ed. Julius Schlosser. Frankfurt on Main, 1920.

*Russian and Soviet Painting*, translations and foreword by John Bowlt. The Metropolitan Museum of Art, 1977.

Saint-Simon, Henri de Rouvroy. *Oeuvres de Saint-Simon et d'Enfantin*. Meisenheim on Glan, 1964.

Schapiro, Leonard. *The Communist Party of the Soviet Union*. London, 1970.

Scheibert, Peter. *Von Bakunin zu Lenin: Geschichte der russischen revolutionaren Ideologen, 1840–1895*. Leiden, 1952.

Schiller, Friedrich von. *Sämmtliche Werke*, ed. C. G. Körner. 12 vols., Stuttgart and Tübingen, 1818–19.

Schinkel, Karl Friedrich. *Berlin und Potsdam: Bauten und Entwürfe.* West Berlin, 1980.

Schlegel, August Wilhelm von. *Verzeichnis einer von Eduard D'Alton hintergelassenen Gemäldesammlung.* Bonn, 1840.

Schlegel, Friedrich. *Kritische Friedrich Schlegel Ausgabe,* ed. Ernst Behler. Zurich, 1959–.

Schrörs, H. *Die Bonner Universitätsaula und ihre Wandgemälde.* Bonn, 1906.

Selden, Ray. 'Russian Formalism and Marxism: an unconcluded dialogue', *Literature, Society, and the Sociology of Literature,* ed. Francis Barker *et al.* University of Essex, 1976.

Short, Robert. 'Surrealism and the Popular Front', *1936: the Sociology of Literature,* ed. Francis Barker *et al.* University of Essex, 1979, vol. 1, pp. 89–104.

Simon, Walter M. 'Saint-Simon and the idea of progress', *Journal of the History of Ideas,* 17, 1956.

Smith, Adam. *Wealth of nations,* ed. Edwin R. A. Seligman. 2 vols., London, 1954.

Smith, Bernard. *Place, Taste and Tradition* (1945). 2nd edn; Melbourne, 1979.

Solomon, Maynard (ed.) *Marxism and Art.* New York, 1973.

*Soviet Writers' Congress 1934.* London, 1977.

Staden, H. von. 'Nietzsche and Marx on Greek art and literature', *Daedalus,* 1976.

Städtke, Klaus. *Ästhetisches Denken in Russland.* Berlin and Weimar, 1978.

Stalin, Joseph. *Problems of Leninism.* Moscow, 1947.

Tagg, John. 'The idea of the avant-garde', *Artery,* 12.

Tatarkiewicz, Wladyslaw. *History of Aesthetics,* ed. D. Petsch. The Hague and Paris, 1974.

Taylor, Keith (ed.) *Henri Saint-Simon (1760–1825).* London, 1975.

Taylor, Richard. *Film Propaganda: Soviet Russia and Nazi Germany.* London, 1979.

Trier, Eduard and Weyres, Willy (eds) *Kunst des 19. Jahrhunderts im Rheinland,* vol. 3, *Malerei.* Düsseldorf, 1979.

Trotsky, Leon. *On Literature and Art,* ed. Paul N. Siegel. New York, 1977.

Umanskij, Konstantin. *Neue Kunst in Russland, 1914–1919.* Potsdam and Munich, 1920.

Valkenier, Elizabeth. *Russian Realist Art.* Michigan, 1977.

Vasari. *Lives of the Painters, Sculptors and Architects.* 4 vols., London, 1963.

Vaughan, William. *German Romanticism and English Art.* New Haven and London, 1979.

Vázquez, Adolfo Sánchez. *Art and Society: Essays in Marxist Aesthetics.* London, 1963.

Vischer, Friedrich Theodor. *Ästhetik der Wissenschaft des Schönen.* 6 vols., 1846–57.

Wackenroder, W. H. *Herzensergiessungen eines kunstliebenden Klosterbruders.* Stuttgart, 1961.

Walicki, Andrzej. *A History of Russian Thought, from the Enlightenment to Marxism.* trans. Hilda Andreas-Rusiecka. California, 1979.

Wees, William C. *Vorticism and the English Avant-Garde.* Manchester, 1972.

Werckmeister, O. K. 'Marx on ideology and art', *New Literary History*, Spring 1973.

Whelan, Richard. 'Fragments of a shattered dream: the Russian avant-garde, 1910–1930', *Portfolio*, September/October 1980.

Willett, John. *The New Sobriety: Art and Politics in the Weimar Period, 1917–1933.* London, 1978.

Williams, Raymond. *Keywords.* Glasgow, 1977.

Williams, Robert C. *Artists in Revolution: Portraits of the Russian Avant-Garde, 1905–1925.* London, 1978.

  *Russian Art and American Money, 1900–1940.* Cambridge, Mass. and London, 1980.

Wolfe, Tom. *The Painted Word.* New York, 1975.

  *From Bauhaus to Our House.* New York, 1981.

Wolff, Janet. *The Social Production of Art.* London, 1981.

Wollen, Peter. 'The two avant-gardes', *Studio International*, 120, November/December 1975.

# Index

AARR, *see* Association of Artists of
  Revolutionary Russia
Academies of Art
  Berlin, 43
  Düsseldorf, 8, 13, 43
  St Petersburg, 103, 113, 114, 115,
    184n.11, 185n.17
  Soviet, 151, 152
Achenbach, Andreas, 113
Adorno, T. W., 165, 197n.4
Ahlborn, Wilhelm, 52
Akh(R)R, *see* Association of Artists of
  Revolutionary Russia
Albert, Prince, Prince Consort of Queen
  Victoria, 92–4, 181n.15,16
Alexander II, Tsar of Russia, 116
Alienation of the senses and art
  Feuerbach and, 24–33, 68, 71–2, 96,
    170n.4–5, 171n.8, 178n.26
  Marx and, 68–70, 71–8, 79, 95–6
  relation to concepts of artistic
    production and avant-garde, 69–70,
    71–8, 79, 95–6, 156–7, 163, 165, 166,
    190n.8, 197n.46, 198n.6
Altenstein, Karl, Freiherr von, 40
Althusser, Louis, 165, 197n.5, 198n.6
Alton, Agnes d.', 39
Alton, Eugénie d', 39
Alton, Johann Eduard d', 36
Alton, Joseph Wilhelm Eduard d', 34–43,
  92, 173n.2,3, 181n.15
Ancillon, Jean Pierre Friedrich, 52–3
Andrews, Keith, 181n.15
Angelico, Fra, 9
Antal, F., 181n.14
Anthropomorphism in art, 24–33, 63, 66,
  67, 68, 72, 120, 171n.8, 171–2n.13,
  177n.26
Arkhipov, A. E., 144
Arnold, Matthew, 16
Artist as priest, 5, 8, 29, 82, 100, 131,
  183n.5, 190–1n.13

Artist as producer, *see* Art and
  technology; Productivist aesthetics
Art and technology
  in Constructivism, 1–2, 76, 100–1, 118,
    120, 122, 123–56, 162–3, 167
    Introduction n.1, 190n.8, 191n.15,
    191n.17,18
  in contemporary Soviet art, 156–7,
    162–3
  in German Idealist aesthetics, 73,
    74–6, 82–3, 87, 103, 155
  and Lenin, 129, 140–1, 192n.11,
    193n.13
  and Marx, 73, 82–3, 87, 155–6, 179n.10
  in nineteenth-century Russia, 99–103,
    118–19, 182n.2, 184n.15, 188n.32
  in Saint-Simon, 11–13, 82, 100, 163,
    167n.1, 168n.11, 182n.2, 190n.8,
    192n.11
  in Soviet Socialist Realism, 155–6,
    194n.25
Arvon, Henri, 189n.36
Association of Artists of Revolutionary
  Russia, 118, 141–2, 150, 151, 152,
    193n.15, 17
Avant-garde
  and Communist Party, 135, 136–9,
    163, 196n.45
  and Constructivists, 1–2, 96, 99–163,
    165, 167n.1, 190n.5, 195n.32,
    196n.45
  and critique of feudal relations, 5, 6,
    11, 12, 13, 16, 21, 24, 32, 69–70, 77,
    91, 96, 99–101, 138, 164, 165,
    182n.17
  and Lenin, 136–9, 140, 141, 190n.2,
    192n.11
  and Marx, 1, 2, 6, 32–3, 34, 74, 77,
    95–6, 124, 125, 164, 182n.17,
    196n.44
  and proletariat, 96, 100, 119, 136–9,
    145, 182n.17

208